LEADERSHIP
at Your Fingertips

To Ron,

with best wishes!

Jan

LEADERSHIP
at Your Fingertips

Proven Ways to Handle Your Challenges

Ian Jacobsen CMC, FIMC

WESTCHESTER
PUBLISHING COMPANY

Los Altos, California

International Standard Book Number: 0–917010–97–3

To obtain copies of this book, contact
Jacobsen Consulting
1.877.407.8001
ian@jacobsenconsulting.com
www.jacobsenconsulting.com

Westchester Publishing Company
342 State Street, Suite 4
Los Altos, CA 94022

Preface

My intent in writing this book is to create a useful reference of effective practices for leaders to deal with the challenges they face in organizational life. I have discovered that leaders who are pressed for time will read a page or two at a "teachable moment" to help them through a perplexing situation. In this age of "just-in-time" work processes, this is "just-in-time" information to help you with your challenges as a leader.

Inspiration Have you ever seen a bumper sticker that states, "The worst day fishing is better than the best day at work"? For many people in this world, that is their reality. It is not that everyone enjoys fishing that much. You can substitute almost any other activity for fishing to tailor this statement for a different passion. I, however, have been lucky. I have generally enjoyed my work. I have had interesting and important assignments and have worked with people I respected, trusted and liked. So when I founded my consulting business in 1983, I focused it to help my clients create a work environment where people would actually enjoy and look forward to work. There is no fundamental reason why work cannot be as enjoyable as pursuits like golf, fishing, etc.

The critical ingredient for having a motivating and productive work experience is to have good leadership. People who have interesting and important work to do, but who lack good leadership, are unhappy. People who perform jobs that a lot of people might not want to perform are reasonably pleased with their jobs when they have a leader who meets their leadership needs. So in my quest to create work environments that bring out the best in people, I have focused on coaching people to become effective, credible leaders.

In the diverse settings where I have worked or consulted, executives, supervisors, managers, individual contributors and team leaders have come to me to get help resolving people-related issues. It has been this way my entire career. They keep thanking me for my help, getting the results they want, and then returning for help with other issues. Though each situation is unique in its own way, there are a number of leadership challenges that most leaders face at some time.

To help the people in my network with their challenges of leadership and organizational life, I launched a quarterly letter for them in 1990. Little did I realize that I was beginning to write this book! Subsequently I discovered that they were making copies of my quarterly letter, *IanSights,* for their colleagues and saving their copies in a binder for future reference. In other words, they were creating a book of my *IanSights.* Then, some of them suggested that I should assemble my *IanSights* into a book. What you are now holding in your hands is the book they asked for.

Approach Readers of *IanSights* have told me that they want practical help with their issues of leadership and working in an organization. They want something they can pick up and grasp quickly. Theory is fine when there is more time, but they want something immediately useful. Thus, that is my approach to writing this book.

Approximately 5000 people have contributed to this book. They are people I have interviewed or who participated in focus groups. They have told me what it takes to attract them to a company, retain and motivate them, and what absolutely turns them off. I have distilled their feedback and applied what I have learned from them.

"New economy" relevancy In an age of economic turmoil, the nature of business is changing, and the pace, like the clock speed of computers, is getting faster and faster. You might then ask of what relevance is the material in this book to a "new" economy business. What I am writing about is basic human interactions that leaders face in organizations. While the "new" economy creates some challenges that are different from those in "bricks and mortar" businesses, leadership is about leading people, and the needs of people for outstanding leadership transcend the distinctions between "new" and "old" economy businesses. To use an analogy from physics, the needs of people constitute the first harmonic, and the nature of work is the second. The need to work with people you respect and trust is equally important in either situation.

Basics first In my experience, most leaders who get into trouble stumble on the basics. Many organizations for which I have consulted got into trouble when they tried to implement leading edge systems without having mastered the essential elements of sound leadership. It is like a situation I saw recently while hiking in Tuolumne Meadows in Yosemite. I saw a tree about 75 feet tall that was uprooted and blown over. It was on solid granite. It had a firm foundation, but its root system did not have the grip to anchor it in a fierce wind. Similarly, leaders and their organizations need both a firm foundation and the mastery of the basic issues of organization and leadership to give them the grip they need to weather their storms.

Getting the most from this book It is possible to sit down and read this book from cover to cover in a short time. But that may not be the way you get the most out of it. Like John Heider's *The Tao of Leadership,* I recommend reading one or two topics at a time, and using it as a reference source. When reading about each topic, stop to think of how it applies to what you do. Does it make sense? Does it reinforce what you do? Does it suggest something different from what you do? What might you do differently?

I hope that what you read in this book will help you to navigate safely the minefields of leadership that you face. I hope that you will become more effective in bringing out the best in the people with whom you work. And, I hope that reading this book will enable you to face your challenges of leadership with greater confidence and composure, and fewer headaches. Enjoy!

Acknowledgements

I am blessed with many people who have encouraged and supported me in writing this book. My wife, Bonnie, has encouraged me and has read and commented on many drafts of the chapters. I am indebted to her and to Linda Grossman and Richard Pike for their suggestions that have made my writing more understandable and readable. Emil Sarpa was the first and most persistent reader to urge me to package my *IanSights* into this book. Chris Smith, Richard Kharibian and Karen Hoxeng have masterfully helped me through the publishing process. And last, but not least, many clients and friends have asked for my help with their challenges as leaders. It has been through helping them with their challenges that I have been able to test and hone the content of this book.

Contents

Organizational Leadership for the 21st Century

1.1

Assertions About Leadership and Organizational Life

In writing about how leaders survive and thrive in organizations, I am making some underlying assertions. An assertion is what I believe to be so. It is not a scientific principle, a law of nature, or a proven fact. My assertions are based on what I have found that works during thirty-five plus years in leadership roles myself, and in working through the challenges of organizational life with leaders from a wide variety of backgrounds in a wide variety of settings. These assertions permeate what I say about specific issues later on.

Organizations

- ❏ 90+% of the leaders I know who have lost their jobs have lost them because they were inept in dealing with the realities of organizational life.
- ❏ Organizations are here to stay. Any time two or more people need to accomplish something together, they need a way to organize and distribute the work.
- ❏ Organizations of the future will need to be organized differently than they have been. The purpose of an organization is to facilitate people working together to achieve a common goal. The Internet and technology are changing the way people communicate and work.
- ❏ Keep your organization as simple as possible. The fewer the people and the more focused the purpose, the less formal an organization needs to be. The larger and more complex an organization is, the more time people devote to organizational issues, and the less they devote to achieving the organization's purpose and mission.
- ❏ Organizations, and hence, teams, experience a predictable sequence of challenges in their life cycle. Leaders who understand these phases, and can help their organization (team) through them, can minimize the time it takes for a team to become effective.
- ❏ Every organization has its own culture and political system. Even those that say they don't, do. You need to understand these systems to navigate through them.
- ❏ Whenever two or more people work together, conflict is inevitable. Conflict can be healthy when it is a competition of ideas. It can be

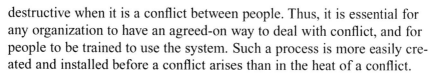

destructive when it is a conflict between people. Thus, it is essential for any organization to have an agreed-on way to deal with conflict, and for people to be trained to use the system. Such a process is more easily created and installed before a conflict arises than in the heat of a conflict.

❑ One reason task forces and cross-functional teams fail is that they have the wrong people on them. Every critical stakeholder needs to be represented – no more, no less.

❑ People judge themselves by their intentions and others by their actions.

❑ People see what they look for. Those who look for problems will find them. Those who look for the good find it. What you choose to focus on will define your experiences.

❑ People need and want timely feedback on how they are doing. Information systems need to be designed to provide the people who can benefit most from feedback with what they need, when they need it.

❑ What gets measured gets attention. Pick measures carefully.

❑ The most effective controls are created and implemented by the people who have to live with them. Controls developed and imposed by someone who will *not* have to live with them day in and day out tend to be ineffective and circumvented.

❑ The most competent person in the world you can hire is still new to your organization and deserves the courtesy of and investment in a thorough orientation.

Staffing

❑ Hire people who are more competent than you in their specialty so you won't have to perform their job in addition to your own.

❑ When you hire, you hire a whole person. It is naïve to assume that people leave the rest of their life on the doorstep as they come to work. Organizations need to be prepared to help employees deal with the challenges they face off the job, too, in order for them to be effective on the job.

❑ Hire people representative of the customers you serve. They will strengthen the ability of your organization to understand and serve your customers, and build your business.

❑ "Hire in haste, repent at leisure." It is easier not to hire a problem person than to have to deal with his/her problems. (You can train or educate people more inexpensively and effectively than you can change their basic values. Yes, values are important!)

Leadership

- ❏ The role of a leader is to inspire and enable people to achieve common goals in support of an organization's purpose and mission.
- ❏ A leader is not a leader without people to lead. Leaders are entrusted to serve the people they lead. Leadership is a privilege earned through being credible to the people one leads and represents, and competent to resolve the issues. For people to commit themself to you is an act of faith. In other words, "followers" need to have faith and trust in you in order to commit themselves fully.
- ❏ A good leader also needs to be a good team player. Many people in leadership roles are also on other teams where they are not the leader, but where they can make significant contributions as a good team player, helping their leader to be effective.

Power

- ❏ Power, in an organizational context, is the ability to influence others to action. While authority comes with position and carries with it a certain amount of power, it is not a substitute for the power enthusiastically accorded to a respected and trusted leader.
- ❏ The more of your powers you share with others, the more you have.
- ❏ Abuse of authority or power is a sure way to engender hatred and destroy credibility.

Change

- ❏ Some people welcome change and some resist. People find that change threatens their sense of mastery of their work, and their power and position in an organization; but people are less resistant to changes they have been a party to creating. Changes that can be introduced as an experiment are less threatening because people perceive that they can have some influence on the outcome.

- Life is about learning lessons. You are enrolled in a full time school called life. Each day you will be presented with opportunities to learn what you need to know.
- There are no mistakes – only lessons. Growth is a process of trial and error and experimentation. You can learn more from failure than from success.
- Past success can be your greatest barrier to future success. It can delude you into thinking that you possess the "magic formula," when in truth, there are no magic formulae.
- A lesson is repeated until it is learned. A lesson will be presented to you in various forms until you have learned it. When you have learned it (as evidenced by a change in your attitude and behavior), you can go on to the next lesson.

Work-life Balance and Employment Security

- Achieving a balance between work and the rest of one's life is an important and elusive goal for most people paid a salary. It is almost impossible to achieve on a daily basis. The best you can hope for is to achieve a balance over the period of a week or a month. There will always be more work that you could do.
- The only true employment security comes from investing in yourself, in the knowledge and skills that you need in order to be continually sought after in the job market.

Communications

- A message sent, but not received, is not communication.
- Informal communications get more attention than formal. People listen more to gossip than they read memos. While you can't rely on gossip as your sole communications strategy, plan how you will deal with it.
- When there is any opportunity for doubt, people believe what they want to believe.

❏ When delivering unpleasant news, get to the point in the first sentence. Don't keep people in suspense.

Ethics

❏ Give credit where credit is due.

❏ Accept responsibility for your actions. Most people know who is responsible and look up to someone who is honest and willing to accept responsibility for his/her actions.

❏ If you would be embarrassed to see your picture on the front page of the newspaper, or would feel uncomfortable having Mike Wallace interview you about what you are considering doing, don't do it.

❏ If there is the possibility that something you are considering doing could be viewed as a conflict of interest, talk through the situation with the people who would be affected by it before you decide to do it.

❏ Speaking ill of others behind their back ("talking stink," as they say in Hawaii) only reflects poorly on the speaker. Most people who engage in this have no idea that all they are doing is "shooting themselves in the foot."

❏ Seeking to engage in sexual relations with the people with whom you work is highly likely to backfire on you. Love can be fickle. In a work setting, when a relationship ends between two people working together, it almost invariably leads to the departure of one.

1.2

Creating a Focused and Flexible Organization for the 21st Century

The marketplace of the 21st century will be intense and competitive, not only for products and services, but also for talent. However, relations with employees, vendors and strategic allies will need to be collaborative. Such an environment will require focused and flexible leadership. We have only begun to see the effects of the information and internet revolution. The "new economy," despite temporary setbacks, promises to come on faster and have more impact than the industrial revolution. In such an environment, the ability of people to work together flexibly and globally to achieve common goals will be a deciding factor in the success of an enterprise.

What does it take to lead in such an environment? First, let's consider leadership. Leadership needs to create an environment that *inspires* and *enables* people to perform at their best in the pursuit of common goals. (This applies to virtual organizations and strategic alliances, too.) Leadership is more than a charismatic person with a cadre of followers. It is essential at all levels and in all areas of a business. It used to be that people in data processing were information "czars." Then the model changed. Now everyone has a PC or workstation. Information technology is now distributed throughout the organization. Leadership needs to be distributed similarly so that people at all levels can take action to better the entire enterprise.

Do leaders need to be charismatic? No! Charisma can get in the way when an organization is focused around a leader rather than on building a strong organization. An infectious passion for the organization's goals, values consistent with the culture, caring, fairness, support for people in their pursuits, credibility, accountability, and the ability to build an organization that achieves its goals are much more important for a leader than charisma.

Every organization has its own culture—values, purpose, mission, vision, and ways in which people relate to their work and each other. In a start-up, the founder determines these. Before a business grows beyond the scope of its start-up team, the team needs to define its culture. When Bill Hewlett and Dave Packard started their business, they hadn't thought much about such issues. As their business grew, they realized that there was more to it than making oscillators. They defined their underlying values and the way they wanted to do business - "The HP Way."

As a business grows, the role of the founder changes. Initially the founder's focus is on establishing the business. As the business grows, the founder becomes a conductor who orchestrates the performance of the entire organization. Orchestrating an entire organization requires attention to these key issues:

1. Business foundation Know what business you are in. Do your market research. What is the outlook for your industry? How does it fit into the "new economy?" What quantum changes could redefine it dramatically? Who are your customers? What do they want/need? What motivates them to buy? Who is your competition? What strategic advantages do you have (or seek)? What "Achilles heels" do you need to work on? Had the railroads seen themselves as in the transportation business, they might not have missed out on trucking, busses, and airlines.

The people who work for you can create your competitive edge. Think of your business in terms of their competencies, not just products, services, and markets.

Honda started out in the motorcycle business. Their competency was in building high performance engines. That opened the door for them to make cars, generators, outboard motors, ATVs, etc.

2. Organization Designing an organization usually receives less attention than designing products or services. That is short sighted. A well designed, scalable organization will outlast most products and services, and is a key for the continuing creation of products and services that will sustain the business over time.

- ❑ What structure, facilities, technology, policies, and systems and processes are needed to focus attention on the critical issues and tasks?
- ❑ How fast paced is your market?
- ❑ How much structure do you need to enable people to succeed in your market?
- ❑ What is the nature of the work needed to fulfill your purpose and mission?
- ❑ What are the mindsets and competencies of the people you need?
- ❑ How will you deal with intergenerational and intercultural differences?
- ❑ How much of a physical organization is needed? What can be "virtual"?
- ❑ How will you create a sense of community among people in multiple locations?
- ❑ What work environment do you need to recruit, retain and motivate people?

Physical space influences how people interact. If your organization depends on creative problem solving, create places conducive to dialogue and teamwork. Pacific Bell, in their San Ramon, CA, facility, has conversation areas that invite people to meet, brainstorm and dialogue.

To promote market responsiveness, keep business units as small and focused as possible. Large, bureaucratic organizations in today's world are like the Exxon Valdez or Titanic. They were not mindful of their environment. When they finally recognized danger, their communications system was too slow, and they had too much inertia to change course and avoid disaster.

3. Hiring Hire only those people whose values are consistent with those of your organization, and who can help grow your business. People whose values are at odds will always be out of sync. It is presumptuous to think that they will change their values. It is easier to hire the right people initially than to have to deal with the subsequent problems of people who don't work out.

If you want a "gold medal" in the "Olympics" of your market, hire "Olympians"—people with the potential to "bring home the gold."

4. Team training   Teams are a fact of organizational life, and will continue to be. Most complex issues require the diversity of perspectives and opportunity for buy-in afforded by a team. Teams can be incredibly productive, but 90% of them that have *not* had team training fail to meet their objectives. For teams that have been trained on how to work together, the failure rate drops to 5%. Teams for "career-defining" projects need such training, and sometimes need a coach.

While training is valuable, coaching creates learning at the "teachable moment"—the critical time for learning. People typically develop greater skill faster with individualized coaching.

People want to master what they do. As technology changes, or as people are expected to gain new proficiencies, they need education, training and support. I was on the Board of Directors of the Sunnyvale School District Education Foundation when it introduced multimedia technology into classrooms. One reason for the program's success was that, not only did we provide teachers with the hardware and software they wanted, we also provided training and a support group. Lacking such training and support, efforts elsewhere failed.

5. Organizational climate   Treat employees as "customers" for your leadership and work environment. Most, whose skills are in demand, have a choice of where they work. In deciding to join your business, or stay, they consider not only monetary issues, but also the quality of leadership and the desirability of your work environment. In treating employees as "customers," you will need to do "market research." Find out what is most important to help bring out the best in them. Then provide what will attract them, keep them and foster motivation.

People want to work for an organization that they believe in and can be proud of. Create a sense of purpose and belonging, and communicate a consistent message of respect, trust, ethical behavior, caring and appreciation. Eliminate fear. Trust is impossible in an atmosphere of fear. People need to feel valued, important and included.

Class distinctions demotivate people who are treated less favorably than others (FACULTY and staff, TOP MANAGEMENT and employees). No one wants to be "second-class." The harm of such distinctions far exceeds their value as a recognition factor for a few people.

Show employees respect by treating them as business partners. Involve them in issues that affect them, such as the design of the work processes they use. People who help design their work processes understand them much better, and have more commitment to making them work. Share performance and financial information widely. Determine which measures are needed for self-management. After employees have been trained in how to understand and use such information, make it available so they can track their progress. Yes, there is a risk in sharing it.

Someone might leave to work for a competitor. However, people who are treated as business partners are less likely to leave and more likely to perform better while they work for you.

Create guidelines that are simple and make sense. Define a strong set of values and a philosophy of business by which your business can live. Communicate it to job applicants in their interviews. Communicate it again in new employee orientations. As you create policies and work processes, make sure they are consistent with your values, and act consistently with them. Your credibility depends on how well you live up to the standards you espouse.

Communicate clear, high expectations, and test for understanding. Emphasize those aspects of work that are most important to customer satisfaction, and to the success of your business. Involve people in setting goals that prompt them to stretch and grow. To make sure that you are on the same wavelength, ask them to paraphrase their understanding of goals and expectations in their own words.

6. Conflict Establish a way to deal constructively with disagreements and conflict. When two or more people work together, conflict is inevitable. It is resolved more quickly and with better results when a process for dealing with it has been established before an issue arises. Unresolved conflicts undermine morale and productivity. I know a number of outstanding people who have changed jobs only because there was no accepted way to resolve issues that were important to them.

7. Pay Pay for results. Split compensation between base pay and pay related to results. Everyone can have some affect on growth and the bottom line, and needs to be included in a pay system that recognizes their effect on results. People pay attention to what is recognized, measured and rewarded, so choose measures carefully. Use base pay to cover ongoing obligations and incentive pay for what adds joy to their lives and motivates them. While stock and stock options can be very powerful motivators in publicly held businesses, cash bonuses can be, too, in privately held and not-for-profit businesses.

8. Change It is natural for people to resist change when they have not been a party to it. Thus, involve people in designing changes that will affect them. One reason why people resist change is that during the transition period they move from competence in the old ways to temporary incompetence with the new. Just think how long it takes to become proficient with a new software package.

To minimize resistance to change, introduce it as an "experiment." An experiment tests a hypothesis. The experimental environment frees people to try a change, knowing that it will be revisited. They are more open to new ways when they are involved in the process and have some influence. If an experiment works for them, they will strive to make it succeed and be adopted. I have seen people embrace a change introduced as an experiment that they would never have accepted had it been introduced as a *fait accompli.*

9. Effective use of time Your time is limited and precious. Use it in ways that give you the best return. Get competent people (staff or consultants) to handle responsibilities that do not make the best use of your time or talents. If you are not in control of your use of time, get a coach to help you.

The business environment of the 21st century will continue to be intense, competitive and chaotic. Businesses will have a core workforce and a satellite of people they call on as allies. Teams will be a basic unit for solving problems. People will need to be skilled as leaders and team players, as they will serve in both roles on different teams. To succeed in this environment, people, and their ability to work together flexibly for common goals, will be a major deciding factor in the success of an enterprise. Attracting, retaining and growing "Olympians," and creating a motivational work environment for them, will be an art form that distinguishes the winners from the losers.

1.3

Leadership and Management

Leadership is the art of inspiring people to undertake an adventure in the pursuit of a common goal. Management is the disciplined process that provides the infrastructure that enables people to achieve the goal. Leadership and management are different from each other, but they go together hand in glove.

Leadership is visionary, big-picture and more right-brained. It challenges and encourages people to look beyond the immediate to change the way things are. Leadership inspires them to strive for a bold, common goal, a desired future, and take the actions needed to get there. Leadership sets the tone, the direction, and models the behavior for people to achieve extraordinary results. It is about the head and the heart. It arouses people's passions. Leadership is getting people to *want* to do something—the "right" thing. Martin Luther King, Jr. was a leader. So was John F. Kennedy. They inspired others to action, to pioneer, to see themselves differently, to blaze new trails, to achieve breakthroughs.

Management is about structure, process, discipline, predictability, control and results. It is more left-brained. It enables people to pursue their dreams through marshalling and deploying resources. It is about the details and monitoring progress to keep people focused and on-target. It seeks innovation, refinement, incremental improvement and predictable results, but no breakthroughs. Management is concerned about doing things right.

Management without leadership preserves the status quo, and encourages complacency, bureaucracy and mediocrity. Many "well managed" businesses have languished for lack of leadership. Even a well-run business like Hewlett-Packard had to have Bill and Dave return from retirement to shake them up. Though management may not be as glamorous as leadership, *the devil is in the details.* While great ideas are essential to an enterprise, 85% of them never get implemented because of faulty execution. Great management gets things right with consistent high quality.

Leadership without management may inspire people to strive for a goal, but then frustrate them by not enabling them to achieve it. Many start-up hi-tech companies achieve a high score on inspiration and a low score on management. Talented people come on board to pursue an exciting vision. Then they beat their hearts out when they find that the infrastructure to support them is not in place. They encounter allocation of resources by whim, duplication of effort, *ad hoc* procedures, and inattention to important issues, while details are micro-managed. They are expected to achieve great results, but lack access to the support they need. Within a year, their great hopes and enthusiasm are dashed. They leave feeling disillusioned, or stay for stock options that lock them in to pursuing an ever-receding pot of gold at the end of the rainbow.

Synergy To compete successfully in the New Economy, and in the Old, an organization needs both leadership to inspire people and management to enable them. Both skills can be developed. Market leadership and sustained growth and profits come only when there is a healthy synergy of leadership and management.

Giving Meaning to Work: Purpose, Mission and Vision

2.1

Giving Meaning to Work

Work, for many people, is more than just a way of making a living. It is an expression of their purpose in life and adds meaning to what they do. It is like a "calling." For other people, work is just a way of paying the rent and buying the groceries. They might like to have a higher purpose to what they do, but there is nothing apparent.

Purpose, Mission and Vision give meaning to work. They help inspire people to pull together to accomplish an important goal.

Purpose is the reason an organization exists in the first place. It is enduring. It emanates from the core beliefs and values of the organization (frequently those of the founders). It is different from "to make a profit." Profit is a result of what you do to satisfy your customers. NASA's purpose is essentially to extend mankind's knowledge of outer space. This remains constant over time.

Mission is what an organization sets out to accomplish over a period of time. It is usually a bold, overarching goal that focuses the efforts of the organization on a specific result. Once it has been accomplished, it is supplanted with a new mission. In the 1960's, NASA's mission was "to put a man on the moon and return him safely before the end of the decade." It was bold. It was inspiring. It focused the efforts of NASA for a period of time. They accomplished their mission, and a new (less bold and compelling) one supplanted it.

Vision is a long term depiction of what it will be like when the Mission is accomplished. It needs to be expressed in graphic terms, so that people can picture a desired future in their mind's eye. It needs to create a tension between the future and the present to mobilize people to move forward toward accomplishing the Vision. The vision of a desired future contributes to the focus and discipline of a team and helps sustain and motivate them through tough times. One of the more famous expressions of a vision was in Dr. Martin Luther King, Jr's. speech, "I have a Dream."

Why are Purpose, Mission, and Vision important? "Where there is no vision, the people perish." (Proverbs 29:18). Once people's survival needs are met, they begin to look for meaning in what they do. They hope to pursue something they really believe in and to which they can commit themselves. Does this make a difference in how an organization performs? You better believe it does! It is the difference between just playing the game and being the winning team. A team with a vision of being Superbowl winners is much more likely to do what it takes during the season to get into the playoffs and win than a team with no such vision.

Does your business have an articulated Purpose, Mission and Vision? Can everyone describe it quickly and enthusiastically? If it doesn't, your business is not achieving its full potential.

Creating a Purpose, Mission and Vision is a sequential exercise for which a facilitator is useful. I recommend using a task force that includes directors, managers, employees and customers. Ten to twelve participants should provide a variety of perspectives, and yet be manageable. Each person should add an important perspective and should also be able to look at the organization as a whole. People with a narrow perspective or an axe to grind may paralyze the process by fixating on their own special interest.

Have the task force address these questions. *The answers for my business are in italics.*

- **Core beliefs** What are the key beliefs and values that shape our business?

    Mutual respect and trust are the cornerstone of effective working relationships.

    People contribute more when they are treated as partners.

    Bringing out the best in people is a "win-win" proposition.

- **Purpose** What is the underlying reason for which the organization exists?

    To create work environments that attract, retain and motivate talented people.

- **Mission** Considering your answers to the above, and the environment in which your business operates, where do you want it to be in its market in 5-10 years? What do you want to have achieved?

    To be regarded as one of the leading experts in the USA on issues of employer attractiveness and motivational work environments.

- **Vision** What will it look like when you achieve your Mission?

    Our clients will be leaders in their industries and sought after as desirable places to work.

    Our clients will experience significantly lower employee turnover than the averages for their type of business.

    We will be quoted frequently in articles on issues of leadership and organization.

> *Qualified prospective clients will seek us for our expertise and reputation for results.*

Have what the task force produces reviewed by the constituents of the organization. Encourage people to question and comment over a set period. After the close of the period for comments, have the task force review the comments, incorporate those that make sense, and resubmit their results for further review and comments. You need at least a couple rounds of review and comments in order to create a sense of ownership in Purpose, Mission and Vision. The stronger people identify with these, the greater their power to inspire and motivate people to pull together.

Many people come to work and perform their work in an uninspired way. Many businesses get by with this level of dedication and commitment. In order for people to turn in inspired performance, they need a source of inspiration and focus. That is what Purpose, Mission and Vision provide.

2.2

The Value of Shared Values

The culture of every organization is shaped by its set of values. Sometimes they are created consciously and communicated formally. Sometimes they are merely inferred from the behavior of leaders. And sometimes there is a "disconnect" between what is said and what one observes. Sears Tire and Auto Centers used to say, "We install confidence." The implication was that they were competent and trustworthy. Then they were convicted of consumer fraud.

Aren't values just "fuzzy stuff?" What place do they have in business? How can they be of value? People see a paycheck or direct deposit receipt once or twice a month. They *live* in the organization. The organization's values are what support them in their work, or what gets in their way. If individual and organizational values are in tune with each other, they help inspire people to perform at their best. They serve as a guiding star for making decisions for which there is no policy. If they are at odds, they create stress and inappropriate behavior. When values are implied rather than explicit, people may act inappropriately. In 1972, President Nixon's goal was to be re-elected. He achieved his goal. The problem was how he and his people went about doing it.

Not only do core values guide behavior, they also define an organization's purpose (or reason for being) and mission (what it sets out to accomplish over time). When they have not been defined, clarified, communicated, and "bought into," people can flounder. Why is that important?

Example

The owner of a young business in Silicon Valley assumed that all his employees shared his values. He was dismayed when he discovered them doing things that clearly violated his values.

An organizational review revealed no common understanding of his values, or employee commitment to them. That not only created confusion about what was appropriate behavior, but also about the purpose and mission of the business.

I facilitated meetings of a task force to explore, clarify and create consensus for a set of shared values. The committee included the owner, managers and employees. Participation in the discussions was lively. We accomplished our task, prepared a two page Statement of Values, and conducted meetings in each department to explain and discuss the values.

Terminations "for cause" dropped 33%. Voluntary terminations dropped 25%. Grievances dropped 38%. Productivity increased 18%. Employees "bought into" the values. They were relieved to have them clarified and communicated. The values have become a way of life. When faced with sensitive decisions, it is now common for employees to discuss issues in relation to the values? The values also serves as a recruiting aid. Some excellent applicants have accepted job offers, in part because they believe in the shared values.

Comment

Shared values may seem like a "soft" aspect of the business, but a set of shared values, for which management sets the example, can really affect financial performance. Key to the success in this example was the "buy-in" created by the group process, the willingness of the owner to rethink his values, too, and his setting an example with the new values.

2.3

Policies That Make Sense

What is your instinctive reaction when someone tells you, "you can't," "don't," "no" and other such admonitions? If you are like most people, you resent being told what you can't do. "What do you mean?" you say defiantly, "I'll show them!"

Policies define the workings of an organization. People understand that when you have two or more people working together, there have to be some rules or policies. Policies need to enable people to work together in a manner consistent with the organization's core values and applicable laws. Positively expressed policies help people to work together. In my experience, negatively expressed policies are more likely to bring out the worst in people.

Several years ago, I was asked to conduct a workshop on personnel policies with a group of HR executives. I asked them to bring a copy of their organization's personnel policy manual. After we developed criteria for effective policies, they broke up into small groups to review the policies of their colleague's organizations. Most found that their policies were more appropriate for a prison than the organizations they represented.

Example

A rash of complaints from disgruntled clients of a property management business convinced its president that it was time to confront problems of absenteeism, employee morale and turnover. In my interviews with employees I discovered that they felt that the policies they had to work with were inconsistent, confusing, and always negative. My review of them confirmed that they were a "crazy quilt" of "thou shalt not" statements extracted from various books of "canned" personnel policies. They almost dared employees to disobey!

First, I met with top management to clarify the core values, purpose and mission of the business. Then, I met with a task force of supervisors and employees. We critiqued each policy in light of the clarified values, purpose, mission and operational needs. I then redrafted the policies to eliminate inconsistencies and refocus them into positive expressions of expectations and consequences. The task force and top management approved the revised policies that were then incorporated into a revised employee handbook. Training sessions with supervisors and employees were used to communicate the revised policies and answer questions.

Employees now see how their work fits into the purpose and mission of the business. They accept and understand the policies that govern them, and feel that they are fair and appropriate. Absences are down by 43%. Turnover is down by 38%. Grievances are down by 67%. Morale has improved noticeably, and client complaints are now rare.

Comments

While there were other issues besides negative policies, they were symptomatic of the lack of thought accorded to creating a work environment attuned to the special needs of this group. Employees wanted and needed clear policies that enabled them to perform their jobs, not just policies that told them what not to do. In addition, the participative process used to revise and communicate policies strengthened employee buy-in and understanding.

2.4

Getting Results With Ground Rules

"Why do we need ground rules?" the task force member asked. "I don't want anything that confines me!"

"OK," I said. "Let's forget about ground rules. Instead, let's list what you have found that helps you work together in a task force, and what hinders you."

After ten minutes we had a flip chart page of what the members found had helped them, and one page of what had gotten in the way of accomplishing their mission on past task forces. I then asked members whether they would be willing to "live with" the behaviors on the positive list, and avoid the behaviors on the negative list. A couple of items were crossed off both lists before we had consensus adoption of what amounted to be their ground rules.

Whenever two or more people need to work together over a period of time, it helps to clarify and confirm the arrangements they need to help them be productive. These are more immediate than the policies of the organization as a whole. They are custom designed by the team to meet their needs. But wouldn't it be more efficient to create a set of ground rules for all teams? Yes, it would be more efficient, but less effective. The value in a group of people creating their own ground rules is that it requires them:

❑ To think about what it takes to create a well-functioning team, and then

❑ To commit to live by those rules.

Many of the rules they establish will be the same as they have had on other teams. That's OK. They are proposing them rather than having them imposed on them. They have the ownership of them. They understand the need for them. They commit to them. If someone doesn't abide by them, then it is their team members to whom they are held accountable.

What do ground rules need to cover? They need to cover whatever is important to the group for helping them work together. Typically they cover at least the following:

❑ How meetings will be conducted.

❑ How the group will communicate with each other between meetings.

❑ How conflicts or dissention will be addressed and resolved.

❑ Who, if anyone, will stand in for a group member when he/she is unavailable?

❑ How commitments and deadlines are to be treated.

In working with task forces, I find that it helps to ask one member to review the ground rules with the group at the start of each meeting and at its conclusion. It helps to remind them of what they created. It enables them to modify anything that isn't working for them, and to resubscribe to them. A review at the end of a meeting helps build accountability and helps the group learn how they can work more effectively together in the future.

Leadership is about inspiring and enabling people to work together to achieve a common purpose. Creating ground rules that help people work together effectively is a key component of enabling people.

2.5

Planning—A Tool or a Trap?

Do businesses that plan have any better results than those that don't?

Planning is worthwhile when you create a shared vision for your business and use it to inspire your team to create a shared future. A well-executed planning process can create buy-in, commitment and coordinated accomplishments. A plan is a waste of time if it isn't used or is irrelevant. It is harmful if it is used rigidly to stifle creative opportunities consistent with long-term goals.

How can you make planning a worthwhile tool? These are my observations from facilitating strategic planning sessions with clients (see planning diagram):

The Planning Process

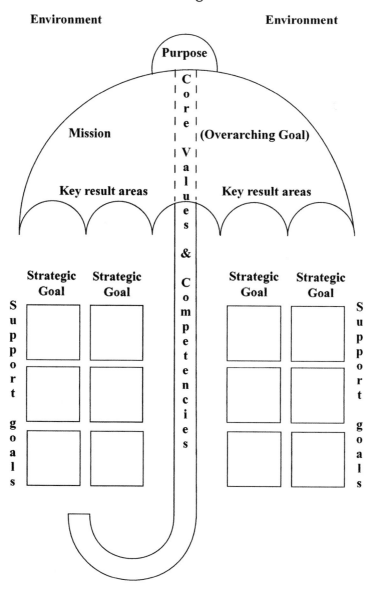

1. Involve people in the planning process who will be held accountable for implementing the plan. I have not seen vital, dynamic, effective plans without such participation. Involvement is necessary if each person accountable for results is to understand the context of what they are taking on to accomplish.

2. Distinguish between your Purpose and Mission Clarify both. Your Purpose is derived from core beliefs and values. It communicates why your business exists. (Example: "We exist to help clients create a workplace that attracts, retains and motivates talented people.") Your Mission is an over-arching, long-term goal to be accomplished in a set period. (Example: "To put a man on the moon and return him safely to earth before the end of the decade.") Missions change; purpose remains constant. Both help focus attention and effort on what is strategically important for your business to accomplish. Review your Mission as the competitive environment changes to make sure that it is still valid.

3. Separate sessions Separate in time the creative visioning process from proposing, prioritizing and defining goals to implement the mission. The goal-setting mindset requires analysis, planning and budgeting—skills that are different from visioning.

4. Create a coordinated set of goals for each year in support of your Mission. Your Mission provides long-term direction; goals provide more immediate direction and serve as milestones for measuring your progress.

5. Set team goals and individual objectives Team goals provide the focus for team members to set their individual objectives. People setting objectives need a picture of how their objectives support the larger goals, as well as how they interrelate with each other.

6. Individual action steps Have the people responsible for accomplishing goals include their action steps and timetables. More time is needed for planning to anticipate this level of detail, but people are more apt to accomplish an objective when they can pursue it one task at a time.

7. Conduct periodic progress reviews Where most planning fails is in the implementation. Ideas are easy, follow-up action is harder. Without periodic reviews, action can slip beyond the point of recovery.

8. Stay flexible and adapt! You cannot anticipate everything, especially with the quantum changes occurring in technology. Unanticipated events will require ongoing readjustment of the plan. That's OK. Remember that changes create opportunities. You'll survive change better with a flexible plan that facilitates opportunism than if you have no plan at all.

2.6

Joy in the Workplace

Is joy in the workplace an oxymoron? No! It is essential for creating a high-performing organization. The CEO, the principal, or the shift supervisor can never realize the full potential of the people they lead without the existence of a sense of joy. A workplace with a *joy deficit* is severely handicapped.

But isn't money more important than joy? People with little employment opportunities may sublimate their need for joy in order to put food on the table, but the need is still there. People who have options leave. Several years ago my wife, an elementary school teacher, took a $10,000/year salary cut to change school districts in the hope of regaining joy in her work. Close to 50% of the people I know who have changed jobs have done so in order to gain a measure of joy that was missing in their work.

How do you recognize joy in the workplace? You see people energized by pursuing goals that they consider to be meaningful. You see them pulling together for a common purpose. You see them volunteering to help each other. You see a "can-do" attitude, optimism, smiling faces, and you hear laughter. You find people who look forward to coming to work. You see supportive leadership and people creating positive experiences out of performing mundane tasks. You see them celebrating success. You hear them telling others about the great place where they work. You see creativity and extraordinary results from inspired people. If you don't see such behavior in your organization, there probably is a joy deficit—and that can be fatal!

Isn't such behavior uncommon? Yes! But it is what people crave. What is all too common is the micro-managing martinet who behaves like a prison guard when, instead, he/she should empower people. Controlling, authoritarian leaders bring out the worst in people, and everyone loses. A leader who does not inspire and enable people to achieve their goals with joy is misusing the organization's resources.

How do you create joy in the workplace? Joy is a by-product. In order for there to be joy, the people you lead need to experience a deep-seated belief in them. They need to see that you are there for them. They need you to look for the good in them, and to bring out the best in them. They need to experience your infectious enthusiasm for accomplishing important goals, and have the freedom to "own" what they set out to accomplish. They need to be recognized for their successes and for taking risks.

Technology was the defining influence in the world of work in the 20th century. While it will continue to be influential in the 21st, the real gains in what organizations can accomplish will come from leadership that unleashes the full potential of the human spirit. For too long organizations have been hiring whole people, yet benefiting from only a fraction of their potential. The organizations that will thrive in the 21st century will be those whose leadership bring out the best in people, and in the process, create a sense of joy. Invest only in companies where there is an abiding sense of joy.

2.7

Nourishing Others With Praise and Gratitude

Who have you praised or thanked recently? In a training session with 17 managers, 15 acknowledged that they did not praise or thank the people with whom they work as much as they could. They were much more apt to criticize, even though they knew that criticism has limited effectiveness in helping others to improve their performance.

Why are praise and gratitude underutilized? Several people in the session said that they were uncomfortable giving praise or expressing gratitude because they considered it manipulative. Others said they had never learned how to give or accept praise or thanks. Still others said that they found it difficult to say anything positive to people who were less than perfect, even when they did something noteworthy. Their answers were not unique.

Are praise and gratitude manipulative? Yes, if they are expressed for an ulterior motive. When they are sincere, they are a nutrient that helps people to thrive and grow. They acknowledge something noteworthy and reinforce one's sense of self worth. They communicate that you noticed and cared enough to express praise or gratitude.

How can you tell if praise or gratitude is sincere?

❑ It is tied to a specific act and is expressed in a timely manner.
❑ It includes the specifics of what is noteworthy.
❑ It is believable. You can recognize the truth in it.

> *"Mary, congratulations on negotiating the deal with Medmax! Not only is that an additional $1,770,000 in sales for us, but also having them use*

our XV30 enhances our market position. Their requirements were tough to meet. You did a superb job of working creatively with Engineering and Manufacturing to meet their needs while preserving our margins."

Gushy praise for no apparent reason (*"You are just sooo great!"*), lacking specific feedback, comes across as insincere. It destroys credibility.

How should you respond to expressed praise or gratitude? A gracious "Thank you!" is all that is needed. If you want you can add, *"Thanks for noticing and taking the time to let me know!"* Some people respond to praise or gratitude by saying, *"Oh, that was nothing!"* The implication of saying that is that the person expressing praise or gratitude was mistaken to do so.

Comment

Research indicates that people actually learn faster and better through praise. Criticism slows the functioning of the brain and impedes learning. People's mistakes often receive more attention than their accomplishments. It doesn't have to be that way.

You see what you look for. Look each day for what your colleagues do that is worthy of praise or thanks. Determine why what they did is worthy so that you can include specific feedback in your praise or thanks. Then praise them on the spot. They'll appreciate that you noticed what they did, and that you went to the time and effort to let them know. You can make a difference!

Building an Organization

3.1

Building an Organization or Team

If you were asked to build an automobile, would you combine a Dodge Minivan body, a Porsche engine, a Honda transmission, Mercedes brakes, and Jeep wheels? I hope not! While these components may work well in their intended vehicles, and may have much to recommend them, they are mismatched for working together.

Yet, there is a tendency for people to build organizations piecemeal as an amalgam of available spare parts when what they really need is a unified structure to create a total system. Even copying the best practices of other organizations typically falls flat. The lungs from the best penguin are inadequate when transplanted into a quarter horse.

Organizations are a series of complex, interrelated systems and processes. They need to be designed for the performance of the organization as a whole, and be in keeping with its spirit. That requires defining and designing the organization as a whole before building and installing its component parts. These are some of the questions that need to be answered to set the context for organizational design:

- ❑ Why does the organization exist?
- ❑ What are the characteristics of its market?
- ❑ What are the different countries and cultures in which it operates?
- ❑ What is it trying to accomplish?
- ❑ What are its underlying values?
- ❑ What are its strategic goals?
- ❑ What resources does it have?
- ❑ What technology and tools are needed?
- ❑ What systems and processes are needed to enable everything and everyone to work together seamlessly?
- ❑ What are the characteristics of people needed to make it work?
- ❑ What technology is available to bring people together who need to work together?
- ❑ What performance measures and systems are needed to monitor performance?

Many businesses neglect to answer these questions when they start out, and so create an organization by default. Their initial focus is, understandably, on getting customers and survival. Before they grow beyond what the founder can deal with personally, they need to define and design their organization. A frequently used approach is to copy what has worked well elsewhere without reference to the above questions. But, that approach generally creates a monstrosity like the auto in the first paragraph—a hodge-podge of systems that fit together awkwardly at best. It fosters people looking for ways to work around the systems, or leaving in frustration. It leads to the organization being "in the shop" frequently for "repairs." And that costs more in the long run than investing in good design.

In a robust market, a business may be able to hobble along on a piecemeal organization. But when the market falters, the crutches splinter and the business stumbles.

Organizations have to last longer than most of their products or services. Fully as much attention needs to be devoted to the design of an organization as to the design of its products and services. A well-designed organization, aligned with its business' purpose and market, comes through good times and hard times better than its competitors. It can accommodate the strains of growth, and can align more rapidly with the market as it changes. A well-designed organization creates a formidable competitive advantage!

3.2

Well-Functioning Organizations

The comic strip, Dilbert, depicts organizational life as a form of to Hell on Earth. Millions of people read Dilbert because what is depicted strikes a chord. So, in spite of Dilbert, is it possible to have a Well-Functioning Organization—one that achieves it intended results and where people enjoy their work? Yes! Here are the common themes of a Well-Functioning Organization:

- **Results** First and foremost, a Well-Functioning Organization accomplishes what it sets out to, and within an agreed-to time period.
- **Action orientation** People are action-oriented - no "paralysis of analysis!" Problems are identified and corrected rapidly. Conflict is easily confronted seeking "win-win" solutions.
- **Shared vision** People buy-in to a shared vision of an important purpose and mission to accomplish.
- **Create value** There is a consistent focus on the customer (client), quality, and creating value for customers.
- **Clarity of expectations** Roles, assignments, ground-rules, expectations and authority are clear, and goals are measurable quantitatively or qualitatively.

- ❑ **"Can-do"** People look for ways to make things happen. They are encouraged to take well-thought-out risks. Change occurs as an "experiment."
- ❑ **Competent and disciplined performance** People are well trained and perform with disciplined competence. They strive to perform at their best.
- ❑ **Resources** People have the tools, staff and support they need to perform their jobs effectively and efficiently.
- ❑ **Respect and care** Mutual respect, trust and commitment prevail with everyone treated as partners. Everyone's views and feelings are important. There are no class distinctions.
- ❑ **Supportive atmosphere** The atmosphere is relaxed, informal and comfortable. People and teams are learning, growing and flexible. Accomplishments, even small ones, are celebrated. Rewards foster and reflect accomplishment.
- ❑ **Rapid assimilation** New members are welcomed and quickly integrated.
- ❑ **Communications** Communications are direct, sincere, open, honest and timely. People get the information they need to perform their work and monitor their progress.
- ❑ **Ethics** Ethical conduct is modeled by top management, encouraged and rewarded. People do the right thing, at the right time, and for the right reason.
- ❑ **Involved partners** People who have a stake in a problem are involved in resolving it. Decisions needing buy-in reflect consensus and are implemented with support.

How can you tell if your organization is functioning well? You can conduct an organizational review in relation to these themes. You can conduct it internally using a task force or using an independent consultant who specializes in such reviews. Using an internal task force involves less out-of-pocket expense, but diverts people from other priorities. Using an independent consultant involves more out-of-pocket expense, and provides a level of objectivity that is seldom possible when the people on a task force have vested interests in the organization.

3.3

People—Are They an Asset or an Expense?

"Employees are our greatest asset," proclaims the annual report. Two months later a press release states, "Our expenses are out of line. Payroll is our greatest expense, so we are cutting our workforce by 20%." Are these mixed messages? You bet!

Assets People create wealth. I have yet to see a machine create a new technology, product or market by itself. Machines can augment people's efforts, but information, ideas, strategy, systems, even financing, are created by people. People are assets—investments that yield a return. When managed effectively, people create wealth while increasing their value in the process—a "win-win" situation.

Expenses People become an expense when their cost exceeds the value of their contribution. This can happen through:

- ❑ Unclear performance expectations.
- ❑ A mismatch between what the work requires and the people assigned to it.
- ❑ Work that doesn't add value.
- ❑ Ineffective work processes.
- ❑ Insufficient training.
- ❑ Policies that undermine creativity, risk-taking, and performance.
- ❑ Leadership that is incompatible with people's leadership needs.
- ❑ Inappropriate incentives.

Though a business has to pay for a whole person, only a fraction of one's full potential may be utilized. This is a losing situation that leads to the demise of a business, and obsolete employees.

Risk Isn't there a risk in investing in people who may leave to work for a competitor, or start their own business? Yes, you can't lock them in a safe to prevent them from leaving. But people who are well recognized for their contributions, and who enjoy their work, are less vulnerable to the siren calls of other opportunities. Even if they leave, you still gain if they are full contributors while they work for you. Your business will suffer if you focus on minimizing your losses when people leave, versus maximizing your return on investment in people.

Mind-set Treating people as assets, and investing in them, is a different mind-set from treating them as an expense: long-term vs. short-term. Instead of quarterly profit per share, focus on long-term return per employee. Ask questions like, "What is the estimated return on investment in work systems redesign, education, training, etc., over the next 5 years?" "What value will Fran add over the next 5 years? What is the estimated value of his/her anticipated accomplishments? What will we need to invest? What is the return?"

Change Unless people are treated as assets, they don't create a sustained competitive advantage. Businesses that treat people as an expense will have problems competing in the information age. They won't get their money's worth from their payroll dollars. They will need to change!

How are people in your business viewed? Is your work environment one that brings out the best in them? If people are viewed as an expense, you are not getting full value for what you pay.

3.4

Strengthening Your Organization Through Diversity

California and Hawaii are harbingers of the future for the United States: there is no longer one racial or ethnic group that comprises "the majority." Everyone in these states is part of a minority group. We are becoming a much more diverse society. In Sunnyvale, CA (Population, 120,000), there are 59 mother tongues other than English in their elementary schools. It is only a matter of time before the rest of the U.S. becomes this cioppino of cultures and languages.

Opportunity View diversity as an opportunity to strengthen your organization. In a global market it is essential to understand the cultures and people with whom you do business. By creating your organization as a microcosm of the people you serve, you add perspectives and knowledge that can help you to create products and provide services attuned to your markets.

Challenge Leading people with different values, customs, language and outlooks can be jarring. If you are an "its my way or the highway" leader, then you probably don't welcome questions, explanations, differing views, input and building consensus. If you are a participative, inclusive leader, then what it takes to lead a diverse team will be nothing new. From the classroom, to the shop floor, to the boardroom, this is what it takes to bring out the best in a diverse team:

1. Look for the best in people You see what you look for. Think of each person as a unique gift from our Creator. Remember: the gift is inside the package. People can be of various colors, sizes, ages, nationalities, degrees of masculinity and femininity, etc. Those characteristics are part of their packaging. It is what is inside that counts. Their gift, as with any other wrapped gift, is inside the package. As with other gifts, there is no guarantee that you will like their gift once you discover it. However, you are cheating them and yourself if you do not at least look for their gift.

2. Get to know the people on your team Help them get to know each other, too. Have them tell about their values, culture, traditions, what they take pride in and what they are sensitive to. When you show interest in them and respect them for whom they are, you begin to build trust and bonds.

3. Prize people for who they are and what they add to your team. Let them know that you appreciate them, and what you appreciate about them. Forget about tolerance; it is not enough! Would *you* only want to be tolerated? You probably would rather be welcomed, appreciated, and made to feel special for who you are. Make others feel that way.

4. Forget about stereotypes Fortunately, people are much more diverse than their stereotypes. Others don't like to be stereotyped any more than you do.

5. Be sensitive to your cultural conditioning and to that of the people with whom you interact. There is no one "right" culture. "American" culture is derived from the many cultures of the people who have participated in the building of our country. It is changing as you read this, and will continue to evolve.

6. Exercise an open mind and good sense of humor—especially about yourself. It is inevitable that at some point someone will unintentionally offend you, and that you will offend someone else. If you are offended, don't take it personally. Chances are 99/100 that it is unintentional. The chances are, too, that if you look for the humor in the situation, and share it with others, it will be easier on everyone. Displaying a sense of humor about yourself eases tensions and helps everyone to move forward. Humor, however, should *never* be at someone else's expense.

7. Create a way to deal with conflict and misunderstandings Work with your team to create a process that everyone buys into. Conflicts and misunderstandings are a natural phenomenon when people of different backgrounds, cultures, ages, and mother tongues work together. A process for dealing with such issues is more apt to be used, and used more effectively, when the people for whom it is intended have had input into its design.

As your business becomes global, you will need to work effectively with an increasingly diverse cross section of people. In order to have a strong organization, responsive to your customers, you will need to build teams of people from diverse backgrounds. View the need to build a diverse organization as an opportunity to strengthen your business. Enjoy your adventure!

3.5

When is a Group a Team?

"Work is no longer fun. We call ourselves a team, but you'd never know it. We've lost our sense of purpose, direction and teamwork. We're mired in debate and inaction."

Not all groups are teams, nor do they need to be. A team is a "group of people working together in a coordinated effort." A team is distinguished from a group by:

1. A common goal and shared values A common goal creates a sense of purpose. It is part of what inspires people with shared values to work together. It focuses their effort and gives meaning and direction to what they do. It is what enabled our country to put a man on the moon.

2. Interdependence Working together is the only way a team can achieve its goals. People are brought into the team because their special abilities, which, when combined with the rest of the team, make the whole team greater than the sum of its parts. One person, no matter how smart and creative, cannot achieve the same results as people working collaboratively toward a common goal.

3. Commitment to the team and honoring each member for what he/she adds to it. For a team to win, members need to place the success of the team above personal interests. This is not easy! There is a temptation for exceptionally competent people to want to show others how good they are at the expense of team performance. One of Phil Jackson's real challenges when he became coach of the Chicago Bulls was to get his star players to work as a team. It boiled down to this: no one wins if the team doesn't win!

Not all teams or groups are effective. To be effective a team also needs:

1. Standards and processes Ground rules and a conflict resolution process enable people to work together in a disciplined manner. Conflict is inevitable. A team needs to create a process for dealing with conflict before it is needed, and use it.

2. Clear expectations, roles, responsibilities and authority What are we expected to do? Why? By when? To what standards? With what resources? Within what constraints? For a well-orchestrated effort and result, everyone needs answers to such questions.

3. Performance information Semi-annual performance reviews are ineffective for monitoring progress. A team needs more immediate information to keep on course. That means having key goal-related indicators to monitor their progress in "real-time."

4. Leadership Effective leadership keeps a team focused, on-task, and pulling together. Someone needs to lead/facilitate meetings, help the team resolve issues, represent them, and develop the team. Leadership can reside in one person, or it can be shared (as in a self-directed team). Leadership attuned to the team's goals, tasks, and relationships is essential. An outside coach is often useful.

Not all tasks require a team. For those that do, there needs to be a common purpose, interdependence, and mutual respect and commitment. For a team to be effective it needs leadership, information and processes that enable people to work together toward their goal.

3.6

The Life Cycle of Teams

As sure as swallows return to San Juan Capistrano, California, every spring, most teams experience a predictable sequence of stages that they pass through in their lifetime, if they don't self-destruct first. This is comforting in that it helps leaders and teams understand that some of the issues they experience are perfectly predictable and normal. It can also be disquieting to realize that to some extent, even the most perfect team experiences these challenges. However, well-functioning teams to some extent, pass through their difficulties faster and with less grief.

Every team, like every other living organism, has a life cycle. Teams are assembled for a purpose and to accomplish certain goals. Eventually they accomplish their purpose and goals, and disband or morph into a team with a different purpose.

B.W. Tuckman wrote an article, "Developmental Sequences in Small Groups," (Psychological Bulletin, Vol. 63, 1995) that has spurred various models of team behavior. I use a variation on his theme. These are the stages of the life cycle, what typically happens in each, and the leadership support needed to move the team forward.

Stages of the Life Cycle of a Team

Stage	*What happens*	*Leader support needed*
Birth	Members selected Orientation "Honeymoon" Low team competence High commitment to purpose	Set direction, train in team skills Create common purpose, goals Clarify expectations Define mission and roles Establish ground rules
Revolution	Question leadership, goals, roles, structure, processes Overwhelmed by what needs to be done Infighting, apathy, withdrawal Low team skills and commitment to team	Identify and confront issues Restructure, as needed Build technical and interpersonal skills, two-way communication Align expectations with reality Highlight strengths; build on them
Resolution	People learn how to work together, develop sense of "we" Fragile harmony, trust, respect, morale	Encourage; confront "groupthink" Facilitate problem solving, decision making and group process Share or relinquish control
Production	High competence, commitment, performance and productivity Collaborative relations; high morale and team spirit	Set goals, provide information Create linkages to other teams Distribute leadership; let team manage itself
Completion	Mission accomplished; team dissolves or morphs	Celebrate, reminisce, grieve Post mortem, lessons learned

So what does this all mean? It means that the team behavior in the "What happens" column is typical. It also means that in order to advance the team in its development, the leader (or the leadership in a self-directed team) needs to provide the support indicated in the "Leader support needed" column. If that support is not provided on a timely basis, the team will not be able to advance to achieve its full potential.

When a team member leaves or a new one is added, the dynamics of the team change. When that happens it is common for the team to revert to the Revolution stage as relationships and roles are redefined.

Some teams become totally dysfunctional in the Revolution stage. Neither the leader nor any team member provides the leadership support to move to the next stage. In effect, the team becomes terminally ill or commits suicide.

Every member of a team should be aware of these stages of the life cycle of teams. It helps them place the team's behavior in perspective and helps them evolve by contributing needed support. Such support is especially important in virtual or self-managed teams where leadership is distributed, often at considerable distance. Every member has a responsibility to ask, "Where are we in the life cycle of our team, and what must I do to support the development of our team?"

Teams are an essential ingredient of organizational life, yet most fall short of achieving their full potential. By understanding that a team experiences predictable stages of its life cycle, and taking appropriate action to advance your team through Resolution to Production, you can contribute greatly to its success.

3.7

Bringing Someone New on Board—The Acculturation Process

"John is a nationally recognized expert in his field. Why does he need an orientation?"

Anyone new to your business, including a new CEO, needs to learn how to "swing through the jungle" of your unique organization. Someone who is a world-renowned expert in his/her field still is a "babe in the woods" regarding the culture and intricacies of your organization, and needs to be brought up to speed. Very few people want to make mistakes. Without an acculturation process to acquaint new people to your unique organization, you unintentionally set traps for them and guarantee yourself headaches.

If your business does not have an acculturation process, create one. If it does, review it to make sure it is working for you. As every organization is unique, an effective process needs to be tailored to the specifics of your organization. Nevertheless, it should probably cover:

- ❑ **Context** History, legends, values, purpose, mission and vision of the business.
- ❑ **Current issues** Special challenges to the business.
- ❑ **Organization** Organization charts including both the big picture and immediate organization; names of people one is expected to recognize, chain of command, informal organization, etc.
- ❑ **Unique attributes** Acronyms, special vocabulary, traditions, etc.
- ❑ **Goals** For the unit and teams in which one will work; and for which one will be responsible and held accountable.

❑ **Progress reviews** When, how and by whom progress will be reviewed, including review criteria and people who will have input into the review process.

❑ **Introductions** People with whom one will work, both every day and occasionally.

❑ **"Words to the wise"** Hints for working effectively with one's boss, coworkers, customers, etc.

❑ **Decisions** How decisions are made, communicated and implemented; decisions one is authorized to make without review, and how to get decisions for the other issues.

❑ **Organizational politics** How the organization actually works, who has power, etc.

❑ **Ethics** What is important for doing "the right thing" in the context of your organization.

❑ **Questions and problems** Who to turn to and how to get answers or action.

❑ **Conflict resolution** How to deal with sensitive issues, sexual harassment, etc.

❑ **Company property and services** How to use them, personal use, etc.

❑ **Supplies and equipment** Where and how one gets what one needs.

❑ **Forms and reports** Those one is expected to use.

❑ **Facilities** Restrooms, copy center, break rooms, cafeteria, etc.

❑ **Policies** The most applicable, and others of which one needs to be aware.

❑ **Finances** The budget process, financial reports, controls, authorizations, etc.

❑ **Absence** What to do if one is unable to come to work.

❑ **Safety/accidents** Hazards, safety procedures, accident reporting, etc.

❑ **Pay** When and how one will be paid.

❑ **Incentive plans and benefits** How they work and when one will be eligible.

❑ **Confidentiality** What is considered confidential and what can be shared.

❑ **Media** How to respond to media requests for information/interviews.

Acculturation is something that occurs over a period of time. Most people are not prepared for, nor can they absorb, an information dump on their first day. Thus, determine when, how and by whom each step in the process will occur. Create a time-phased map so that participants can see the larger context, what is coming and who will be involved. Have each phase signed off by the new employee and the person responsible for conducting it. Have each person completing the process interviewed by the next higher level of management to review how it went and find out what was learned. A well designed and implemented process will help your business recruit, retain and motivate top talent, and spare you the embarrassment of unwitting mistakes.

"If you think the cost of education is high, consider the cost of ignorance!" New people in an organization have only limited effectiveness until they know how to "swing through the organizational jungle." Yes, it takes time and money to acculturate them. But it's a lot less expensive than the cost of mistakes and decreased motivation resulting from ignorance.

3.8

Pruning Your Organization for Health and Growth

Organizations are living organisms, like trees and shrubs. You prune trees and shrubs to remove dead wood, shape growth, and improve health and vitality. For similar reasons, organizations need pruning, too.

Changing needs As an organization grows, the knowledge and skills required for its future growth change. Methods that work in its infancy do not suffice through puberty and into maturity. Some people excel in start-ups, others at growing an emerging business. Some people can't make a transition from one stage of the business to the next. In addition, even with careful hiring, not everyone works out.

No formulas Pruning an organization by a specific percentage (eliminating the bottom 5%) is not the answer. It may be greater or less than what is needed. The basic issue is who has "what it takes" to meet your organization's needs in the immediate and longer-term future. That requires a strategic plan that defines future direction and assesses the current talent vis á vis anticipated needs. Some people will have significant long-term potential. Others may be fine for the next year, but come up short for the longer haul. And some may already be holding you back.

Who to prune The people to prune are those who are holding you back and those whose jobs are outgrowing them. If they have what it takes to add strength in another role internally, redeploy them. If not, help them to move elsewhere so your organization can be strengthened, and so they can operate within their zone of competence.

Is it cruel to let someone go who may have worked faithfully, to his/her capacity, but who no longer meets your needs? No, not if he/she is treated fairly. Nor is it a kindness to keep someone in a job for which he/she is a marginal performer and is slipping. People who are in above their head usually know that they are and become preoccupied with their survival. They frequently have lost the respect of their coworkers, and the stress of the situation affects their health. What is kindest is to deal honestly with them about their strengths and opportunities, and help them once again to be in a situation where they are competent, respected, and appreciated.

How is pruning perceived? It depends on how it is communicated and carried out. Employees are quite perceptive and realistic about who adds value and who doesn't. How pruning is perceived also depends on the organization's culture. Where pruning has met with success, employees are viewed as mature adults who are investing part of their life in the organization. Everyone understands that the needs of the organization change over time. Some people will continue to add value longer than others, but eventually, everyone will leave. During their stay, they will be prized and appreciated for what they contribute. When it comes time to leave, they will be treated fairly and given support in making their transition to their next opportunity.

Organizations need to be pruned to enable them to grow and be healthy. Pruning is not whacking away with hedge trimmers. It is examining the structure needed for the future and cutting with care. Pruning, well done, is an art form that yields healthy growth in the right places and shapes the organization for the years to come.

3.9

Restructuring Your Organization

Why Your organization is the framework in which the work of your business takes place. As your business changes, so must its structure and infrastructure. The foundations for a cottage will not support a skyscraper. Thus, at some point, growth, mergers, acquisitions, cutbacks or market changes will require you to restructure your organization.

When You could wait until you are in a crisis. However, the best decisions are seldom made in a crisis. You could also take steps now to prepare for when you will need to restructure. I recommend reviewing your organization at least every two years, or when you anticipate the addition or deletion of significant products, services, staff or locations. Major additions of employees need to be prefaced with a review to make sure they are needed and will be utilized effectively. Major cutbacks need to be done in the context of who will be needed to accomplish the remaining work, and to lay the foundation for your future. Changes to any part of your organization are bound to have repercussions elsewhere—everything is interrelated. Whenever you are going to make a change to one dimension of your organization, look at the organization as a whole.

Who I recommend forming a high-level task force with a strategic perspective. Consider people with extensive knowledge of your organization from the following areas, depending on the nature of your business and the scope of restructuring:

Marketing
Sales
Operations/manufacturing
Research and Development
Finance
Information Technology
Facilities
Human Resources
Purchasing and Contract Services
Investor Relations (Donor Relations in public service corporations)
Public (Government) Relations

Some of these people may already be on your management committee, so why create a separate task force? I have found that a task force generally works better than the management committee for this task. It is more focused because it has a more focused charter than that of a management committee. A management committee is apt to get distracted by other issues. In addition, there may be significant players not on the management committee who also need to be involved in a restructuring. A task force enables them to be full participants in the process. Whoever you choose needs a firm grasp of your business as well as a strategic perspective. In order to make it work, you also need to include the people on the task force who will have to buy into the restructuring.

How The charge for a restructuring task force is to define and redesign your organization structure for a spectrum of possible scenarios you may face. The process I recommend begins with clarifying the underlying principles, values, purpose, mission and major goals of your organization, in other words, what it is all about. Your organization has strengths, weaknesses, opportunities and threats that can help or hinder its progress. Thus, I recommend an assessment of your present organization in its current competitive environment, as well as in several possible future scenarios in which it may have to operate. Given the probable changes and opportunities in the competitive landscape, and the purpose and mission of your business, create a vision of the future 5-10 years out. When you compare your present situation with your vision, you define your gaps for goal setting.

Once you have the vision to provide direction for your organization, and several scenarios of routes to get there, then assess the organization and structure you will need to achieve your vision. Address these seven interdependent dimensions:

1. Organizational unit This is typically portrayed on an organization chart based on functions (marketing and sales, R & D, manufacturing, human resources, finance, etc.), markets, products or services. This is frequently referred to as the formal organization. It depicts reporting relationships. Sometimes the reporting relationships and scopes of organizational units are all that is considered, but the six other dimensions need to be considered, too. What are the organizational units you will need? What are the reporting relationships that enable them to perform at their best?

2. Cross-functional or interdisciplinary teams Because the parts of an organization are interdependent, issues that transcend organizational units or disciplines need to be addressed by teams of key stakeholders. For example, new product development typically requires people from R&D, engineering, manufacturing, purchasing, marketing and sales, customer service, and finance. For what cross-functional or interdisciplinary issues will you need teams?

3. Structure of work For work to be accomplished, you need work systems, tools, technology and processes that enable people to work together in coordination. These are the key processes that determine workforce utilization, productivity, quality and profitability. Re-engineering is a process to redesign the structure of work and its interrelationships. What are the simplest work processes you can use to achieve your goals for productivity, customer service, quality and profit? What tools and technology are needed? Given the skills of people in your available workforce, how do you need to structure work? What training is needed to bring people up to speed and keep them ahead of the obsolescence curve? What configuration of information is needed to enable them to perform their work effectively and efficiently?

4. Space Space (including location and facilities) affects organizational design, work process design, and the interactions of people. It can aid communication or make it more difficult. You may decide to have manufacturing done off-shore while keeping R & D and engineering at home. You may choose cubicles over offices. Whatever you choose has ramifications for the other dimensions. Space affects the structure of work and the way people work together. Considering the markets you choose to serve (from your strategic plan), what location(s) are needed to serve them effectively? How should space be configured in each location to facilitate work processes and communications?

5. People This dimension includes the values, culture, knowledge, skills, leadership and personal characteristics of what it takes to make everything else work. The tasks and technology from the Structure of Work dimension drive what is needed for people talent, but the characteristics of people affect the nature of work, too. Frequently the people dimension is not consciously designed; it is just allowed to happen. Considering the work to be done, what are the values, knowledge, skills, abilities and motivations of the people you need? What type of work environment is needed to attract, retain and motivate them? What leadership do they need to bring out the best in them? What infrastructure do they need to enable them to be productive?

6. "Virtual (outsourced)" Some services make sense to have on-staff, or in-house, and others make more sense to purchase. Expertise that a business needs occasionally may best be "outsourced." So may services that are outside a business' core competences. Services such as payroll, maintenance or technical services, legal, and security are frequently purchased. In some cases, manufacturing is purchased, too. Though virtual services need to be viewed as part of the extended organization, they are not part of the headcount. What are your core competences? How will you capitalize on strengths and manage weaknesses? What expertise do you need only occasionally? What is the quality of virtual services available to you? If you outsource, how will you maintain control over what you purchase? What are the costs of in-house versus outsourced services?

7. Financial Everything requires money and has financial implications. How should you structure your debt? What are the cash flow patterns and how do they affect the business? If your business is privately financed, should it go public? Life is never the same in a business once it becomes a publicly traded company. What are the most relevant measures of financial performance for your business, and how can these measures be shared to facilitate better self- monitoring throughout your business?

Most people want to work for a healthy business. They look to management to take the actions that foster strategic positioning and growth consistent with a strategic plan. Moving through the transitions from your current business to an envisioned future can be stressful. People accept such transitions when they understand the context and need for what they are experiencing, and buy into the future benefits. Thus, the success of restructuring hinges not only on the soundness of the plan, but also on the process used to create and communicate it.

Attracting and Selecting Talented People

4.1

What People Consider in Evaluating Their Employment Choices

Employees are customers for your work environment. They don't have to work for you. Those with knowledge and skills in short supply have choices. In order to attract and retain them, you need to know what's important to them, and do a better job of meeting their wants than your competition. What do they consider when making job change choices?

In interviews and focus groups with 5000+ employees, I have sought to find out what is important to them in deciding where to work. I have identified 26 factors they most commonly consider when they evaluate whether to stay or accept a job elsewhere.

Regarding Work Itself

- ❑ Important/meaningful/interesting work
- ❑ Clear direction and realistic expectations
- ❑ The resources needed to do the work
- ❑ Well-maintained current tools/equipment
- ❑ Reasonable freedom to perform one's work

Regarding Relations with Others

- ❑ Mutual respect and trust
- ❑ Supportive leadership
- ❑ Helpful and friendly co-workers
- ❑ Honesty and openness to differences
- ❑ Recognition
- ❑ Sense of participation and partnership
- ❑ Feeling of being "in" on what happens
- ❑ A way to resolve issues productively

Regarding the Organization

- ❑ Credible leadership (who know what they are doing and who "walk the talk")
- ❑ Policies and rules that make sense

❏ Fair treatment
❏ Esprit de corps - pride of being associated with the employer
❏ Sense of control over one's life (balance between work and the rest of life)

Regarding One's Career

❏ A feeling of competence/mastery
❏ A mentor - someone who takes interest in them and their career
❏ Opportunity for and support of professional growth
❏ Growth of one's value in the job market
❏ How one sees oneself in one's career in relation to one's peers

Regarding Compensation and Benefits

❏ Competitive and fair pay
❏ Benefits tailored to one's needs
❏ Tax-sheltered way to build wealth (401[K] or stock options)

Other

❏ Housing (commute, cost, schools, etc.)

Where is job security as a factor? In the past decade, it has been supplanted by the desire to continue growing and gaining value so as to be readily employable.

How important is each factor to the people who work for you? How well is your business providing what the employees you want to hire and retain are looking for? What do you need to do to assure the attractiveness and competitiveness of your business for the staff you need? I recommend surveying employees periodically using a comprehensive instrument. They are your "customers" for your work environment. A comprehensive survey can tell you what they consider to be important, how well you are doing in meeting their needs, and how you compare with your job market competitors. A quick and inexact alternative is to provide the people on your team with a copy of these factors and ask them to rank order them in order of importance to them. The composite picture of their rank ordering will give you a snapshot of what is important to them.

In boom times, you need to attract and retain talented people. Some people think that retention is not an issue during down times. That is not so! Especially when having to let people go, you need to make sure that the survivors (people who remain), are on board and not seeking to jump ship in despair. Knowing and providing what is important to your particular team is critical.

4.2

12 Tips for Selecting People for Your Team

As a leader, your success depends on your team. With the right people, you can accomplish miracles. With the wrong, your accomplishments will be limited and your headaches many!

Too often, managers feel pressured to fill a job vacancy quickly, so they cut corners. As a result, hiring mistakes are the most common cause of terminations. Here are 12 tips to help you improve your hiring process and your "batting average" in selecting people for your team:

1. Don't feel pressured to fill a job just because it is vacant. If it is essential to have it filled immediately, get a contract employee or someone from a temporary agency. That takes the pressure off of you. People are available at all skill levels on a temporary basis.

2. A track team or a basketball team? In selecting people, a lot depends on the sort of team that you need. On a track team, you have specialists who require little integration with each other. On a basketball team, although each player has a defined role, all have to work in unison. If your team must work in unison, hire people who are committed to helping you win—as a team.

3. Don't clone yourself! Part of the strength of your team is in its diversity of views and talents. Analyze the outlooks, abilities and motivations you need to make your team complete. You can't have a winning team with only quarterbacks. You need talented people for the rest of the roles, too. Get people with a variety of perspectives and abilities who have "fire in their belly" for your team's mission. Your team will undoubtedly confront some trying situations, so you'll need people with dedication and commitment to your mission, and to working as part of your team.

4. "Inherited" people When you become a leader of an established team, you "inherit"' people. If you were part of the team before being promoted, then you know the people you will lead. (See chapters 8.3 and 8.4.) If not, you will need to get to know the people you lead and what they do. Either way, interview them as though you were selecting them. In effect, you are. You need enough information to ensure that you have the right complement of people to accomplish your mission. Determine not only their competence, but also whether the leadership you can provide and their needs for leadership are compatible. You may want to change some assignments, as well as people. However, for the sake of your credibility, hold off on making changes until you can demonstrate that you know the team as a whole, the issues you face, and each member as an individual.

5. Define job requirements and expectations carefully   What does the job really involve? What specific abilities (aptitudes, knowledge and skills) do you need? What motivators are best for this type of work? With whom will the applicant work? What personal qualities are best suited to work for you, and with people who will be frequent contacts? How important is each requirement? Which ones are critical? What is the minimum level you can accept on each? You need a firm grasp of the requirements to screen applicants effectively.

If your business has a personnel or HR department, they can help you recruit and screen. If it doesn't, consider using an employment agency or contract recruiter. A good pro can save you time, and may have sources of applicants you are unaware of. If you plan to advertise and screen with no intermediary, at least ask a sample of your employees to review the ad copy. Ask if the proposed ad: a) depicts the job accurately, and b) will attract the applicants you want.

Post the job internally. It may be of interest to a current employee. Also, current employees are sometimes your best source of referrals for applicants.

Whether or not you have an affirmative action plan, look for applicants who will help the composition of your work force represent the community your business serves. Not only is it part of your social responsibility, it is good business to have people who can relate to the circumstances and needs of your customers.

6. Team interviews   The people you select will have to work with others on your team, and they may have to interact with others in your business. Ask colleagues who understand the job, and who will work closely with it, to help you screen and interview. Share the job requirements with them so that they know what you are looking for, and can evaluate applicants on the same requirements. Assemble the people involved to orchestrate the interviews, and subsequently to discuss with you the candidates they interviewed. Each will have a different perspective, so you will have a richer picture of each candidate than if you had done all the interviewing yourself. In addition, when you choose a consensus candidate you will have better buy-in and peer support for the person you choose.

7. Plan the interviews   Plan your interview questions to focus on the critical job requirements. While you don't need to ask questions in a rigid sequence, a list of questions is like a shopping list: it reminds you of what you are "shopping" for so that you don't forget anything important.

Though interviewing is a two-way process, you want to make sure you get the information you need for a fair decision. Asking the right questions in the right way is critical. (For interview questions, see chapter 4.4, "Planning Interviews to Select the Right Applicant.")

People answer questions not only with what they say, but how they say it, and with their "body language". Listen carefully with your eyes and ears for their spoken and unspoken answers.

To reduce the chance of discrimination charges arising from interviews, avoid questions that could be interpreted as dealing with race, color, national origin, religion, age, sex, provisions for child care, physical handicap, veteran status, or sexual preference. One is permitted by law to seek information, and make employment decisions, only on factors that can be demonstrably related to predicting job performance.

8. Applicant evaluation On a blank sheet of paper draw a dozen horizontal and vertical lines to make a matrix. List the most critical requirements on one axis. Enter the names of applicants on the other. As you interview applicants, evaluate them on each job requirement. 10 points = ideal, 5 = acceptable. This creates a profile of strengths and weaknesses. It increases the objectivity of your applicant analysis. Eliminate anyone you rate less than a 5 on a critical requirement.

9. Check references of previous employers for the top candidates. It may be difficult to make contact with people who actually know the applicant, but it is worthwhile. Ask, "What does it take to bring out the best in (applicant)?" "What brings out the worst in (applicant)?" Answers to these questions can give you some helpful insights. Evaluate reference information carefully, as well as biases of the person giving it. (See chapter 4.5)

10. Choose carefully! It is improbable that you will find someone who scores 10 on each requirement. Analyze the candidates on the matrix for the best profile of strengths, and the most manageable vulnerabilities. Avoid anyone with a vulnerability for which you can't compensate. Select people who will blossom in the role you have to offer and with your leadership. Compare your analysis with your intuitive evaluation and the team interview feedback. Choose the candidate who, based on all things considered, has the best chance of success.

11. Extend your job offer In offering a job, communicate that you really want the candidate by making your best offer. Have good reasons for the terms you offer and explain them. The objective is to communicate that you really want the applicant and have put together an attractive offer. Avoid dickering. If an applicant is inclined to dicker, he/she may want to dicker about all sorts of other matters. Confirm your offer.

12. Thank applicants Thank everyone who applied, either by letter or phone. Many employers treat applicants like dirt. If you want to attract top employees, treat applicants the way you would want to be treated. An applicant you turn down today may be someone you want to hire later on. You want to leave a good impression of your company as an employer, and you as a leader.

Hiring is an art. There are many variables in terms of job requirements and applicant qualifications and desires that must be balanced. You reduce the risk of hiring a problem person when you involve the people with whom an applicant will have to work as part of your hiring process.

4.3

Selecting an Effective Leader

"Select in haste, regret at leisure."

Effective leaders inspire and enable people to perform at their best in the pursuit of common goals. Leadership requires an infectious passion for achieving goals and results, values consistent with the organization's culture, fairness, caring and support for the people one leads, and above all, credibility.

Whether a leader is effective depends on the alignment between his/her values and leadership style, the goals to be accomplished, and the values and needs of the people to be led. A leader's constituents include not only the people who report to him/her, but also peers and higher-ups. Think of them as "customers for leadership." If a leader's "customers" don't buy into his/her leadership, then instead of supporting their leader, they may engage in subversion. In other words, a leader at odds with his/her "customers," can be not only ineffective, but also counterproductive. Thus, alignment and mutual support between a leader and his/her "customers" is essential for a leader to be effective and for a team to accomplish its goals.

Why are fewer than one in five leaders in my surveys rated as truly effective? The primary reason is because leaders typically are chosen more for their knowledge of the goals to be achieved than for their ability to lead others. People assume that someone who is respected for his/her technical know-how will also be a good leader. While a leader has to be knowledgeable in the field of endeavor, being too knowledgeable can lead to micro-management and ineffective use of time and resources. An effective leader must have enough technical knowledge to understand the issues, ask insightful questions, provide direction and monitor progress. He/she must also have leadership skills consistent with the needs of the group.

Involve "customers" in selection If you want better selection of leaders, involve the people in the selection process who will have to work with him/her. When they have helped choose their leader, they have an ownership stake in making the relationship work. Not only does this empower the people, it also creates a higher level of accountability on the part of the leader to the people with whom he/she will have to work. This is the process I recommend:

1. Before screening begins, create a selection team including the "customers." Have them define, as a group, their needs and expectations, and the leadership qualities they need to bring out the best in them. These will become the factors for applicant evaluation and selection. Though you will want a list tailored to your specific needs, you will probably want to consider some of the following:

- ❑ Knowledge of the challenges the leader will face
- ❑ Passion for dealing with the challenges and achieving the goals
- ❑ Self confidence (without being conceited)
- ❑ Values consistent with the organization and appropriate for the challenges
- ❑ Willingness to face up to and work out the tough challenges
- ❑ Willingness/ability to look at issues creatively and from a variety of perspectives
- ❑ Honesty, openness, integrity and credibility
- ❑ Ethical standards
- ❑ Ability to earn trust and commitment among his/her constituents
- ❑ Ability to inspire and empower the people he/she will lead
- ❑ Ability to listen attentively, and express oneself clearly and persuasively
- ❑ Ability to balance the needs of the organization and team members to get results
- ❑ Ability to sort through competing priorities and focus on what's important
- ❑ Ability to balance the need for action and consensus in decisions
- ❑ Follow-through on commitments

2. Create an applicant evaluation matrix (See chapter 4.2, #8) using your selection factors to profile and compare each applicant.

3. Draft interview questions to elicit the information needed, both for personal and reference checking interviews. (See chapter 4.4, Interview Questions to Select the Right Applicant.)

4. Train the selection team in interviewing skills, if they have not had such training. For interviews in which more than one selection team member is present, orchestrate the questions to be asked so that each member is responsible for some. Make sure that each knows his/her role.

5. Have the selection team interview the top candidates, individually or in small groups, and record and report their findings to the rest of the team in a subsequent team meeting.

6. In a facilitated meeting of the selection team, discuss the evaluation profile of each candidate. What are his/her strengths, and what causes concern? Values and leadership style are both difficult to change and critical to leadership credibility.

7. Strive for a consensus decision. Seldom will you find a candidate with whom someone doesn't have a concern. Explore their concerns and try to get answers for them. The question is whether they can "live with" and support the candidate. Don't appoint anyone team members cannot "live with."

Yes, this process takes extra time. Is it worth it? Most definitely! Its value is in the multiple perspectives brought to the selection decision, the understanding of a leader's "customers" of the demands of the job, and in the support and cooperation a leader will have who has been selected this way.

4.4

Planning Interview Questions to Select the Right Applicant

Hiring the right applicant is critical. Hire the right person and your problems are half solved. Hire the wrong person and your problems have only begun!

The challenge is to hire the "right" person, someone who has both the ability to perform the job, and the motivation to perform it in your work setting. Both are essential. Ability is a combination of aptitudes, knowledge and skills. Motivation is related to short and long term goals, values and traits.

What resources do you have to help determine who to hire? The application or resume provides data on education, experience, and accomplishments. In some cases, validated tests can be used to determine job knowledge and skills. Interviews of the applicant and references are used to delve further into knowledge, skills and experience, and to gain insight into the goals, values and traits that shape attitude.

Behavior on the job is influenced by values, attitudes and the social sanctions of the work place. The social sanctions, usually expressed as values or policies, define what is considered appropriate behavior. While you can establish certain standards of behavior, it is difficult to change one's values and attitudes. Sometimes attitudes change to conform to required behavior, but it is easier to hire people whose basic attitudes are reasonably consistent with the behavioral expectations of your organization.

Interviews with applicants and their references are the most common way to assess knowledge and skills, and determine attitudes. The success of interviews depends on asking the right questions, and interpreting answers correctly.

Planning

Prior to conducting interviews, prepare a description of the position you seek to fill, including expectations, and analyze it. Determine the education, skills, experience, goals, values and personal traits that are essential for success. Determine what information you can obtain solely from the application or resume, and what you seek to discover from interviews. In a sense, this is like creating a shopping list. It helps you organize your questions so that you don't forget one. Draft a script of questions to use in your interviews. You will probably not follow the script exactly, but the fact that you have formulated the questions you want to ask will improve how you ask them, and will serve as a check to make sure that you ask them.

Questions

A question should have a purpose. It should be designed to provide you with the information you need to evaluate an applicant for a specific job.

There is an art to asking questions. You need to understand the types of questions, which to use for a given purpose, and how to state a question. Also, questions posed to an applicant or an applicant's reference should be stated in a way that avoids implying the desired answer. The objective is to get as close to the truth as possible. If you give clues to the answer you want, the applicant may bend the truth. These are four basic types of questions:

1. Closed questions seek a brief, factual answer. *(In your career, who is the best supervisor for whom you have worked?)* They are appropriate for verifying data, confirming one's understanding, and for prefacing a probing question.

2. Open questions seek to draw out the applicant's views. *(What aspects of your job did you enjoy most?)*

3. Probing questions prompt the applicant to expand on a previously stated answer. *(And what did she do to help bring out the best in you?)* This type of

question can be useful in clarifying one's understanding of a previous statement.

4. Test questions pose a situation the applicant may have to face in the job, and ask how he/she would handle it. *(While in the cafeteria, you see a friend grab a candy bar off the rack and stuff it in her purse. What would you do?)*

Questions must be related to the actual job, and posed to all applicants the same way to avoid discrimination.

There is no "magic" set of questions that you can use with all applicants in all situations. Questions need to be tailored to the circumstance to be appropriate, but the following may help you think of questions you want to ask:

- *Why did you leave your last job? Or, Why are you considering leaving your present job?*
- *What new knowledge and skills did you learn from your last job?*
- *Describe for me what was one of your most challenging assignments, and how you met the challenge.*
- *Describe a situation that did not turn out as you planned. What was your reaction? What did you learn from it?*
- *What was the most difficult (or unpleasant) part of your last job?*
- *How do you feel about (some unpleasant aspect of the work)?*
- *What were some of the pressures you experienced in your past jobs? How did you deal with them?*
- *What are your career goals? How do you see this job fitting into your career?*
- *What has given you a sense of satisfaction in your last three jobs?*
- *What would you have changed, if you could, about your last three jobs?*
- *What have your previous supervisors done to help bring out the best in you?*
- *What have your previous supervisors done that made your job more difficult?*
- *What has been your experience in working as part of a team? What do you find satisfying about being part of a team? What problems does being part of a team create for you?*
- *What have you learned about working with people from your previous supervisors, co-workers, customers or clients?*
- *Please describe a situation at work where someone created a problem for you. What did you do to resolve it?*
- *Who has had the most influence in shaping your work habits? How?*

❑ *A friend with whom you work has been reprimanded for too many late arrivals and is on warning. Another late arrival this month and she may lose her job. A few minutes before the start of her shift she phones you to say she will be fifteen minutes late. She asks you to clock in for her so that it will not look as though she was late. This is contrary to policy. How would you handle this?*

❑ *What information do I need to know about your references to understand the point of view of the people giving them?*

❑ *Is there anything else I need to know in considering you for this job?*

General Tips

The interview consists of an opening, information exchange, and closing. The opening is to put the applicant as ease, as much as possible, with "small talk." The body of the interview is the information exchange. That is when you pose your planned questions, answer those of the applicant, and make your pitch to "sell" your job and organization, if you are interested in the applicant. In the close, you thank the applicant for his/her time, and indicate when and how you will be in further contact.

Give the applicant your undivided attention. Take brief, key-word notes during the interview. Save writing your more detailed notes until afterwards.

Sometimes an applicant will say something to which you take exception. If that happens, don't argue (unless your objective is to see how the applicant behaves when confronted). Your objective in the interview is not to convince the applicant of your view. If the applicant's statement is pertinent to your evaluation, you can say, *"I'm interested in your statement about _____. Can you tell me more?"* If the applicant asks for your views, you can say, *"Our time together is limited. If I explain my views now, we may not have time to accomplish the purpose of this interview."*

A risk in asking open or probing questions is that the applicant may not know when to stop answering them without some clues from you. The key is to interrupt the applicant politely, communicate that your question has been answered, and move on to the next one. It is more polite to interrupt at the end of a sentence, but you can also interrupt in mid-sentence. Say, *"Let's move on to* (your next question)." As you interrupt, raise your wrist inconspicuously so that the palm of your hand faces the applicant to signify "stop." This "body language" reinforces your message.

People express themselves not only with words, but also with intonation and "body language," and what they choose *not* to answer. Listen with your ears as as your eyes for their spoken and unspoken messages. Look for changes in voice, wording, eye contact, posture, hand movements, etc. as they answer your questions.

Interviewing applicants and selecting employees to work for you is one of your most important management responsibilities. Your success, your organization's success, and the success of the people you hire are based on obtaining valid information and using it to make sound judgments. Interviewing is one important tool available to you to obtain the information you need. Planning your interviews increases the probability that you will obtain that information.

Interviewing is a skill. Like the development of other skills, it requires practice to gain proficiency.

4.5

Reference Interview Guide

References can provide valuable information about an applicant, but they may be difficult to obtain. Some people have sued their former employer because of reference information they thought was false or harmful. As a result, the Human Resource department is reluctant to do more than confirm minimal information about past employees. If you contact HR for reference information, you may only verify dates of employment and job titles. Moreover, they typically don't have the perspective to provide you with the information you need to evaluate how the applicant might work out in your job.

Sources of information In checking an applicant's references, the most significant information about the applicant can usually be obtained from former supervisors and coworkers. To obtain first hand information, ask the applicant for the names and phone numbers of former supervisors and coworkers. Phone them directly. Indicate that you were given their name and phone number in order to check the applicant's references.

Purpose The purpose of the reference interview is to verify information, and to get views on how the applicant performed and behaved in other jobs. The information you obtain should help you evaluate how the applicant will adjust to your environment.

The interview When you begin a reference check interview, state who you are and your reason for calling. State that you are authorized by the applicant to obtain reference information. Ask whether the person with whom you are speaking has time to talk with you.

"Hello! I am (your name) of (name of organization). I have been talking with (applicant) about a job we have for (job title). He/she authorized me to phone you for reference information. Any information you provide me will be confidential. My decision to hire, or not to hire, ____ will take into account what you say, but will not be based solely on that. Do you have a few minutes now to talk with me?"

If the reference has time to talk, ask your questions. If not, schedule a time to phone back.

The reference may say that he/she is not at liberty to discuss the applicant because of company policy. The following may get the reticent to open up:

"I'm sorry about that. I don't want to get you in trouble. I'd like to emphasize that whatever you say will be treated confidentially. With your knowledge of _____, you are in an ideal position to advise me on how to help _____ succeed in our job."

Questions to ask The kind of questions to ask depend on what information you need to obtain. If you missed specific points on the application or during the interview, now is the time to get them. To make sure that you cover all the points on which you want information, it is helpful to have a list of questions. Some general questions for probing about the applicant are as follows:

- *In what capacity do you know ____?* (This question is intended to find out whether the person was a supervisor, a friend, a colleague, or what.)
- *When did he/she begin working for you?*
- *What were his/her duties and responsibilities? Were there any changes in his/her duties and responsibilities while he/she reported to you?*
- *What types of assignments could he/she handle independently? In what situations would he/she be required to seek your approval before taking action?*
- *How did he/she respond to guidance and constructive criticism?*
- *What progress did he/she make in learning from you?*
- *How accurate was his/her work? Did he/she learn from mistakes? How defensive was he/she when an error was detected?*
- *Please describe his/her relations with your customers? With you?*
- *If he/she worked as part of a team, what was his/her affect on teammates?*
- *What were ____'s best qualities?*
- *What would you have liked to change about ____?*

❑ *How many days of unscheduled absences did he/she have in the past two years?*

❑ *How frequently was he/she late to work? For what reasons?*

❑ *Did he/she do anything that caused concern to you or others in your business?*

❑ *What were the circumstances leading to his/her leaving your job?*

❑ *Under what circumstances would you re-employ him/her?*

❑ *What reference information did you get on him/her? How accurate was it?*

❑ *Is there any additional information that I should know about _____ before deciding whether to offer _____ our job?*

For a perspective on the applicant in your job, describe it briefly:

Let me tell you about the job for which we are considering _____. (Give a brief description.) What strengths would _____ bring to this job? What reservations might you have about him/her in this job? If we hire _____, what additional training or coaching do you recommend to improve his/her chances of success?

The information you obtain may correspond with what you obtained from the application and your interviews, or there may be some differences. If there is a discrepancy between what the applicant told you and what the reference said, say:

"(Applicant) told me _____, and now you have told me something different. How do you account for the difference?"

In closing ask
"Do you have any other words of wisdom for me in considering _____ for our job?"

Thank the person for providing you with reference information. He/she has placed trust in you to use the information wisely, especially if some critical comments were shared.

Making sense of your information While reference information can be helpful, it must be treated as just another piece of information. What you get may be accurate, or it may be biased. Be sure to evaluate this information as carefully as you evaluate the information from the employment interview. Small discrepancies do not necessarily indicate that one person or the other is lying. They may only indicate differences in perception. Large discrepancies should be investigated, as mentioned above. It is sometimes necessary to talk with another reference to obtain a third-party view of a discrepancy.

If the information you get from one source is negative, don't disqualify the applicant solely on that basis. Check further. Find out more about the person who gave you negative information. Sometimes seemingly negative information from one person is actually positive when you delve further.

An applicant's most recent supervisor usually has the most up-to-date picture of the applicant's abilities and personal characteristics. However, occasionally an applicant's most recent job has been the wrong one for him/her. Sometimes a person will be a star employee in one work environment, and a problem in another. In that event, you need to check with other previous supervisors. When you get mixed reviews on an applicant, you have to figure out which are most applicable to your work situation.

When a pattern of negative reports about an applicant supports your observations from your interviews, dismiss the applicant from further consideration.

Communication with applicant When a consistent pattern of reference information prompts you rule out an applicant from further consideration, your decision must be communicated very carefully to the applicant. You don't want to get yourself and the references in trouble with a defamation of character suit. Wait to communicate with the applicant until you have selected the applicant you want. Then say:

"We have made a hiring decision for our _____ job. You had a lot of competition. We have offered the job to the applicant we believe is best suited to our needs. We really appreciate your time, interest and patience."

If a rejected applicant asks why he/she did not get the job, avoid attributing your decision to the references. In all probability, the pattern of references only underscores concerns that came out of the interview. Instead, emphasize:

"You were a serious candidate. As strong a candidate as you were, we were very fortunate to have a candidate who meets our needs even better than you."

You need all the information you can get to make effective hiring decisions. You are unlikely to "bat 1000." But, valid reference information intelligently used can improve your batting average substantially, and save you grief.

4.6

Providing Employment References

Current legal opinions typically warn employers against providing reference information for former employees, other than verifying employment dates, job title and salary. The safest route is to accept current legal advice. Some people have been successful in court proving that reference information from a former employer denied them an employment opportunity.

In some organizations, a policy limited to verifying employment dates and job title is appropriate. It is consistent with the way people are managed, and provides prudent legal protection. Providing additional information could expose the poor quality of their leadership, employment practices, or their HR staff.

What is safe from the legal perspective is not necessarily good for managing people. I'll explain.

In this day and age, employment security comes from being attractive in the job market. Few people look to a career with one employer, so they want reference information that will support them when they are competing for another job.

A verification-only reference policy seeks to protect an organization from the occasional problem employee. In so doing, it treats all employees as potential problems. Good employees resent being lumped in with problem employees. As a result, they figure ways to circumvent HR so that prospective employers can have direct access to the people who will speak well of them. In spite of company policy, supervisors and coworkers give reference information "off the record" because they know that "what goes around comes around." In other words, a verification-only policy may be counter-cultural and ineffective.

An alternative to a policy of verifying only dates of employment, salary and job title is used successfully by some organizations. They treat terminations as a natural event. They recognize that employees will eventually leave, and that they should be prepared for such events. They let employees know what kinds of information will be provided for references when they leave, so employees know in advance what they can expect. Employees know that preparation of a reference letter is included as a planned part of their out-processing when they leave.

Negotiated reference   When an employee leaves, the supervisor and a member of the HR staff typically meet with the employee to draft a reference letter. The objective of the letter is to provide factual information about the employee's history with the organization to help both the employee and prospective employers. Not only does it contain dates of employment, salary history, and job titles, it also contains such information as:

- A description of job responsibilities and career moves
- Special skills or knowledge used on the job
- Special accomplishments
- The number of unplanned days absent in the past two years
- Accident history, as appropriate
- Sales rankings for the past two years, as appropriate

❑ Other quantifiable information of significance
❑ Disciplinary actions taken, if any
❑ Grievances filed, if any, and their outcome
❑ Reason for leaving, as appropriate

The employee receives several copies of the reference letter to use in his/her job search. The letter's contents also serve as the basis of information used by HR and past supervisors to answer reference requests. A copy is included in the employee's personnel record with his/her signature authorizing the organization to share the information with prospective employers authorized by the employee.

The reference letter "negotiated" by an HR representative, the supervisor and employee is viewed positively. Employees know while they are working what information will be included in a reference letter when they leave. It has a positive effect on performance. The process of creating the reference letter also gives the employee a feeling that he/she has had input into what will be remembered and said about his/her employment. It is the essence of "no surprises" management. It actually provides greater control, fairness and consistency than a verification-only approach. I have not seen a successful legal challenge when this approach is used properly.

When to use A policy of providing reference letters, as described, is appropriate only in organizations that believe that policies should be designed for the 95% of employees who are good, and are willing to accept some legal risk for the sake of good people management. (You can never protect yourself adequately with policies for the 5% of your employees who are your problems. If you try, you may create an environment that turns good employees into problems!)

What posture should you take regarding reference information? That depends on the nature of your organization. Do most of your employees perform well? Are your supervisors generally well respected? Do you seek and employ career-minded employees? Are you willing to accept a little risk for the sake of creating a work environment that brings out the best in people? If you can answer, "*yes*" to these questions, then this approach to reference information may be a real alternative. If you have to answer "*no*" to some of these questions, then just verifying employment dates, salary and job title is the "*safe*" approach.

5

Involving the People You Lead to Bring Out the Best in Them

5.1

Decision Making — Command vs. Consensus

Can an organization really be run by consensus? Does consensus = unanimous agreement? Isn't it appropriate to give orders sometimes?

Command The goal of command decisions is immediate response. The person giving an order has the authority to give it, and is assumed to know what he/she is doing.

Command decisions are appropriate when the person in charge knows more than the others, and when fast action counts. A pilot in an emergency must act quickly. There isn't time, nor is it appropriate, to hold a meeting with the crew.

Consensus The goal of consensus decisions is general agreement and sufficient support that the decision can be implemented without delay. It is more inclusive than majority rule (51% for, 49% against). Unanimity = 100% agreement, and that's not always possible. Consensus decisions seek sufficient agreement and buy-in from stakeholders to acheive a workable outcome.

The consensus process is appropriate for issues where multiple perspectives need to be considered. It presumes that no one person knows as much about the issue as all the stakeholders know as a group. It also presumes that stakeholders need to buy into a decision for maximum acceptance. A revision to a sales incentive system needs input from people who will administer it, and those whose behavior it is intended to influence, to avoid resistance in implementation.

Choosing an approach An effective leader uses each approach appropriately. The first task of a turnaround manager is to stop financial "hemorrhaging." That requires quick decisions, but bringing an organization back to health requires actions that have broad-based support. That requires a consensus.

To decide which approach to use, ask:

1. Is this a life/death issue needing an immediate decision/action?
2. Do I have all the relevant information I need to make an informed decision myself?
3. Who are the people affected by this, and what do they know that I might not?
4. Who has an important perspective on this issue and a stake in this decision?
5. Who has to implement (live with) this decision? How are they apt to accept it if they have no input?

For consensus decision-making, a respected representative of each critical "stake" should be invited and encouraged to participate.

Negotiating consensus Consensus building is a form of negotiation. The key is to find an alternative that people can "live with." This may not be the one that is technically the best, but it is one for which there is sufficient support to make it work. It is a repetitive process for which facilitator skills are helpful. *"John, if I understand your position, you have problems with _____ because of _____. Is that correct? If we changed _____, could you live with it? How about everyone else? If we make this change, can you live with it?"* When the critical stakeholders can "live with" a decision, you have consensus.

The practice of management is an art. Nowhere is it more evident than in making decisions. Consensus, where it is not needed, can constipate an organization. It can also be a crutch for managers who are paralyzed when having to make a decision. Command decisions where consensus is needed can also constipate an organization from resistance by stakeholders who have been excluded from the process. Achieving a balance between command and consensus is an art that is aided by intuition and perfected through learning from experience!

5.2

Taking Responsibility for Your Decisions

Some time in the next year, you will make a decision that you will subsequently regret. No, I can't guarantee that you will, nor would I wish that on you. But, there is a high probability that you will. Life is a series of decisions—most work out, but not all. I hope those that don't will be lower on the scale of seriousness than "life-threatening" or "career-defining."

Every decision carries with it an element of risk. I have yet to meet someone who gets up in the morning and says, *"Today I plan to make a really bad decision!"* Most decisions that go sour are not willful endeavors to cause harm. They result from faulty assumptions, not involving appropriate stakeholders, and frequently, inattention. The treacherous center divider along curvy Highway 17 between Santa Cruz and Los Gatos, CA, is a monument to decisions that did not work out!

George Washington reportedly cut down his father's cherry tree. When confronted by his father about the truncated tree, he said he could not tell a lie. He owned up to his deed. Although his father was not pleased to lose the tree, he was pleased that George accepted responsibility for his actions. This story is taught in grammar school, but some people just don't get it. Richard Nixon probably would have remained President if he had said, *"Oops! I really goofed! We shouldn't have broken into those offices. I apologize. What can I do to set things right?"* Although taking responsibility for his actions immediately would have been difficult and embarrassing, he could have saved himself and his country a lot of agony. The same applies for President Clinton.

People can accept a mistake, even one as repugnant as President Nixon's. But, what instantly drains their reservoir of good will is denial, deceit and cover-up. As difficult as it may be, telling the truth initially is easier in the long run than living with a lie. So you get caught speeding. Is it the police officer's fault? Probably not. Is it worth stretching the truth about? No. Own up to it. *"I'm sorry, officer. I guess that I let my foot get too heavy on the gas pedal."* Who knows, he/she may be so stunned by your honesty that you get off with a warning.

At work, one of your decisions backfires. Do you try to blame others? If it was your decision, take responsibility for it. If you attempt a cover-up or to blame others, you "shoot yourself in the foot." You can't fool others most of the time. If you try, the only person you're fooling is yourself. Your credibility is enhanced when you own up to what people know is your responsibility. *"Oops! This didn't work out as I had hoped. I guess its `back to the drawing board!'"*

Guidelines Here are guidelines I have found helpful:

- ❑ Use the resources available to you. If possible, before making a decision, consult the people who have a stake in it.
- ❑ Don't do things that would "give you heartburn" if you saw them reported in the headlines of the newspaper.
- ❑ Pay attention to details. Most great plans that fail do so because of faulty execution. "The devil is in the details!"

It isn't worth "losing your tail to save your face." No matter how careful you are, you're bound to make some mistakes. In most cases, your credibility hinges more on how you take responsibility for them than on the mistakes themselves.

5.3

Encouraging Healthy Dissent

"I knew what would happen. I could have saved us at least $750,000. But I also knew that it would be career suicide to raise my questions about that decision. No one wanted the tough questions asked. Their minds were made up."

Is "healthy dissent" an oxymoron like "jumbo shrimp" or "friendly fire?" To some people, dissent is to be avoided. It potentially threatens power, control and ego, and can derail pet projects.

One symptom that an organization is in trouble is a lack of expressed dissent. That is not to say that everyone agrees with all proposals and actions. It only means that people who can see through the "emperor's new clothes" have learned that expressing their views is risky and unappreciated. So even though they can see a mistake in the making, they keep quiet. They have seen or heard of the consequences of dissent. Their self-preservation instincts keep them quiet.

A healthy organization encourages and rewards people for "finding the flies in the ointment." All decisions have pros and cons, and both need to be addressed in order to arrive at an informed decision. It is less expensive to discover the dark side of a decision before it is made. You may still decide to proceed with it, but at least you can plan how to minimize its consequences.

Every organization has a political system, though some are more intense than others. People learn quickly what is politically correct, and what may destroy their career. Most of the people I have interviewed during organizational reviews prefer to work in an environment that encourages and rewards them for expressing honest and genuine dissent. But, most are reticent until they have seen that raising tough questions is actually safe, appreciated and rewarded.

How are people treated when they raise tough questions or express dissent? Should you even care? Unless you want to be "captain of the lemmings" (who follow their leaders to the sea unquestioningly and drown), you need a broad spectrum of views on issues critical to your business. You need people who really care about your business, and who feel free to call "time out," when they question what's going on. As Crosby, Stills and Nash sing, "You've got to speak out against the madness." And like it or not, people sometimes get caught up in the madness and lose sight of reality. As the above quote indicates, you can make expensive mistakes when people think they will be ostracized for asking tough questions. You can't afford that!

Take Stock

- ❑ Observe your meetings. Is there balanced discussion of both the pros and cons? Are the "what if" questions being asked?
- ❑ Have you been surprised about the resistance with which a decision was received?
- ❑ Has anyone who raised questions or expressed dissent been "banished to Siberia?"

If people refrain from asking tough questions, or expressing dissent, you may be "captain of the lemmings." That is a distinction you don't need!

5.4

Delegation—Empowering People for Accomplishment

As a leader, your role is to inspire and enable people to achieve a common goal. You do not do all the work yourself. You must rely on others, even though you are still responsible. That means that you need to have people:

- ❑ Who you trust
- ❑ Who know what is expected of them
- ❑ Who are competent
- ❑ Who have the resources, freedom and support to accomplish their goal
- ❑ Who provide you with the information you need to support them in their endeavor

Most people really want to perform at their best. Here are some tips to help you empower your team to accomplish important goals.

Set the goal Delegation is enlisting/enrolling/empowering others to accomplish a goal that is of value to you, your business, and the people to whom you delegate. Everyone involved needs to derive a direct or indirect benefit from participation. Thus, in presenting an opportunity, focus on the outcome and potential benefits that will inspire others to commit to it. Explain the goal to be accomplished, the time in which it needs to be completed, and *why* it needs to be done. People need to understand the "whys" in order to place the assignment in context.

Choose the project team The people who need to be part of a project team are:

- ❑ People who add the perspective of the key stakeholders affected by the work of the team.
- ❑ People who will be involved in the implementation.

These are the people who need to have "buy-in" for the project to succeed. All need to be invited to participate. Some may not need to participate, so long as they believe that someone is watching out for their interests.

Encourage buy-in People commit to what they identify with and feel they can contribute to in a significant way. The more their involvement in designing the process by which they work toward their outcome, the greater their sense of ownership and commitment. Thus, in delegating, it is important to paint a clear picture of the desired outcome and provide enough "space" for the people who will be following through to become owners/partners in the venture.

Test for understanding Ask, *"What is your understanding of this assignment?"* to verify that you have a mutual understanding. If they can describe what they are embarking on to your satisfaction, then you are on the same wavelength. Don't ask, *"Do you understand?"* It is an ineffectual question. Some people are unaware of what they don't understand or do not want to admit that they don't understand.

Clarify the approach Ask how he/she plans to approach the assignment, and what challenges he/she anticipates. You don't want to micro-manage, but sometimes the "hows" are critical. The ends don't necessarily justify the means, as President Nixon painfully discovered with his Committee to Re-elect the President in 1972. It is important for people to understand the critical values and ethical issues, and for you to understand enough of their plan that you can live with their approach. Knowing and approving a game plan is not micro-management. Constantly fiddling with it is.

Confirm understandings in a plan When you delegate you are still responsible and accountable for what you have delegated. You, however, cannot personally be in control, yet you need to be sure that there are controls. For any project of some length, ask the project team to develop a project proposal or plan confirming their understanding of the assignment. This is a way for the team to work out their approach and confirm their understanding of the desired outcome with you. It should include:

- ❏ The goal and anticipated approach to achieving it
- ❏ The criteria/standards by which their work will be judged
- ❏ The resources they will need
- ❏ The support they need from you as the sponsor
- ❏ The anticipated schedule
- ❏ The updating and review process to keep you informed and avoid surprises

Team training If the project you are delegating is assigned to a team, provide team training. Every team has its own personality and team dynamics that affect how it works. Most cross-functional teams need at least one session on how they will work together as a team.

Support It is natural for project teams to get "stuck" at some point. They may not know how to deal with resistance from people who don't want the project complete. Internal conflict may cripple them. Others may want to change the focus or scope of the goal. In any event, you need to find out when they become "stuck," and be there for them to help them get "unstuck."

Celebration and learning   The completion of any delegated assignment needs to be celebrated and the team recognized for their accomplishment. Celebration does not have to be big. Even coffee and donuts in honor of completion will do. This is necessary to recognize the people on the team and to bring closure. A natural and valuable follow-on to the celebration is to review how the project went:

- ❏ What went well?
- ❏ What could have gone better?
- ❏ What was learned?
- ❏ What learning needs to be passed on to others as "organizational learning?"

Organizations that fail to conduct such a review and learn from it are doomed to make the same mistakes repeatedly.

The people to whom you delegate are your allies. They want to succeed, and in the process, "look good" themselves and make you "look good." They need to know what is expected and why. They need to have reasonable freedom to exercise their creativity and judgment in order to feel a sense of ownership and pride in what they do. They need the resources and support to accomplish their goal. You need enough information to know when to contribute your help, and to be confident that your team has matters under control.

5.5

Staying on Course — Monitoring Progress

Let's say that you decide to drive across the USA. You will need some road maps or perhaps a global positioning system. You may have your vehicle checked before the trip to reduce the chances of a break down. You may make reservations for places to stay. All of this requires some planning. You may need to make some detours because of road conditions that were not apparent when you planned your trip. You may become diverted because you discover an attraction you want to see. To reach your destination, you will need to monitor your progress and adjust your plans.

The same is true in business. If you want to take your business to the next level, you need a plan, and you need to monitor progress and make adjustments.

Vision without implementation gets you nowhere. In my experience, the stage at which most strategic plans fail is in their implementation. Why? Most frequently, the people charged with implementation of a strategic initiative have not bought into it, or thought through what it takes to implement it. Their days are filled with responding to "urgent" matters; important initiatives languish.

Making sure that important initiatives don't languish is not "rocket science," but it does require some disciplined follow-up. This is what I recommend:

1. Confirm expectations and arrangements Ask the person (team) responsible for the initiative to summarize his/her understandings of the desired results, the resources available, and the timing for progress reports and completion. If the expectations and arrangements summarized correspond with your understanding, then you are on the same wavelength. Yes, it is better to have it in writing. Memories fade faster than ink.

2. Determine the key measures that you need to monitor progress towards your goal, and who needs to monitor these measures. These vary for each organization and for each initiative. They need to be relevant to the initiative, measurable, and provided on a sufficiently timely basis that they enable people to control the process in real time. Think of four to ten metrics. With fewer than four, there is a chance that something important is being neglected. More than ten, and you may become distracted by measures that are of lesser relevance. Create a facsimile of a dashboard, a scorecard, or a set of meters on which to depict the data for easy, focused attention. Share these graphic representations with the people responsible for taking action.

3. Determine monitoring frequency How often do you need to check your "dashboard" in order to make timely corrections? This will probably be a function of how frequently you can get updated performance information and the risks involved. It will also vary depending on the information. For example, when you drive, you need to check your speedometer more frequently than your gas gauge.

4. Schedule periodic reviews of progress with your team. Ask them how frequently you need to "touch base." Though it may be tempting to cancel or reschedule a "touch base" session, don't. There is an adage: "If you expect, you've got to inspect."

5. Support versus interference Management is establishing the strategic direction, providing strategic guidance and resources, and monitoring progress to assure success. Micro-management is meddling in the details and second-guessing. Management is essential; micro-management undermines ownership of the process and results, and generally brings out the worst in people.

6. Provide team training Provide a team responsible for an initiative with training to help them work through the challenges of working together. The most frequent reason initiatives fail is that team members did not work together and didn't ask for help when they got stuck.

7. Be flexible As in any long trip, situations change from what you anticipated initially. Be flexible and prepared to capitalize on opportunities that are consistent with achieving your goals. Be prepared for detours. Cancel the initiative if it no longer makes sense.

8. Celebrate milestones completed and results achieved. Celebrations help build *esprit de corps* and recognize people for their accomplishments.

9. Look for learning Always conduct a "lessons learned" session for each strategic initiative. Learn from both successes and failures, and pass on what you learn to others so they may benefit from your experiences and learning.

Thousands of important goals or strategic initiatives flounder because of careless and inconsistent implementation. When you want to accomplish something important, create a monitoring system to provide you with the information you need to reach your goal. The monitoring system should be simple and relevant so that it will be used, and so that it will illuminate where corrective action is needed.

5.6

Getting Results From A Task Force

The task force has become a regular part of organizational life. Task forces are formed to solve multidimensional problems that require stakeholder input and buy-in in order to find a solution that can be implemented.

Some task forces work well and accomplish their purpose. Others flounder. Here are 12 tips to create a productive task force.

Composition Include 6 - 12 people who understand the issues and who will have a role in implementing the solution. Complex problems generally require at least six—more than 12 can be unwieldy.

Purpose Establish a clearly defined purpose for the task force, and a target time for completion of its task. Write this on easel pad paper and prominently display it at each meeting to keep people focused. Clarify the resources and authority of the task force. Will it just be recommending, or will it be implementing, too?

Launching At the first meeting, confirm the purpose of the task force, and the reason each member was selected. Ask people to introduce themselves and state:

- ❑ What they bring and how they can benefit from participation
- ❑ What behavior of others on a task force helps bring out the best in them
- ❑ What behavior of others on a task force really annoys them

Ground rules Brainstorm ground rules (chapter 2.4). Then ask people if they can "live with" them. Work on the ground rules until you have a set that everyone will commit to. Post them at every meeting. Review them at the start of each meeting to refresh people's memory, and at the end, in the meeting review.

Facilitator Choose an open-minded person with good facilitation skills. The facilitator's role is to help the task force move forward. Someone who is seen as trying to sway the group toward his/her position will have limited effectiveness.

Agenda Each meeting needs an agenda with a set time for each item. All task force members need input into the agenda. The agenda should be distributed before a meeting so that people can prepare for it.

Participation For a task force to achieve its goal, everyone needs to participate. The facilitator is responsible for drawing out people who are reticent and limiting those who are talkative.

If someone is repeatedly absent, does not participate, or asks to drop out, let him/her leave. Replace him/her with someone who will participate and add value.

Alternatives Seek creative alternatives. There is seldom only one possible solution. People sometimes grasp at the first alternative that seems viable. Explore options before choosing one.

Consensus Consensus decisions are typically a task force goal (chapter 5.1). Consensus is not unanimous agreement. It means that critical stakeholders can "live with" a decision.

Process monitor Group dynamics are a key to what a task force can accomplish. Appoint a process monitor to observe how the group interacts. Include a report of his/her observations during the meeting review to help improve how people relate to each other. Rotate this role through the group from meeting to meeting.

Meeting review Devote 5–10 minutes at the end of a meeting to review how it went.

❑ How did we do in relation to our ground rules? In relation to the purpose of the meeting?

❑ What worked well today?

❑ What should we change to have a more effective meeting next time?

Notes Meeting notes clarify, record and communicate points that need to be remembered. Appoint a recorder to write and distribute notes on a timely basis.

When a task force is composed of the right people, energized with an important purpose, and focused in well-run meetings, creative results can be achieved while people have fun.

5.7

Getting Results From Committee Meetings

An old adage says, "A camel is a horse designed by a committee." Are committees that bad? Is it possible to have an effective committee? From my observations working with committees, and feedback from committee members, I will highlight what makes them succeed.

Composition The composition of a committee reflects the nature of an organization, its stage of development, and the committee's purpose. A management committee typically includes an executive and the people reporting to him/her who are responsible for a significant part of the organization. Also included are people who add a unique and important viewpoint to decisions.

Purpose For a committee to be effective, it needs a purpose that members view as important, and members need to subscribe to the value of group process. Typical purposes include:

❑ Coordination and communication among key people

❑ Solving interdepartmental or cross-functional problems

❑ Getting a variety of perspectives for decision-making

❑ Providing for continuity of operations.

Conditions Committees work best when their purpose, the role of each member, and the committee's authority and accountability are discussed and agreed to on a consensus basis by members. That does not mean that the purpose has to be redefined whenever a new member joins, but any new member needs to be briefed on the committee's purpose and operating rules.

Committees need a set of mutually agreed-upon guidelines to govern their operation. They needn't be Robert's Rules of Order, but they do need to address:

- ❑ Who will prepare the agenda, who has input to it, and when it will be distributed
- ❑ Reason for each agenda item, and the action required
- ❑ Time estimate for each agenda item
- ❑ Who will preside in the chair's absence
- ❑ Who should attend, and whether "stand-ins" may represent people absent
- ❑ When meetings will start, and how latecomers are to be treated
- ❑ How strict the chair should be in keeping the meeting on track
- ❑ What happens when participants are unprepared to discuss an issue
- ❑ Who will prepare the minutes, their level of detail, and when they will be distributed
- ❑ Information that is sensitive or confidential
- ❑ Information that should be communicated, and how to communicate it
- ❑ The approval process to extend a meeting beyond its scheduled conclusion
- ❑ Criteria for reviewing meeting content and process at its conclusion

Agenda In preparing an agenda, the person responsible needs to determine whether each item really belongs on it. Is it an issue on which broad input is needed? Is it an issue requiring interdepartmental coordination? Is it an issue on which the organization needs to present a common position? If it were an "information only" item, would a memo be better? If in doubt, it is usually better include it. Then, during the meeting review, ask whether it was appropriate.

Building bonds Each committee has its unique purpose and group dynamics. One responsibility of the chair is to bring out the best in the committee members. That means getting to know each as an individual and helping each to discover and build bonds with colleagues. One bond needs to be a commitment to the committee's purpose. The potential for other bonds can be explored during introductions, either when the committee is formed, or when a new member is added. Introductions should cover:

- ❑ A brief explanation of each person's area of responsibility
- ❑ Why the person is on the committee

❑ Special areas of expertise and unique perspectives to help the committee
❑ Prior experiences that may be relevant or of interest .
❑ Prior committee participation that brought out the best in the person
❑ Special sensitivities ("hot buttons") that may trigger the person

Monitoring process Another responsibility of the chair is to monitor the group process. That means:

❑ Encouraging the reticent to speak and the loquacious to listen
❑ Seeking clarification when there is misunderstanding
❑ Identifying areas of agreement and disagreement
❑ Facilitating brainstorming or problem solving
❑ Keeping the group focused on its purpose

Sometimes it helps to appoint a committee member as process monitor for a meeting. The person with that responsibility generally is someone who, during the appointed meeting, can concentrate on how people live up to the ground rules. During the meeting, review the process monitor reports on his/her observations. Rotating this assignment among committee members enables everyone to develop observation and feedback skills. It strengthens the group as a whole.

Problem behavior Sometimes a chairperson is reluctant to confront problem behavior because of concern about how to constructively deal with sensitive interpersonal issues. In such cases, a consultant or facilitator can help. A consultant can observe meetings, share observations and suggestions, and coach. A facilitator can facilitate a meeting to clarify purpose, develop meeting review criteria and feedback methods, and can also coach.

Achieving buy-in In interviews with me, managers have told me about decisions made that were never implemented. Research into these situations uncovered that one or more people who were supposed to have "bought-into" a decision, in fact, had not. Not all their questions and concerns had been answered. The committee chair had assumed that silence = agreement, felt pressed for time, and assumed consensus. A helpful question to ask each committee member before making a group decision is, "Can you live with this decision?" If the answer is, "Yes," fine. If the answer is, "No," find out what he/she can live with.

Communicating decisions Meetings are typically used to sort through alternatives and arrive at decisions. The process is not complete until the following points are resolved:

❏ What needs to be communicated?

❏ Who needs to know? Who has no need to know, or should not know? Why?

❏ How should the decision be communicated to achieve desired results?

Meeting review A meeting review just before adjourning only takes a few minutes, and is time well spent. It provides the chair with feedback on his/her leadership. Equally important, it gives committee members feedback on how they affected the group process. As such feedback can be critical, it helps for the members to create the review criteria as a group. That way, there can be up-front discussion and understanding regarding the meaning of the criteria, plus agreement on how critical feedback can be presented constructively.

Managers typically spend at least 20% of their time in meetings. When meetings have a clear purpose and are conducted well, they can energize and focus participants to get things done. When a meeting's purpose is uncertain, when it starts late and runs over its time, when discussions stray, when decisions are postponed, when politics subvert the group process, people become disillusioned and unproductive. Too much of an organization's success depends on effective meetings for them to be anything less than effective!

Formal Meeting Review

Meeting for review _____ Date _____

Purpose To assess a recently completed meeting on 25 attributes of effective formal meetings.

Instructions Please consider each statement in relation to the meeting you have just attended and rate your agreement with it using the following scale. Leave blank anything that does not apply.

5 = strongly agree   3 = partially agree   1 = strongly disagree

1. I had sufficient notice to prepare for the meeting.	1	2	3	4	5
2. I received in advance the materials I needed for preparation.	1	2	3	4	5
3. There was a stated purpose for the meeting.	1	2	3	4	5
4. There was an agenda indicating the purpose of each item.	1	2	3	4	5
5. The agenda included only items appropriate for this meeting.	1	2	3	4	5
6. We had ground rules that we agreed to live with.	1	2	3	4	5
7. We adhered to our ground rules.	1	2	3	4	5
8. The meeting started within two minutes of the appointed time.	1	2	3	4	5
9. Each agenda item had a time estimate.	1	2	3	4	5
10. Time estimates were adhered to, or modified by group consent.	1	2	3	4	5
11. The meeting ended by the agreed-to time.	1	2	3	4	5
12. Everyone who needed to attend was present.	1	2	3	4	5
13. Everyone was prepared for what was expected of him/her.	1	2	3	4	5
14. Reports were clear and to the point.	1	2	3	4	5
15. I expressed my views and feelings as much as I needed to.	1	2	3	4	5
16. No one dominated the discussions.	1	2	3	4	5
17. We listened to each other with courtesy and respect.	1	2	3	4	5
18. Discussion stayed reasonably on-course.	1	2	3	4	5
19. The meeting was not delayed by interruptions.	1	2	3	4	5
20. A consensus was achieved for each item needing consensus.	1	2	3	4	5
21. Decisions and points to remember were recorded in the notes.	1	2	3	4	5
22. Follow-up and accountability were established for each item needing follow-up.	1	2	3	4	5
23. Confidential information was identified as such.	1	2	3	4	5
24. A communication strategy was established for decisions to be communicated as a result of this meeting.	1	2	3	4	5
25. We accomplished in this meeting what we set out to.	1	2	3	4	5

5.8

Getting Results From a Self-Managed Team

According to an old adage, "When everyone is responsible, no one is responsible." To some people, the idea of a self-managed team sounds like the adage. Though some teams deteriorate to that condition, many function quite effectively.

A self-managed team is one in which the responsibilities and tasks of leadership are distributed among the team members instead of being concentrated in one person. This is not new. For ten years, I was on the Program Committee of the Northern California Chapter of the Institute of Management Consultants. We were all busy, experienced professionals responsible for the programs at monthly chapter meetings. One person arranged for our facilities, another publicized the events, another handled the program evaluations, another the reporting to and liaison with the Chapter Board, and another facilitated the meetings and took the notes. Each took responsibility for arranging for presenters for a specific event. No one was the designated leader. Everyone shared in making the team function.

Many teams with a designated leader have a hard time being effective, so how can a team with distributed leadership be effective? Here are five keys to the success of a self-managed team:

1. Unifying purpose and mission There needs to be a clear and compelling reason for people on a self-managed team to work together. They need to see that only by working together can they achieve a goal that makes a difference to the business, and to them.

2. Look for, use and value each other's strengths One of the benefits of a self-managed team is that it typically contains a broader range and greater depth of abilities than one leader is apt to possess. Everyone's strengths can be used for the benefit of the team. In order to do so, people need to look for the strengths of their team members and have them fill roles that play to their strengths. They need to value their colleagues for what they bring, and realize that their team is healthier for its diversity of abilities.

3. Clear roles, responsibility and accountability With the distributed leadership of a self-managed team, there is the potential for confusion regarding roles and responsibilities. Thus, the team, needs to work out everyone's roles and responsibilities in order to keep people from tripping over each other or letting things "slip between the cracks." It helps to create a matrix of management tasks and team members and indicate who is ultimately accountable for each, who has primary responsibility, and who is back up. These assignments need to be reviewed periodically, especially when there is a change in team members, to keep them current.

In addition, because a self-managed team does not operate in a vacuum, people within the organization and key outsiders need to know who to contact for their interactions with the team.

Coordination and communication A challenge of distributed leadership is to keep everyone in the loop for the information they need. When roles and responsibilities are parceled out, a communication matrix also needs to be created. Such a matrix needs to show each member's information needs and preferred communication method to feel informed and to be able to execute his/her responsibilities knowledgeably. In addition, the team needs to meet periodically for planning, coordination, problem solving, monitoring progress, and other issues of team management.

Rewards that encourage teamwork Making a self-managed team function effectively requires an extra measure of dedication on the part of the team members. Distributed leadership adds to the complexity of each member's work and the impact each has on the team's success. Thus, rather than rely on incentives that reflect only individual performance, basing at least a portion of compensation on team performance rewards people for pulling together.

People who participate in a well-managed, self-managed team typically enjoy their added responsibility. They feel more a part of the team and the organization, and feel that they have greater influence on matters that affect their work and life. They develop skills that stand them in good stead in their career. Their employer benefits from:

❑ Greater leadership capacity in the organization
❑ Greater identification of the team members with the organization
❑ A higher level of motivation among the team members

Any team in the forming stages deserves an investment in team training. A self-managed team, because of its greater complexity, can benefit from training tailored to making it self-managed.

5.9

Getting Results From a Virtual Team

"How do I build a team among people who are scattered over the globe in different time zones, and who may never meet each other face-to-face?" Welcome to the world of virtual teams!

Virtual teams are not new, but their use has increased. The globalization of business has created a need for people in dispersed geographic areas to solve problems together. Technology (e-mail and video or teleconferencing) has made it easier and faster to share information and build relationships at a distance.

Virtual teams face the same issues as teams where people work in the same place. However, when team members are not present physically, they may experience greater difficulty communicating and building the bonds that create an effective team. When people are sitting around a table in the same room, there are visual clues (facial expressions, level of attention, who sits where, body language, etc.) that create and communicate a context that is difficult to pick up on when people are in dispersed locations. Is it possible for team members to bond and communicate effectively under such circumstances? Yes! However, extra effort is needed for relationship building. Besides, people need something inspiring around which they can form a common bond; they also need conditions that enable them to work together. Here's what I've found that helps overcome the challenges of distance, dispersion and competing priorities:

- ❏ **Team members who will have a stake in the results of their work.**
  People whose future will be affected by the work of a virtual team have a greater stake in making the team a success and accomplishing a mission that can be implemented.

- ❏ **A clear, compelling and critical mission** to which team members will commit. If the team's mission seems less important than day-to-day demands, members will find reasons to procrastinate and slip deadlines.

- ❏ **Clear expectations and accountability, roles and responsibilities.** In others words, they need to know what they are to accomplish, by when, with what resources, who will do what, and how their results will be evaluated.

- ❏ **Mutual respect, trust and commitment** are the glue that bonds team members together. People need to feel that they are an integral part of a team and that they are valued for what they add to it. Thus, invest time having people get to know each other. If you can't get them together in one location initially, then have them prepare and share the following electronically (e-mail, video or teleconferencing, or multimedia meeting services).

Their background and current responsibilities.

Their perspective on and stake in the team's mission.

Why they are participating.

What they hope to accomplish as a part of the team.

What brings out the best in them working as part of a team.

What makes them come "unglued" working as part of a team.

A picture of each so they can associate a face with each name when team members have not met face-to-face.

While this may seem like "soft stuff," follow-through on commitments is based on relationships. The stronger the bond, the better the results.

Ground rules define how the team will work together. As a team will need to live with them they need to create them if there is to be mutual commitment. They need to include:

How the team will work together across different time zones.

How they will resolve or manage differences and make decisions.

How they will share and document information and decisions.

Meeting protocols (agenda, self identification, being recognized, interruptions, punctuality, stand-ins, side-talk, minutes, action items, etc.).

❑ **Management support** Even the best of teams can encounter issues for which they need someone to champion their cause, or to help them get "unstuck."

❑ **Appropriate recognition and rewards** need to reinforce the importance of what the team is accountable for accomplishing. Incentives (bonuses, stock options, etc.) need to be based on total team performance.

Thanks to technology and better knowledge of how teams work, effective virtual teams are now possible. The challenges of time zones, distance and competing priorities can be overcome using technology, so long as effective team building and team management principles are applied.

6

Building Performance

6.1

Creating Inspired Performance

"I'm looking for someone to speak to our team. They need to be pumped up. Can you improve their motivation?"

Such phone calls are not unusual. After all, my business is that of coaching leaders who want to create a work environment that inspires and enables people to perform at their best, as individuals and in teams. But, sustained motivation and performance are not a "just add water, mix and bake" matter.

Inspired performance is possible when people:

- ❑ Believe fervently in what they are doing
- ❑ Are committed to an important goal
- ❑ Are supported in their efforts

If any one of these ingredients is missing or shorted, trying to "pump people up" is like trying to inflate a tire with a leak—it won't last.

Beliefs and values People's beliefs and values are central to inspired performance. Someone who sees no value in striving for a gold medal is not apt to be on an Olympic team. To "go for the gold," select people who not only have the talent, but who share that value.

Something to believe in Most people hope for more than just a job. They want to do something that is important in relation to their beliefs and values. They are willing to go above and beyond the call of duty when they can see the potential for results consistent with what is important to them. Inspired performance requires commitment to a cause.

In business, a cause equates to the team's or organization's purpose (its reason for existence) and mission (what it endeavors to accomplish). Reportedly, when Apple was courting John Sculley, Steve Jobs asked him whether he just wanted to sell sweetened water (Pepsi), or whether he wanted to change the world. He chose the latter. A business can have an important purpose, but if people don't buy into it, you miss out on commitment. Why is that important? Because there is usually much more to do than there is time for. People have to make choices in their use of time. Commitment is what gets them to follow through on what's needed to "go for the gold."

For an organization to achieve inspired performance, it needs a purpose and mission that are consistent with the values of its people and to which they will commit. In hiring people, make sure they know the purpose and mission of your business, and that they will commit to them.

Support is critical Even the most noble purpose and exciting vision can be undermined by lack of support. People committed to a compelling mission only become frustrated and "bail out" or "turn off" when their efforts are met with lack of resources, unclear/changing expectations, too many/unrealistic requirements, and controls that don't make sense. These are only a few indicators of a lack of support.

Inspired performance could be the norm, but it is the exception. Like making a soufflé, the recipe is not that complicated, but it is exacting. With proper execution, a soufflé rises, and is fluffy and light. But when one cuts corners, it falls flat and is tough. With the pressures of organizational life, there is a temptation to cut corners. And as with a soufflé, performance falls short of its inspired potential.

6.2

Winning Through Disciplined Performance

Whenever you see a team that wins consistently, chances are that they are also well disciplined. Disciplined performance starts with mastering the basics. That is why professional baseball or football players begin their training camp each season throwing and catching the ball. It isn't that they don't know how to throw and catch. They are undergoing a regimen to build skill mastery, character, self-control and rigorous teamwork in preparation for the rich scenario of situations they will face. It's a lot of work, but it pays dividends in winning the World Series or Superbowl.

Mastery Disciplined performance creates players who have mastered the game well enough to be able to capitalize on opportunities and deal with challenges without missing a beat. They know how to size up a situation quickly and act instinctively. Some people say that in fast-paced competition one can never be prepared for every eventuality. That is true—but a well-disciplined team can grasp the situation quickly and function. A good example of disciplined performance was the grace under pressure performance of the Forty-Niners with Joe Montana as quarterback when they would come from behind to win the game in the final minute.

Disciplined performance is important not only on the playing field, in the emergency room or in the fire department, it is important in the rest of business, too. The competition is as severe as in sports and the stakes are as high. However, people in business seldom devote the level of effort and attention to building performance as you see on the field or in emergency services. There doesn't seem to be enough time, and businesses generally "get by." How come there is not enough time to do things right the first time, but there seems to be time to correct the mistakes?

Creating Disciplined Performance

A shared set of team-oriented values and goals   It is essential for everyone to believe that unless the team wins, no one wins. The San Jose Sharks have lost many a game because individual players tried to be heroes rather than passing the puck to their team members who were better positioned to make a goal.

Role clarity   Disciplined performance requires that everyone knows his/her role and responsibilities. Everyone needs an assigned role. That can change as circumstances change and as people are cross-trained to handle different roles. But there must be no confusion about who does what if there is to be consistent, high-quality performance.

High expectations and standards   Everyone needs to strive for their personal best performance *in support of the team.*

Supportive ground rules and adherence to them   Ground rules, within reason, enable people to work together more effectively and efficiently than without them. They enable people to perform without tripping over others. In our society, we have a rule that people stop for a red traffic signal light. Though some people run the light, most of the time you can count on people stopping for you when the light is red for them. Imagine what driving would be like if you had to stop at every intersection because you were not sure that the cross traffic would stop for you! Just as it is essential to have clarity about who does what, it is also essential that there be some rules of the game to which people adhere.

Useful feedback and learning   A team is a system. Every system needs feedback to keep it on target, and to enable people to learn, grow and improve. Feedback is the life-blood for honing skills and team performance. Disciplined performance requires people to know in "real time" the important measures of team performance for self-monitoring and timely correction.

"Tough love" coaching/leadership   Every team experiences problems—guaranteed. Procrastination and reticence to confront team issues have no place in disciplined performance. Confronting and resolving issues with care, concern, and responsible action is essential.

Team spirit Team spirit builds commitment to the team and its goals. It comes from identification with and pride in the team. "Little things mean a lot." Big victories are more apt to get attention and celebration, but contributing to the big victories are many little ones. Celebrating them as a team focuses on the component parts to creating the big victories. Every victory celebrated as a team helps to build team spirit.

Business has its equivalents of the Superbowl and World Series. Being first to market with a new product or services that will redefine an industry is certainly equivalent. Intel has defined the chip market for personal computers. Sun had defined the market for workstations, Cisco for routers and Solectron for contract manufacturing. Their leadership positions are not a matter of chance. Yes, they have made a few mistakes—and recovered quickly. But they have had a consistent focus and a disciplined approach to creating their winning teams. They, and their stockholders, have been the beneficiaries of winning through disciplined performance.

6.3

Performance Reviews That Help Bring Out The Best In People

Performance reviews are an accepted part of employer-employee relations, but frequently neither supervisors nor employees are enthusiastic about them. Why? Do people naturally resist giving and receiving feedback? Some do, but most people want and need to know how they are doing. They appreciate useful feedback.

Flawed system Negative perceptions of performance reviews frequently reflect negative assumptions about people, and inappropriate roles for both supervisor and employee. All too frequently the supervisor is asked to be "Saint Peter" determining who can enter "Heaven". The supervisor is supposed to be all knowing. The employee is presumed "guilty until proven innocent". The nature of the process establishes the supervisor as a "critical parent" and the employee a "child". To compound the problem, frequently a supervisor saves up criticism to unload on the employee during the semi-annual or annual review, at which point it is too late to be of any usefulness. Finally, many performance review forms focus on employee attitudes rather than accomplishments and job-related behavior. Behavior reflects attitudes, but behavior is observable, attitudes are not.

Change the system Research indicates that most people want to perform well and grow in their career. They want a sense of mastery and the self-satisfaction that comes from personal growth and accomplishment in their work. They are looking to work for someone they respect, someone who is fair, and someone who takes an interest in and mentors them. They resent performance review systems that, and supervisors who, demean them. In most cases, people who are treated as responsible, mature adults behave as such. If the process is designed to protect against problem people, it creates a self-fulfilling prophesy for people to become problems!

Benefits One might ask why try to bring out the best in people? What's the percentage in that? As a rule, top performers are underpaid in relation to their worth, and poor performers are overpaid! When you bring out the best in people, you are getting more than your money's worth. Employees become a strategic advantage over your competition. They do everything they can to make sure that they are on the winning team. That's something you can't buy. That only comes from the commitment that one *voluntarily* makes to do one's best.

The performance review—How to The performance review process cannot, in itself, bring out the best in people. It is just one tool that needs to be aligned with other management processes. Nevertheless, here are some steps that can transform the performance review process to help bring out the best in employees:

1. Transform "bosses" into coaches Coaches naturally assess training needs, provide training, set goals with people they coach, observe performance, provide feedback, and provide the direction and communication for everyone on the team to pull together. The role of supervision is to make sure that the people on the team have the resources they need to do their job effectively. Supervision that is oppressive, condescending or parental is apt to bring out the worst in people.

2. Focus on performance development Performance development is an ongoing cycle of planning, coaching, reviewing progress, and back again to planning. It creates progress and performance reviews as a normal consequence of developing employees to achieve their full potential. While a review can also serve administrative needs, its primary focus should be on developing employees for better performance and career growth.

3. Involve stakeholders Involve people in the design and implementation of the performance development system who will use it. Include a member of the human resources staff on a task force, but it should not be viewed as an HR task force. Effective performance development systems must be seen as management tools, not personnel tools. It is crucial to bringing out the best in people that those affected by it "buy into" it.

4. Establish and communicate standards for quality, productivity, personal growth, and behavior. Emphasize these in the performance development process. Employees need to know what is expected, and the standards for which they are accountable. Use measures that they can self-monitor, so that they don't have to wait for your feedback to know how they are doing.

5. Communicate, communicate and communicate! These are the three most important elements of performance development. You can't be an effective coach without knowing the people you coach. Listening is as important as what you say. You can't inspire people to achieve new goals without communication. You can't reinforce good performance, or help people to change behavior, without timely, caring and honest communications.

6. Show that you care There is no better way to show that you care than by encouraging people when they try, praising them when they make progress, showing them how when they need an example, and supporting when they falter. The ultimate insult is not caring enough about people to try to help them work out a problem. Be honest, constructive and encouraging.

7. Involve employees in setting goals Help them to identify and define goals that make sense to them and to you. They are more apt to strive for goals that they have helped to establish. They become their goals. They will be more inspired to work for goals that they have committed to accomplish.

8. Involve employees in reviewing their progress and performance When it is time to review progress, you need the perspective of the employees being reviewed. Ask them to prepare a draft review reflecting their perspective in advance of preparing your review. (An alternative is to prepare the review jointly.) Seeking their input communicates respect and recognizes that they have important information to consider in the review.

9. Don't "grade by the curve" A bell-shaped curve assumes a "normal" distribution of winners and losers. When you are trying to bring out the best in people, you are seeking to create a better than "normal" team. You are seeking to develop star performers! True, some will perform better than others, but don't demoralize good performers by communicating that they are "below average," especially if your "average" is high. Focus on how they can increase their value to you.

What is the effect of your current performance review system? Does it help bring out the best in people? If it does, great! It's working for you. If it makes people defensive, if it creates grievances, if people are not keeping pace with change, it is working against you. If it is working against you, establish a task force of stakeholders to review and revise it.

6.4

Communicating About Job Performance

Job performance is the reason why you employ people in your business. Everyone's job performance has some impact on the success of your business. One of your prime responsibilities is to help employees develop their job performance so that the performance of the organization as a whole is greater than the sum of its parts.

Basis for job performance Job performance is a combination of motivation, ability, and resources allocated to a job. Slight any of them and job performance will suffer. The resources allocated to a job are generally, but not always, independent of who is in it. What employees add is the ability and motivation, so you need to coach them to develop their ability and inspire their motivation.

In coaching, it is important to distinguish between ability and motivation. Ability is a combination of aptitude, knowledge and skills. Aptitude is innate. Though I love music, there is no way I could become a concert pianist. I don't have the aptitude. No amount of practice will change that. Knowledge and skills can be learned and developed. Motivation is one's will to apply one's aptitude, knowledge and skills to the job. Though you cannot motivate people, you can influence their motivation through your caring and support.

Job performance is a personal statement that reflects ability and motivation. People blossom and grow with positive feedback. Critical feedback is necessary at times, but needs to be expressed in such a way that it is not an attack on one's self worth and so that it does not create defensiveness. How you communicate can be as important as what you say.

Making communications meaningful In communicating about job performance consider these points:

1. Real-time Communicating about job performance needs to be an ongoing activity. An annual or semi-annual performance review does not provide feedback on a timely enough basis to be useful. Such reviews are primarily for administrative purposes.

2. Investment Communicating about job performance is an investment in future performance. It needs to create learning in the partnership between you and the person with whom you are communicating. Both you and your team member need to determine how you, as partners, can add value to the enterprise and commit to a course of action.

3. No surprises When it is time for a formal performance review, there should be no surprises. Any significant aspect of performance should have been discussed on a timely basis during the period covered by a review. Discussions during a review should primarily summarize what occurred since the last one and plan for the next. Problems requiring attention should be addressed as they occur and not saved for the review.

4. Setting Arrange for a time and place where you can talk without interruption. Interruptions detract from the meeting and diminish its importance.

5. Coach Your mission is to help people achieve their full potential in your organization. Acknowledge and build on their strengths. Help them to find and commit to ways to minimize the effects of their weaknesses.

6. Involvement Involve employees in planning and preparing for their review. Either complete the review form jointly in a meeting, or ask them to prepare a draft review beforehand. Strategically, involving employees in preparing their review communicates your respect for them and trust in their objectivity. Nine times out of ten they will be harder on themselves than you are.

7. Do your "homework" Know what you want to cover. Make notes of the points you want to make so that you don't forget them. Script what you want to say about sensitive points. While you probably will not read from the script, scripting enables you to organize your thoughts and determine in advance how you want to express yourself.

8. Listen attentively and without interruption when there is disagreement. Note any points to discuss later. Emotions need to be vented before people will listen to reason. When pent up emotions have been drained, summarize what you heard to confirm that you listened. Only then will an employee be ready to listen to what you have to say.

9. Specific feedback When praising, whether in coaching or in a performance review, tell why the performance is good:

> *"Your report on _____ was complete and concise. You understood the issues and your recommended actions not only make sense, they will save $100,000."*

When confronting a problem, explain what the employee did (or didn't do) that created the problem, and why it is significant:

> *"I know that you want to upgrade your sales. That's great! But telling a customer that she should buy Nina Ricci because Chanel perfume is only for 'little old ladies' insults her, and it demeans one of our products."*

10. Confronting problems When confronting a problem, ask for the employee's view of it, and how to solve it:

> *"How did those errors evade your discovery before the president received your report? What can you do to make sure that doesn't happen again?"*

11. Avoid arguments. They don't solve problems. They only increase defensiveness and polarize people. Accept that views may differ. Aim to prevent a recurrence. The objective is to enlist cooperation for creating new or changed behavior:

> *"I accept that our views differ about who was responsible for Mrs. Jones receiving the wrong medication. We can't turn the clock back and change what happened. We must focus on how to prevent such mistakes from happening again. What are your ideas?"*

12. Course of action Ask for a commitment to a course of action. The best approach is if an employee can identify what needs to be done and voluntarily commits to do it:

> *"What can you do to make sure that you are at work on time henceforth?"*

If the answer you hear is not a satisfactory way to meet your expectations, state what you expect:

> *"I'd hoped that you would suggest a way to make sure that you get to work on time. Since you haven't, I suggest that you: Buy a second alarm clock with a loud bell. Set the first one to ring at 5:45 AM, and the second at 6:00 AM. Get up when the first one rings. If something goes wrong, get up when the second rings. If you're going to be late, call me. I need to know before the start of your shift. Can you live with that?"*

13. Set follow-up times There are two old saying: "If you expect, you've got to inspect," and "What gets on the calendar is more apt to happen." People seldom adopt new patterns of behavior without some coaching and help. If you want to increase the probability of an employee following-up, set the stage by setting follow-up times to review progress:

> *"Let's meet briefly next Monday at 8:45 AM to see how things are going with your new alarm clock and earlier wake up time."*

14. Celebrate success! Coaching is a process of helping people create new knowledge, skills and patterns of behavior. While they may learn from mistakes, they also learn from successes. Help them analyze why they succeeded so they learn from positive experiences. Communicate through a celebration that what they have accomplished is important, appreciated and recognized.

15. Document points that you may need to remember. Memories fade. If there is ever a question about what was said, you'll be glad you have it documented.

Communicating effectively about job performance takes some time and practice to master, but the rewards are worthwhile! As someone in a leadership role, your challenge is to bring out the best in the people you lead. The best way to leverage yourself as a manager is to invest in well-trained staff, and coach them to be top performing, too. When they shine, you shine!

6.5

Performance Goals and Feedback—the "Breakfast of Champions"

Scrap the annual performance review! It may be needed for administrative reasons, but it is a disaster as a coaching tool.

Become a coach As a leader, or as a parent, you are responsible for bringing out the best in people and to help them be all that they can be. That is a coaching role that requires:

- ❏ Showing them how to do what you expect them to do
- ❏ Setting clear performance goals
- ❏ Observing their attempts
- ❏ Giving them frequent, timely, specific, valid and sincere feedback
- ❏ Elevating goals as they gain proficiency

Think of teaching someone to ride a bike. First, you show them what riding a bike is like to create a mental image of what they will be doing. Then you place them on the seat, put their feet on the pedals and hands on the handlebars. You hold them upright as you familiarize them with the feel of the bike. As they gain balance, you give more latitude. Eventually, you remove the training wheels. All the time you give encouragement. *"That's the way! Now pedal a little faster. Watch out for that tree! Now try stopping on this line. Pretty good! You came within two feet."*

This is timely feedback. You don't wait for an annual performance review. You look for what they are doing "approximately right," as Ken Blanchard would say, and cheer them on. When they make a mistake, you bite your tongue. If you say, *"You dumb klutz! How could you fall over?"* you only focus attention on falling, not on learning to ride.

Communicate your expectations In coaching, let people know what it takes to excel. Show them the concentric circles on the performance target and the points you associate with each circle. They will then be able to track their own performance and strive for the highest points. If you don't show them the points, they will assume that the center is the highest value when, in fact, you may value it differently. They can't win if they don't know your rules of game!

Specific feedback Words such as "Good job" encourage, but fail to communicate why it was a good job. Specific feedback is more instructive and helpful. It communicates what was good, and why. Add specific feedback to your encouragement: *"Good job! As you dove off the high board, your arms were together directly in front of your head. Your body was straight, and your feet together. You entered the water with only a three-foot splash. Now if you can keep your hands together, pointed like an arrowhead, you'll make an even smaller splash. Can you try that now?"*

Escalate goals Performance goals need to escalate as competence increases. What was acceptable yesterday is no longer acceptable. You won't win an Olympic medal without continually stretching to higher levels. You should expect and get more from someone with three years on the job than three weeks. People need to know that your expectations will escalate if they expect their pay to escalate, too.

Most people really want to excel. They appreciate help from someone who cares enough about them to be a coach or mentor. They especially appreciate knowing what it takes to become a "champion," and to get feedback that instructs them.

6.6

Using Incentive Compensation to Improve Growth and Profits

WII-FM. Is that a radio station? No, it stands for, "What's In It—For Me?" WII-FM is at the heart of incentive compensation. Whether or not employees ask that question explicitly, it is always an implicit question. For your business to succeed, show employees how they will benefit from helping your business to grow and be profitable.

In order to realize your business' full potential, you need to have everyone working together as though they had an ownership stake in it. Incentive compensation rewards employees for helping your business grow and be profitable. It enables them to see in economic terms, WII-FM. It also provides a meaningful measurement of your business' performance, and can be a rallying point for improved teamwork.

Creating and implementing an effective incentive compensation plan requires careful thought, communication and tailoring to the business. Anticipate the plan's ramifications to avoid pitfalls, of which there are many. Here are some considerations for the design and implementation of an incentive compensation plan:

1. Align with strategic goals Develop objectives for your plan that will support the strategic goals of your business. If long-term growth is important, the plan should reward accomplishment of long-term growth objectives. If current profit is important, it should reward attainment of current profit objectives. If both are important, it should reward a balance of profit and growth. In short, it should be designed to support what's important for your business.

Don't copy another business' incentive compensation plan. Even if another plan is accorded the designation of "best practices," that doesn't mean that it is appropriate for your business in an off-the-shelf form. There may be similarities between organizations, but you will probably find significant differences that will affect the success of the plan in your business. Do your homework and create a plan that fits the strategic goals and culture of your business.

2. Use relevant performance measures Choose your business performance measures carefully. Not only do you need to have an information system that easily provides you with the data you need for measuring business performance, but also the measures must be appropriate to the behavior you seek. For example, don't base incentive pay for sales people only on gross sales. Include returns and allowances, and advertising and promotional costs. Unless these costs are included, you may get a distorted view of what your sales staff is accomplishing, or you may reward behavior that actually undermines your goals.

3. Set a performance threshold Certain levels of company performance (profit, growth, etc.) should be attained before any incentive payments occur. These levels should be adjusted each year to recognize growth that becomes part of the ongoing business.

4. Base incentive payments on attainment of annually determined goals and objectives Avoid strict percentage of sales or profit formulas. You need flexibility to adjust incentive targets as your business grows, and as the business environment changes, without the perception that you are cutting the payout. Some businesses start a commission structure for sales staff with a relatively high rate of commission. As the business grows, they become concerned when the best sales people start earning more than some managers, or even the President. They then cut the commission rates to correct their "mistake." This action is usually viewed as a "cheap and greedy" move. As a result, they lose some top performing sales people, and employee trust. This problem can be avoided with good planning and appropriate use of annually determined goals.

5. Include all the people in the plan who influence the results you are seeking
Don't limit plan participation only to sales staff or top management. They are obvious. Support people may have a smaller direct impact on results, but they need to be included. They can have lower levels of plan participation to recognize their smaller direct impact, but they should be included to foster total team performance.

6. Scale payout potential to impact on business results Set goals for the balance between base and incentive pay. For people with a high impact on business results, you may want as much as 50% of their total compensation leveraged with incentive pay. For people with a smaller impact, 10% of total compensation as incentive pay may be appropriate.

7. Involve people in the plan design who will be plan participants They are the people who are supposed to be motivated and rewarded by the plan, so it is important to gain their input. They will learn about the critical issues of plan design through the process of involvement. Their input will also increase the probability that the plan will truly represent an incentive for them. They can also help sell the plan to others who will be included in it.

8. Keep it simple Keep your incentive compensation plan as simple as you can and still meet your needs. The simpler the plan, the more easily understood it will be. If the purpose of the plan is to enhance performance, people need to understand it and how it operates. Also, the more complex the plan is, the more time and expense is required to administer it.

9. Communicate the plan and provide people with frequent graphic reports on progress toward their incentive goals. Use the incentive plan to develop *esprit d'corps* and enhance teamwork. People need to know how they are doing on a timely basis in order to keep on course.

10. Phase in plan It is usually difficult to cut base pay in order to add an incentive component to compensation. If base pay is already high in relation to the market, you may be able to implement an incentive pay plan incrementally over time. While maintaining base pay relatively constant, you can increase the target amounts of incentive pay each year until you have achieved your desired balance between base and incentive pay.

    If you want to install or revise an incentive compensation plan, and you don't have someone on staff who is experienced in it, seek help. If incentive compensation is worthwhile, it is worth doing correctly. The cost of expertise is insignificant in relation to the benefits your business can derive from an incentive compensation plan that enhances your business strategy and performance, and that reflects the culture of your business.

6.7

Using Recognition to Build Performance

Forget awards such as employee of the month, or similar schemes that single out one person! Though they are usually well-intended attempts to provide recognition, they may backfire. Frequently, all they do is embarrass the person being recognized and turn off those who did not receive the recognition. Why is that?

- ❑ Everyone else who has performed well feels slighted, especially if the person receiving the recognition is not perceived to have performed noticeably better than the rest.
- ❑ Frequently, the criteria used to make the selection are unknown, so the recognition is perceived as a "brown-nose" award or favoritism.
- ❑ Sometimes, awards are perceived as awarded to the "squeaky wheel," to silence him or her. That sets up a counterproductive reward structure.
- ❑ If teamwork is important, individual recognition is inconsistent with teamwork. If the team wins, everyone wins. If the team doesn't, no one should.
- ❑ Sometimes, awards are used to manipulate people into doing something for the wrong reason. I know of an organization that gave a trip to Las Vegas to the person who brought in the most new members. The person who won focused more on winning the trip than on making sure that the people he recruited would derive value from their membership. Of the sixteen recruits, only one renewed the next year.

Don't get me wrong! I believe in recognizing people for their accomplishments when it is done appropriately. Here's what I suggest:

1. Set inclusive criteria When everyone can win, more people will strive to achieve. Yes, you'll be recognizing more people, and that's great. You will benefit from their higher level of performance.

2. Keep raising expectations As more people achieve set standards, they need to increase for people to grow in value.

3. Provide self-monitoring information As people strive to improve, they need timely information. Think of golf. People don't have to wait for performance reviews. They know their score immediately and can recalibrate what they do without being told to.

4. Unintended consequences Before establishing any criteria, look for their unintended consequences. Be sure that the behavior you are recognizing is based on doing the right thing for the right reason, and is in the best interests of your organization. Don't reward people for inappropriate behavior!

5. Cite specifics When you recognize people for their accomplishments, cite specifically what they did and why it is important. Your specific feedback may be more important than any goodie they are awarded. It communicates that you care enough about them and what they do to pay attention and provide specific feedback. That is a genuine compliment!

People flourish on recognition for their accomplishments when it is credible to them and their peers. To be credible, the criteria must be clearly understood and viewed as relevant to furthering organizational goals. Awards need to go to the right people for the right reason.

Communicating About Sensitive Issues

7.1

Communicating About Sensitive Issues

Boss: *"Why you didn't tell me about the cost over-run?"*

Employee: *"I knew it would upset you. I saw what happened last month when Sam told you about the widget problem."*

Boss: *"Maybe I was hard on him, but I need to know about problems."*

Employee: *"OK. How do you want me to tell you about problems? I don't want to be the `messenger who gets beheaded for telling the king bad news.'"*

Natural reluctance Telling people good news is usually not a problem. But how do you tell the "emperor" about his "new clothes?" History, folklore and cartoons depict serious consequences for brave souls who have tried to be honest in telling their boss about what he/she may not be pleased to hear.

"Not even your best friend will tell you," was the tag line of a deodorant commercial. It is a normal reaction to avoid being the bearer of bad news, especially to someone who has substantial influence over one's life, such as the boss. And it is an equally normal reaction to become defensive when confronted with bad news, especially of a personal nature. So when people see more potential risks than rewards, they don't communicate about sensitive issues.

Essential information Sensitive information is generally important information. Careers can be at stake. I have seen both managers and employees suffer because their supervisor did not share important feedback on their interpersonal relations in time to be useful. Their almost unanimous refrain has been, *"If I had known about that earlier, I could have done something about it."*

Gesture of caring Communicating sensitive information, though not pleasant, is a gesture of caring and should be viewed as such. *"This is difficult for me to tell you, but I care enough about you to risk upsetting you with information that you need to know."*

I have had to be the bearer of unwelcome news, both as a manager, and as a consultant. I have a few scars, but for the most part, my honesty and the way I presented the message have been appreciated. Here's what has worked for me:

1. Set the stage Before you find yourself in a situation where you need to communicate sensitive information, discuss how he/she wants you to do it.

"At some time I may have information that you need to know about, but which may be upsetting to you. I realize that I have a responsibility to you to share such

information, and I want to fulfill my responsibility as best I can. I have found that when I know that someone really wants to know about sensitive issues, and we have worked out beforehand how to communicate it, it makes it easier for both of us. How do you want me to approach you to communicate such information?"

When you need to share information that may be upsetting, harken back to your conversation. *"Remember our conversation about sensitive information and how you want me to communicate it to you, well I need to now. It this a good time?"* Asking about the timing gives the person a choice of listening now or scheduling a better time. Either way, you are getting the person's permission to proceed.

2. Get to the point quickly People generally prefer to hear the news quickly rather than be led to it along a suspenseful path. It also helps to describe what happened free of emotionally charged words. *"We need to correct a bug in our DeskSet 4.1 software. It freezes the operating system. The only way users can recover is to reboot their computer. We will need to send a revised version to our customers at an estimated cost of $459,000."*

If you need to express yourself on a personal or emotional issue, describe how you feel or felt. You may need to "count to ten" first to regain your composure and choose your words carefully. Describing how you felt is more acceptable, and less threatening, than displaying your emotions.

"I need to talk with you about our conversation yesterday regarding the trip to Raleigh. When you suggested that we share the same hotel room and spend an intimate evening together, I couldn't believe my ears. I got up and walked out because I was in no shape to continue our conversation. Your suggestion was unwanted and inappropriate. I thought of filing a sexual harassment complaint with HR, but decided not to at this time. I decided to let you know clearly that any suggestion of sex or romance is unwelcome. I like you and have enjoyed working with you for the past two years. I hope that we may continue working together as colleagues—no more, no less."

3. Test for understanding Communicating is a closed-loop process. As with a radio station, you can "broadcast" your message, but if the other person is not "tuned in," you have not communicated. Frequently you can pick up visual clues from the person's concentration or body language. Another way is to say, *"What I have just told you is probably not what you wanted to hear. To make sure that we are on the same wavelength, please tell me what you heard."* If he/she missed or misunderstood a point, you have an opportunity to clarify it. *"You got most of what I said. Let me just clarify one point. Making a counter offer to John will not change his mind about leaving. If we had been sensitive to his concerns six months ago, he would not be leaving now. It is too late now!"*

4. Be prepared for reactions Communicating about sensitive issues is not without risk. When you understand what normal human reactions are, you can be prepared for them. Such reactions can be:

- ❑ Acceptance *("I didn't realize I was dominating the meetings. I'll try to change.")*
- ❑ Defensiveness *("What do you mean that I get upset easily?")*
- ❑ Denial *("Nicotine is not addictive!")*
- ❑ Seeking others to blame *("I was only doing what Muriel told me to do.")*
- ❑ Flight *("I can't deal with this now; maybe tomorrow.")*
- ❑ "Killing the messenger" *("Since you are always criticizing the way I lead, maybe you should try working for someone else. You're fired!!")*

If the other person erupts, usually the best strategy is to listen carefully without interruption and jot down key words to remember until he/she has nothing left to say. This is not easy! You may be tempted to interrupt to clarify or disagree, but you cannot make headway until the other person has vented his/her pent-up emotion. After a brief silence, he/she will be willing to listen. Recap your points of agreement, and then explain your position on the disagreements.

("You know, we see _____ and _____ the same way. I now understand why we differ on _____, and _____. This is how I see them, and why. I'm not trying to get you to change your views, but I do want you to understand mine.")

You can't control how others will respond to sensitive information. The best that you can do is to choose how you want to respond, respond accordingly, and document what transpired for future reference. State the facts: date, time, place, who else was present, what prompted the communication, what you said, what the other person said, how he/she reacted, how you reacted, and how you left the situation.

5. Seek help, if needed Whether you are dealing with:

- ❑ The person to whom you report
- ❑ Someone who reports to you
- ❑ A peer or friend
- ❑ A spouse, parent or child

You need to be able to communicate openly and honestly about sensitive issues, and a relationship in which you can't is unhealthy. It eats away at you physically and psychologically. If you can't communicate openly with someone important to you, seek help—for both of you. If, after getting help you still can't, you may need to re-evaluate your relationship. Life is too short to endure a relationship in which you can't communicate about issues that matter to you.

7.2

Helping Others Work Through Problems

"I've got a problem that has kept me awake for the past two nights. Talking it through with you really would help! May I tell you about it?"

You can be a valued resource to the people with whom you work by being a good listener who asks insightful questions. Organizations are full of people who have problems that keep them awake and distract them from performing at their best. Some think it is a sign of weakness to need to discuss an issue with a confidant, but it is actually a sign of wisdom. Wise people recognize that the process of explaining a situation to a good listener often helps them to clarify it. Frequently an insightful question leads to an "ah-hah" that helps you see things in a new light.

When a colleague asks you to listen through a problem, it is a compliment. It signifies that he/she trusts you to listen well, ask good questions, help him/her decide on a course of action, and keep the conversation confidential. Here are some tips to help you create value for your colleague:

1. Block out enough time Ask how long he/she needs. Add a "fudge factor." Most people underestimate how much time they will actually need. If you can't devote that amount of time when asked, schedule a time soon when you can.

2. Privacy Find a place where you can talk confidentially and without interruptions. Part of the value you bring is in focused listening. Distractions and interruption undermine that. In terms of confidentiality, your colleague needs to realize that everything said will be confidential unless he/she tells you about any illegal activity. You may have a responsibility to make sure that the proper authorities find out about anything illegal.

3. Objectives As a confidant, your objectives are to help your colleague to:

    a. Articulate the problem clearly and determine its root cause
    b. Explore alternative ways to solve it
    c. Choose an alternative that will solve it
    d. Take responsibility for solving it

Unless the problem is with you (in which case you are not the appropriate confidant), you can't solve the problem, nor should you try. Your role is to empower your colleague to take the next steps through the process of working through the problem.

4. Strategy Ask questions that help your colleague to gain insight into the problem and its solution. If your colleague makes statements with which you take exception, accept that they are his/her current perspective. Don't argue. That will only place your colleague on the defensive, rather than opening his/her mind. Instead, ask probing questions for clarification and listen. If you believe he/she has been blind to a point, you can ask, *"Have you considered _____? Or "How about _____? That may be worth considering."* Remember, your role is not to solve the problem, but to help your colleague take action to solve it him/herself.

5. Questions Here are some questions to help you through the process:

What is on your mind? (What's been keeping you awake?) After active listening, you should be able to summarize the problem in a few sentences to make sure that you understand it. Problem definition is critical to problem solution.

What are just symptoms, and what is the cause? Frequently, what appears to be a problem is a symptom of another problem. Trying to solve the symptom doesn't solve the problem. You need to burrow down to the root cause before the problem can be solved.

Why is it a problem? If it is a problem, it has adverse consequences for someone.

Who is affected by it and how are they affected? If they benefit from the problem, they may resist any attempt to solve it. If they suffer from it, they will be more apt to lend their support. Whoever is affected needs to be a party to solving it.

Who "owns" the problem? What are their perspectives and positions on it? The people who "own" a problem are those with authority to take action to solve it. They are generally part of the group who is affected by it.

What are consequences of not solving it? One alternative is to do nothing. It has a cost against which the cost of solving the problem must be weighed. Sometimes, the cost to solve a problem is greater than the cost of living with it. Your colleague will have a better chance of getting the problem solved if the consequences of non-action are more costly than the consequences of solving it.

What is your desired outcome? This is your colleague's vision of what life will be like without the problem. Sometimes, people want to get rid of a problem, but have not envisioned the plusses and minuses of life after the problem is solved. A vision is very important for convincing constituents to take action.

What are the alternatives? There always are alternatives. They need to be brainstormed and evaluated.

> *What are their plusses and minuses?* Only through a thorough look at both can your colleague make an intelligent decision.
>
> *What support and resistance can you anticipate for each?* Who will benefit and whose "ox gets gored?" What can be done to change resistance into support?
>
> *Which is best or most workable?* The best and the most workable are not always the same. One alternative may be technically superior, but the organization isn't ready for it. Another may be less technically attractive, yet have support within the organization.

*What are **you** going to do?* As solving the problem is not your business, you need to "put the monkey on the back" of your colleague to follow up. You may need to role-play several scenarios for the follow-up action to prepare your colleague for the challenges of the next step.

> *By when?* Without a time commitment, procrastination may overcome your colleague. You may not want to invest the time in helping a colleague through these questions only to discover that he/she failed to take action. Setting a deadline is essential, as is a time for your colleague to report back to you on what has happened.

If you are viewed as a good listener and objective sounding board, then you will be asked from time to time to help your colleagues work through problems. To be of most value to them, you must not let yourself get sucked in to becoming an "owner" of the problem, too. If you can help a colleague work through a problem that he/she in turn takes action to solve, you will have done him/her and your organization a valuable service.

7.3

Correcting Problems With Behavior or Job Performance

You hire people to solve problems, not to create them. Discovering that a team member is not working out is an unwelcome realization—like discovering that you have termites in your house.

One of the most difficult situations for a manager to face is the likeable person who is an under-performer. Yet, everyone on a team knows who is performing and who isn't. Keeping someone who isn't performing on your team beyond the time it takes to make that determination undermines your team and your credibility. Waiting is a kindness to no one! As a matter of fact, a poor performer and the rest of your team will interpret procrastination as tacit approval of lower standards. You can't afford that!

Performance vs. behavior problems A performance problem exists when the performance you get is different from what you expect (sales below quota, errors exceed standard). A behavior problem exists when someone is doing something that is unacceptable (stealing supplies, threatening a coworker). Though you may be tempted to hope that such problems will just disappear, as with termites, that is not likely to happen without some action. The sooner you confront a problem, and take action, the better.

Objective of process The objective in working with an employee who has a behavior or performance problem is to help him/her correct it and become fully productive. Sometimes you will succeed, sometimes you won't. For situations when your efforts fail, you need a record of your efforts as backup for termination. Thus, you need to make notes of your conversations for future reference, if need be.

The process is basically the same for correcting either behavior or performance problems. To confirm your expectations and diagnose the problem, you engage in an exploratory meeting. To check progress, you have a follow-up meeting during which you assess progress and decide on the next step. If an employee has corrected the problem, you congratulate him/her and the process ends. If he/she hasn't corrected the problem, or made acceptable progress, you continue to explore how to solve it, get renewed commitment for action to solve it, and schedule another follow-up meeting. If, after repeated attempts to help an employee solve a significant problem there is not acceptable progress, you fire him/her or transfer him/her to a more suitable position.

Performance = ability × motivation applied to a task. Ability includes aptitude, knowledge and skills. Aptitude is innate. Low aptitude can be compensated for to a certain extent by extra training and practice, but that may not enough. No matter how much training and practice I have, I will never be a Joe Montana. Knowledge and skills can be acquired through education and training. In diagnosing performance problems, if a person lacks the aptitude to perform the job, then he/she is in the wrong job. If he/she has the aptitude, then the question is if he/she has the necessary level of knowledge and skills, and whether he/she is motivated to perform the work to the required standard. If he/she has the ability and the motivation, then you need to look at the understanding of what is expected, the performance standard, and the system.

Most people want to behave properly and perform well. When they don't, something usually has gotten in the way. You need to discover what obstacles they are encountering. Frequently, the problem is with the system or work process.

Assuming that you hired carefully, you considered the ability and motivation of an employee for his/her job before extending your job offer. Thus, the action to take is to diagnose why there is a gap between what you expect and what you get.

Confronting poor performance   Certainly, you need to give people a fair chance to learn the ropes and demonstrate what they can do. You need to make sure that they understand what is expected, and that they have adequate support from you and their team members. When you see signs that someone is falling short, engage them in problem solving.

Exploratory meeting   When there is a problem, 75% of the time the supervisor and employee have a different understanding of the expectations or standards. In spite of efforts to communicate, there may be a misunderstanding.* Set up a meeting to explore the situation using this format:

- ❑ Restate your expectation: (Supv.) *"I need to talk with you. When we talked during your orientation, I thought that we agreed that you would visit your top 30 customers in your territory by the end of the month."*

- ❑ State your perspective: (Supv.) *"There is just one more week left before the end of the month. As of yesterday, I believe that you have visited only five and have 8 more visits scheduled."*

- ❑ State why this is a problem: (Supv.) *"I promised them that you would visit them within one month of your appointment. It doesn't look like you will make it. I don't want them to think that we don't keep our promises."*

- ❑ Solicit employee's view: (Sales rep.) *"You're right. We did agree that I'd visit them, but I thought that I was to have my visits with them scheduled within a month, not completed within a month. I've contacted all 30 and have all but 9 scheduled. Some of the people have been traveling and won't be available for me to visit until next month."*

- ❑ Ask what it will take to close this gap? (Supv.) *"Well, then, what will it take for you to have all the visits scheduled by the end of next week?"*

---

*Hint: In testing for understanding, people frequently ask, "Do you understand?" Equally frequently, people will say that they do so as not to appear stupid, or because they may not know what they don't understand. A better approach is to say, "Tell me what you understand about _____." If he/she can paraphrase what you said to your satisfaction, then the probability is that he/she understands. If his/her paraphrased understanding is different from yours, you can then clarify the points of misunderstanding. Another way is to ask, "What questions do you have?" This question implies that there should be questions. It makes it easier for someone to ask than if you ask, "Any questions?"

- ❑ Ask what support the employee needs: (Supv.) *"Is there anything I need to do to help you?"* (Sales rep.) *"No. It has helped me just that we clarified our different expectation.*
- ❑ Ask what the employee can commit to: (Supv.) *"What can you have completed by next week at this time?"* (Sales rep.) *"I can complete scheduling my visits by the end of the month."*
- ❑ Set a time for the follow up meeting: (Supv.) *"If you run into problems, let me know. In the meantime, when should we get together next to see how things are going?"* (Sales rep.) *"Let's meet next Wednesday at 4:15."*

This approach reaffirms your expectations, tests for understanding, and engages the employee in devising a course of action that he/she can commit to. As you will need to refer to this conversation in the future, summarize it in a memo to the employee with a copy for his/her file.

Follow-up meeting(s) In your exploratory meeting, or in a previous follow-up meeting, you set a time for a follow-up meeting. Whether or not progress has been made, this meeting needs to occur. If the employee has corrected the performance problem, he/she needs to be acknowledged for his/her efforts and success. (Supv.) *"A week ago I was a little concerned that you were slipping on visiting the 30 top customers in your territory. I am pleased to see that you now have your visits scheduled, and that you have completed 12 of the 30. I'll be interested to talk with you about what you learned form your meetings. Thanks for following up on this priority."*

If the problem persists, pursue further problem solving. The conversation will be similar to the exploratory meeting. However, before concluding the meeting, the employee needs to know the possible consequences if he/she does not meet your expectation.

(Supv.) *"After our meeting last week, I was encouraged that you would complete your scheduling of visits with your top 30 customers by now. How has it gone? Where are you in the process?"*

(Sales rep.) *"I know today is the deadline. I hate to tell you, but I still have five more to schedule. With all I've had to do, I just couldn't seem to find the time to make the calls at times when they are available to talk with me."*

(Supv.) *"I know that you have had a lot on your plate, and that they can be hard to get hold of, but we agreed that this is high priority. Is there anything else getting in your way?"*

(Sales rep.) *"Yes. Six of our customers have been so upset with the repeated breakdown of their 425E Activastors that I've not wanted to talk with our other customers until we have the replacement module ready. When will that be?"*

(Supv.) *"They'll be ready on Wednesday.*

"I'm concerned that you would let upset customers get in the way of setting up meetings. You and Customer Service are our critical first line of defense. If customers are having problems, that's all the more reason to visit them."

(Sales rep.) *"Yeah, you're right. It's just that after only three weeks in this job I don't feel knowledgeable enough about our products yet to answer all their questions intelligently."*

(Supv.) *"You can never know enough. That's OK. Tell them that you'll get back to them with the answer in 24 hours. Then you can ask me their questions and I'll help you find the answers.*

"Now, when can you have the rest of the meetings scheduled?"

(Sales rep.) *"I'll have them scheduled before the end of the day on Friday. Let's meet at 4:45, and I'll show you I can meet the deadline."*

How patient do you need to be with someone having a behavior or performance problem? Violations of important policies, laws or ethical standards don't deserve much patience. Performance deficiencies for which you see promise and progress deserve patience as long as you can live with the rate of progress. Don't keep anyone for whom you have lost hope.

Success is not guaranteed Not everyone with behavior or performance problems can be turned around. In the first place, they need the basic ability (aptitude, knowledge and skills) and motivation. Then they have to understand and commit to what is expected. Additionally, they have to want to change what they are doing, and they need to have a chance with support and coaching. When they succeed they need to be recognized for their accomplishment. If they can't, or won't, then they need to be removed from the job and replaced.

How about reassignment? Can someone who doesn't work out for you be a good employee in another situation? Perhaps! People have different talents. Mozart was a musical genius, but a poor money manager. He composed great music, but you wouldn't want him to manage your money. While some training might have helped him, his real strength was elsewhere. Just because someone doesn't work out for you doesn't mean that he/she is doomed to failure in other situations. The best solution for everyone is for him/her to change to a job where he/she can pursue his/her real talents, and for you to get a replacement who will meet your needs.

Confronting behavior or performance problems is easier said than done. Yet, it is one of the most important functions of leadership. When someone is not working out, others on the team are aware of it and expect you to take action. The longer you procrastinate, the less respect you will have. Your team expects you to take appropriate action. They will support you if you are fair and preserve the dignity of their coworker.

7.4

Confronting Conflict Productively

Conflict in the workplace is inevitable! Whenever two or more people work together, there are bound to be different values, goals and motives, as well as misunderstandings, hurt feelings and unmet expectations. This may sound depressing, but accepting this reality, and acting to resolve conflicts quickly, is critical for keeping your team focused.

Conflict is like the tip of an iceberg. It is the visible manifestation of fear, frustration, loss of control and other feelings that appear threatening.

Conflict is not all bad When it prompts people to explore new ways of thinking and more options, it can be beneficial. It is unproductive when its effect is to undermine mutual respect and trust, divert people's energies from their goals, create "win-lose" situations, and undermine cooperation.

How do people deal with conflict? It depends on their level of assertiveness, willingness to cooperate, stake in the conflict, and the nature of the people involved. While you might be assertive when you have a disagreement with your child, you might be much less assertive with someone who is pressing a loaded gun to your temples. If the issue is about which movie to see, you'll probably be less assertive than if it is about which car to buy; there is more at stake with the car purchase.

When people are *un*assertive and *un*cooperative, they tend to avoid conflict. They typically lack the skills to problem-solve with others for a creative, mutually acceptable resolution. They may even deny that there is an issue. They lose, and so do others because the issue is not confronted and resolved.

When people are *un*assertive and cooperative, they tend to take the "no problem" approach to conflict. *"If that's what you want, no problem. I'll do that."* They want peace and harmony more than they want the best solution.

When people are highly **assertive and *un*cooperative**, they try to win at all costs. They won't accept a compromise. *"I'm right! Therefore you must be wrong (and don't you forget it)!"*

When people are highly **assertive and cooperative**, they tend to seek creative solutions. They know what they want and they are willing to work with others to achieve a solution in which everyone wins.

Goal In confronting conflict, the goal is to create situations where issues are resolved to everyone's satisfaction, and where they believe that they have benefitted from working together. Then they and the organization are better off because the conflict was resolved creatively. Is this possible? Yes! Here's how:

1. As an organization, establish a set of values that clearly communicate that:

- ❑ Conflict is natural and can be healthy when approached with mutual respect.
- ❑ Confronting conflict is to be welcomed as an expression of caring.
- ❑ It is not only OK, but also desirable, for people to have differing views.
- ❑ Conflicts should be resolved as informally, early and peacefully as possible.
- ❑ The goal of conflict resolution is to develop creative solutions that enable everyone to benefit from the process.
- ❑ Conflict resolution efforts that create winners and losers are inconsistent with the organization's values, and will be used only if other means fail.

2. Accept the inevitability of conflict. Discuss how you want to approach it with the people with whom you work. Then when a conflict arises, harken back to your discussion and agreement. This facilitates dealing with the issue because you have a common prior understanding of how to handle it.

3. As an organization, establish a conflict resolution process to use when informal efforts don't work. The following process attempts to change a "head-to-head" confrontation into "side-by-side" problem solving between equals:

- ❑ First, ask each party to the conflict to describe it as they see it.
- ❑ Then, determine the points of agreement between the parties.
- ❑ Isolate the points of disagreement.
- ❑ Have each party state its position, reasons for it and why it is important to them.
- ❑ Have each party describe in their own words the position of the other parties.
- ❑ Have the parties develop a consolidated statement of the core issues.

❑ Ask each party to state what they would consider to be a satisfactory resolution.

❑ Have the parties brainstorm ways in which to meet everyone's needs.

❑ Have the parties narrow the brainstormed alternatives to the top few, and evaluate them.

❑ Create a consensus for which alternative to adopt. If that can't be achieved, refer the recommendations to a higher level for a decision.

4. Most conflicts, especially misunderstandings or hurt feelings, can be resolved on an informal basis if confronted immediately. The longer the time between an incident and a confrontation, the more difficult the confrontation is because of built-up feelings.

5. Some conflicts are more difficult to resolve because an event has happened, and you cannot turn the clock back and live life differently. Even if you can't change history, it may be valuable to confront it (a) to "get a load off your chest," and (b) to reduce the chance of a repeat incident. When a conflict eats away at you, it does you no good. Even if it can't be resolved, the act of expressing how it has affected you generally makes you feel better. Especially if the conflict is based on a misunderstanding, it is important to confront the situation to reduce the chance of it happening again.

6. When you confront someone, first plan what you want to accomplish, and how you want to accomplish it. Your chances of accomplishing your objectives are better with forethought. Also, it may help to discuss your thoughts with a trusted friend or confidant who can help you focus on your objectives and comment on your approach.

7. When you confront someone, cite what has happened, its effects on you and others affected by it, and your desire to resolve the situation.

"I need to talk with you for a few minutes about something that is bothering me. I've thought about it and decided that it is better for us to discuss it, than for me to let it eat away at me.

"This morning in front of my team you bawled me out for not getting the Jones order out by 3:00 PM yesterday. I understand how important it is to you for us meet our commitments, but bawling me out in front of other people demeans me. If I looked unhappy, it was because I was astounded and disappointed that you would chew me out in front of others."

Then, express what you consider to be an appropriate resolution of the conflict.

"We can not turn the clock back and do things differently. Nor will it help either of us for you to apologize to me in front of my team. In all probability, there may be times in the future when you take issue with what I have or have not done. What I would like is your commitment that whenever you take issue with my actions, you will talk with me in private. Can you live with that?"

End by thanking the person for his or her time, consideration and cooperation.

8. There may be times when you are confronted. The first rule is to control your temper and listen, listen, listen. You cannot control what the other person says, but you can control how you respond. When someone confronts you, it is natural to feel at least a little defensive, but defensiveness only makes it more difficult to resolve a conflict.

Listen to what the person has to say until he/she has nothing left to say. When the person has nothing left to say, he/she is then ready to listen, but not one minute before then. The fact that you have listened attentively, without interruption, enhances your position and builds a debt of gratitude on the part of the other person to listen as well to you.

When you start speaking, summarize first your understanding of what the other person said. (Carl Rogers, the noted behavioral scientist, urges not to argue until you can restate the other person's position in your own words to his or her satisfaction.) Then, summarize your points of agreement. That helps build a bond. When you discuss points of disagreement, recognize that reasonable people can see the same thing differently. Say, "Let me tell you how I saw that," and proceed to explain your viewpoint. The more open-minded and non-defensive you are, the more open-minded and non-defensive the other person will be.

Whether or not you come to agreement, thank the other person for having expressed his or her views and feelings. He/she took a personal risk in confronting you. That was an expression of trust and caring.

As stated earlier, conflict is natural in organizational life. When it can be surfaced and confronted, there is a chance of resolving it. If it is present but does not surface, it can become a preoccupation that drains talents non-productively and destroys some people. Even though confrontation has some risks, it is far better for everyone to confront conflict and resolve it creatively.

7.5

Expressing Anger or Other Strong Feelings

Working with some people can try the patience of a saint! Mistakes, excuses, complaining, snide remarks, and people jumping to conclusions can be a real challenge. In all probability, you are not a saint. So how are you supposed to deal with someone who arouses your anger?

Over the past 35 years, I have been a "lightning rod" for managers who have had to deal with people who "pushed their hot-buttons." Here's what I've learned in the process:

Choose your response You *can't* control what others do; you *can* choose how to respond. Approximately 75% of the people I have coached through problems, in reflecting back on how they expressed their anger in the heat of the moment prior to coaching, have regretted how they did so. So, when faced with a situation that makes you angry, **count to 10**. It may seem like a simplistic answer, but it works. Though it may be tempting to fire back reactively, when you do so you lose control of yourself and the situation. You need to have enough time before responding to regain your composure and determine how you want to respond. You can say, *"I am not in any frame of mind to deal with this right now. I need to 'count to ten' and get back to you."* Then ask yourself:

1. What do I want to accomplish in responding to this person about this situation? Do I really want to vent my anger, intimidate and turn off an employee, and appear completely out of control? If your objective is to change an employee's behavior, then a less emotional, problem-solving approach is indicated.

2. What is the best way to get my message across? What gets through to the person with whom I need to communicate? If you are the captain of a prison chain gang, the communication strategy is different from that used if you are in charge of a research and development team.

3. What do I need to do, so that when I look back on this a month from now, I will feel proud of how I handled this situation?

Displaying anger seldom brings out the best in you and others. It diverts attention from the message to the anger, and puts everyone on the defensive. People close down when they are defensive. They are less open to solving problems exactly when they need to be more open. Does that mean you should hide your feelings? Yes and no. In most situations, delay expressing yourself until you can express the message you want. When you have regained your composure and determined your objectives, explain how you felt:

"Yesterday, I was so upset that I was ready to fire you, and I knew that was not the appropriate response. I have calmed down now. Let's see how we can prevent that from happening again."

You can't change someone's behavior. Change comes from within. The best you can hope to do is to influence one to change. Thus, engage an employee in problem solving:

Explain
"This is what I expected." (Explain) *"This is what you did (or what happened)."* (Describe)

"This is how I felt as a result." (Describe how it affected you.)

Ask
"What are your options for `getting the toothpaste back in the tube' (correcting this situation)?"

"What are you going to do to change _____, and what help do you need?"

"When do we need to get together to review your progress?"

Anger is a natural feeling. It is, however, a feeling that can overcome you and distract you from accomplishing your goals. It is difficult to step outside yourself when you are angry to call "time out," or to listen non-defensively to criticism. You will, though, be pleased that you did when you reflect back on how you handled a vexing situation.

7.6

Letting Go of Anger Toward Others

When bad things happen, it is natural to feel disappointment and anger, and to wish for justice or retribution. Bruised egos, misunderstandings and unkept promises are part of organizational life. They can be seeds of anger. Obsessing over them undermines your *joie de vivre,* health, and your team.

Place in perspective "Good" happens! And even though it is not fair, so does "bad." "Bad" can happen intentionally or unintentionally. Someone may hurt you without being aware of the pain you feel. Your anger generally does not hurt them as much as it hurts you and the people who experience its effect on you.

How we deal with anger is part of what defines us. Some people love their anger. Others don't know how to reduce it. But hanging on to anger keeps you focused on the rear view mirror when you need to be looking ahead. No matter how you try, you can't turn the clock back and change the past. Actions to right a wrong still do not change what happened.

Choice You have a choice. You can give control of your life to the person who angers you by hanging on to your anger, or you can forgive and get on with life.

To forgive is not to condone what has happened. It is more like saying, "I don't like what you did. I wish it had not happened. But it does me no good to hold a grudge, so I am going to let go and move on."

Letting go The *basic* letting go process works this way:

1. Accept that there is "bad" in the world and that you will experience some. Part of the challenge of organizational life is to place the events of your life in perspective.

2. There is also a lot of "good." Look for it and you will find it. Focusing on the good fosters a sense of gratitude and helps you place things in perspective.

3. Recognize that continued negative feelings about someone or some event anchor you in the past. Ask yourself these questions and write down the answers:

    a. How is this affecting my work, team, mental outlook and physical health?
    b. How will I benefit by forgiving?
    c. What will I lose if I forgive?

4. Envision what life will be like when you are freed of your anger. Write this down, save it, and commit to yourself to pursue it.

5. Draft a letter to the person you forgive:

Dear ____:

On May 23, 1997, _____ happened. It affected me _____. Because of your role in this I have held anger toward you until now. I still don't like what happened, but I have come to realize that it does no good to bear a grudge. Thus, I would like to forgive you and get on with my life.

6. Sending the letter to the person could backfire on you. Much of the anger reduction benefit comes from writing the letter, so just file it in your "grudge file."

7. With some good friends, ceremoniously destroy your "grudge file" and celebrate your liberation.

Don't let anger control you! You can't control what happens to you in life. You can choose how you respond. The ironical result of a bad experience is to surrender control of your life to the person who inflicted pain on you. For the benefit of you and your team, don't let that happen.

7.7

Reducing Your Risk of Sexual Harassment Problems

Sexual harassment claims and suits are burgeoning. Attorneys' fees can easily cost $300,000 for a *victory*! A loss can run in the millions. Moreover, sexual harassment is devastating to the person harassed, the alleged harasser, and the organization—a true "lose-lose" situation. Can you prevent sexual harassment from occurring in your organization? No! But you can reduce substantially your risk of sexual harassment, overt or subtle, with some relatively simple actions.

Example

In an organizational review for a client with 400 employees, we discovered that they had not adopted and implemented a sexual harassment policy. The president had not wanted to believe that something like sexual harassment could occur in his organization. When he was reminded of a $7 million award by a jury in a prominent sexual harassment case, he agreed to have the issue discussed in his weekly management committee meeting.

The managers were asked to brainstorm what they thought constituted sexual harassment and their answers were written on a flip chart. They offered the obvious behaviors, but were unaware of many of the more subtle forms. As a result, the president and his team realized that they needed a policy and process to reduce their sexual harassment risk. The president appointed a small task force to draft the policy, and to plan and implement the processes for policy promulgation and complaint resolution. The resulting policy draft was comprehensive, and consistent with the organization's values. The complaint resolution process was simple, time-ly, and it assured confidentiality. Five men and women were selected for a pool of potential complaint investigators. An employee with a complaint could choose one of them to investigate. Implementation included training in small groups for all current and new employees. The task force's recommendations were approved by the management committee and legal counsel, and were implemented within three months.

To date there has been one complaint of overt sexual harassment, and two claims of subtle harassment. They were investigated quickly and appropriate action was taken. All the people involved in the process felt that they were treated fairly and appropriately. No one has taken legal action related to sexual harassment!

Comment

What made this approach a success was:

- ❏ Sustained promulgation of the policy and process, and top management support
- ❏ Consistency of the policy and process with the values of the organization
- ❏ A general belief that the consequences are reasonable and appropriate
- ❏ Immediate follow-up on complaint investigation
- ❏ The credibility of the investigators and the process as a whole

Any business with a typical cross section of employees will eventually have to deal with a charge of sexual harassment. It is far less costly to try to prevent sexual harassment, and plan how to deal with it when it occurs, than it is to muddle through once it happens.

7.8

Absenteeism—What You Can Do About It

Absenteeism is an *abuse* of one's privilege to be absent from work for authorized reasons. Occasional use of sick leave is not absenteeism. When an employee would truly endanger his/her health, or infect others by being at work, he/she should stay home.

Absenteeism is usually a symptom of other problems. To control absenteeism, you need to determine the underlying causes of why employees choose not to come to work.

Absenteeism (except for chronic health problems) is seldom found among employees who:

❑ Enjoy their work

❑ Feel their jobs are important

❑ Have a high level of self-esteem

❑ Are recognized for their accomplishments

❑ Feel they have effective supervision

❑ Have esprit de corps

❑ Have reasonable policies defining approved behavior

If your organization provides this type of work environment, you probably don't have organization-wide absenteeism. If you do, conduct a review of your work environment to determine how employees behave, including their decision to come to work.

Conducting an organizational review focused on absenteeism can sometimes be done by internal people. Other times an outsider is needed. For insiders to succeed, they must be open, objective, and be perceived as having no vested interests in the resulting recommendations. While an organizational review may be needed in some situations, absenteeism ultimately has to be corrected at the individual level: between the supervisor and employee.

Guidelines How you handle an absence has a large bearing on how an employee will behave when faced with a decision of whether or not to come to work. Some general guidelines are:

1. Let employees know that they are important, and that when they are not at work, it creates problems for you and others on their team. Make sure they know that you expect them at work when they are scheduled to work, unless coming to work would endanger their health or the health of their team members.

2. When an employee is absent, distinguish between when he or she could have come to work, but did not, and when he or she truly should not have come to work. Also, distinguish between isolated illnesses and chronic or frequent ones. Normal sick leave is to continue earnings when one should not come to work for reasons of health, or to protect the health of others. It is not intended for these problems that require special attention, such as:

❑ Chronic illnesses reflecting genuine health problems (including addiction)

❏ When an employee stayed home to care for someone

❏ When an employee could have come to work, but chose not to

3. When you discover a problem, address the situation:

❏ As soon as you discover it

❏ After you have determined how you want to handle it

❏ With your records and facts in order

Use resources available to you (your supervisor, HR, employee assistance programs).

4. In a problem solving session with an employee, be sure you explain clearly what problems he/she has created for you and others by his/her absences:

❏ Focus on what can be done to improve attendance, now and in the future.

❏ Avoid arguments about whether past absences were justified. (Arguments only make you and the employee defensive.) Focus on how to improve from now onward.

❏ Ask the employee for his or her views on what he or she can do to improve attendance. (No one is closer to the problem than the employee. If he or she can propose a solution, it is easier for you, and the employee is more apt to accept the solution.)

❏ Get the employee to commit to you what actions he/she will take to improve.

❏ Summarize your understanding in a note confirming your discussion. Keep a copy for yourself and give one to the employee. Even with informal discussions, it is important to confirm commitments in writing. They are remembered longer.

5. Monitor attendance. Express your appreciation to employees for coming to work when you know that they are not feeling well, or when you know that there are circumstances that could have kept them from deciding to come to work.

There always seems to be more time for correcting problems than preventing them. In the case of absenteeism, there are some things one can do in an effort to prevent problems:

❏ There is no substitute for a relationship of trust between you and the people who report to you. Trust involves risks, but the risks can be minimized if you know the people. Trust is a lot easier to build before a problem arises.

❏ Get to know people who report to you. Each has a unique background that influences his or her behavior. Show interest in them. Discover their ambitions, interests, etc. You will be better situated to determine the risks of extending trust. When problems arise, having taken interest in them will help you to work with them more cooperatively.

❏ Help the people with whom you work to feel good about themselves, their work, and their team. They want to feel important and needed. (If they enjoy coming to work, they will be less apt to be absent.) Make sure that they have the training, information, tools and work processes to do the job correctly the first time. When they do a good job, let them know you appreciate what they have done. Tell why you consider their work praise-worthy. If they fall short of your expectations, find out why, and help them learn how they can perform better next time.

❏ An open door policy is too passive to prevent problems. Take an active interest in employees. Get out of your office, walk around, and ask employees about what problems affect them and their work (including personal problems). Help them to find ways to solve their problems. Make sure there is adequate follow-up.

One of your prime responsibilities is to get problems solved. You do not have to solve all the problems yourself. Get people involved who are in the best position to solve them.

❏ Let the person to whom you report know which policies and work processes are working well, and which ones create problems or unintend-ed consequences. Though you have to manage within your organization's policies, you may be able to influence them, or help redesign them. Your input is important!

❏ If you anticipate a problem with an employee, or if you find yourself in the midst of a problem, ask for help from HR or your supervisor. They are resources for you.

❏ Choose carefully the people who work for you. Your success depends on them. It is a lot easier not to hire a problem employee than to have to cope with one!

Absenteeism is a reflection of your leadership and management. The people on your team are looking for leadership and management that inspires and enables them to perform their best - individually, and as a team. If you let one person get away with absenteeism, it communicates to others that they can get by with it, too. The people on your team generally suffer when a team member is absent and they must pick up the slack. They expect you to confront absenteeism constructively, and want you to.

7.9

Standing up for What is Important to You

Organizational life is filled with challenges. Organizations are filled with a variety of personalities and not everyone sees ethical issues as you do. In addition, the pressures of fierce competition in the market sometimes prompt people to take, or propose to take, actions that are at odds with your values or organizational values. Standing up to them can be risky, but if you don't, then you risk living at odds with your conscience. That can be a long sentence!

As a manager and as a management consultant, I have frequently had to take a stand on an issue. That "comes with the territory." And I have never been beheaded for standing up for what I believe is right. Here is what has worked for me.

Clarify the other person's position Though it might be tempting to dismiss the other person's position out of hand, such a tactic is apt to be interpreted as uncooperative and is more apt to be met with resistance. In any form of negotiation you first must understand the other person's position, and *demonstrate* your understanding, before confronting it.

"Gee, what you're saying sounds like you want me to advertise for sales clerks for our leather goods store when we don't have any openings. Then you want me to hire them for our factory outlet and place them there. You believe that an ad for our leather goods store will draw more applicants than one for our factory outlet will. Is that correct?"

"Yes, that's exactly right."

Ask for his/her assessment of the risks and consequences of his/her position Asking a question is sometimes more powerful than making a statement. The process of answering the question may create an "ah hah" for the person.

"What are the risks and possible consequences associated with that?"

"I would not have suggested that if I thought there was anything wrong with it. I suppose it might be consider 'bait and switch,' but I doubt that anyone would try to sue us."

"Is anything we do OK, just so long as we don't get sued?"

"No, but I thought I had a pretty clever idea. Do you have a problem with that?"

State your position and preferred alternative Once you have listened and demonstrated that you understand, the other person has a "psychological debt" to repay by listening to you.

"Yes, I do. I'm concerned that it is `bait and switch.' It rubs my ethical sense the wrong way. We might not get sued, but I don't want us to get a reputation in the job market for `bait and switch' tactics. If that were to happen, we would have an even harder time recruiting than we do now. Instead, I propose _____."

Analysis of proposed alternative Once you have proposed your preferred alternative, ask what he/she sees as its pluses and minuses. Asking him/her to come up with and think through the pluses and minuses requires him/her to think about how your alternative would work. Having him/her express his/her concerns lets you know what they are. Once you know his/her concerns, you are in a better position to detune them or possibly turn them into pluses. As in the sales process, you can't counter objections until you know what they are.

Summarize your discussion—Seek permission Summarizing enables you to bring the issue back into context and emphasize the key points. If there still is an undisclosed objection to your alternative, it provides an opportunity for it to surface before you seek to proceed.

"Thanks for taking the time to discuss my concerns about advertising for sales clerks. As you correctly discerned, I have problems with that. I am glad that you understand my concerns. I believe we have settled your concerns about my alternative plan for advertising in targeted community papers. Why don't I proceed with my targeted advertising alternative starting this week end?"

"Go ahead. I was initially skeptical about it, but I think it is worthwhile trying them."

There is seldom just one way to accomplish an objective. By proposing an alternative that accomplishes the objective, you are taking action to accomplish it in a way you can live with.

Fallback position Though the process I have described works in many cases, it may not always work. Negotiations are predicated on both parties wanting to come to an agreement. If the person with whom you want to negotiate doesn't want to negotiate, this process won't work.

Some people have a vested interest in a particular course of action and are not open to alternatives. Or, they may not be sold on your proposed alternative. Either way, if what you are being told to do violates your principles, you may choose to take a stand.

"I've listened to your reasons for advertising for our factory outlet sales clerks using the leather store as the lure. I understand them, but you have not persuaded me that it is ethically correct and in keeping with the values of our company. My conscience won't let me do that."

Sometimes the person will back off. In other situations the person may draw a line in the sand.

"Screw your conscience! I want those ads placed as I originally told you to do."

"I said that my conscience wouldn't let me do that. If you insist, then you'll have to find someone else to do it. I'm prepared to resign, if that's what's necessary. This is very important to me."

You don't take this position very often, nor do you draw a line in the sand frivolously. The principle has to be very important to you, and you have to be willing to accept the consequences. The person with whom you are negotiating, when faced with the prospect of your resigning, may relent. But, your conscience is with you for life. You have to be able to sleep nights.

7.10

Confronting Lying

Lying is rampant in our society. From the Oval Office to the local courtroom, from the home to the work place, and even in school, people manipulate technicalities and make statements that they know are false with the intent to deceive. *"Did you hit Johnny?" "No. He hit me first." "Well, did you hit back?" "Yes, but he hit first!"* In the kid's mind, "hitting" is an aggressive act and "hitting back" is defensive and, thus, not "hitting." Is it any wonder that President Clinton responded the way he did when he was asked if he had sex with Monica?

Confronting lying is tricky No one likes to be called a liar, or to be caught lying. Accusing someone of it is apt to raise his/her defensive hackles and prompt further lying to cover for the original lie. Then getting to the truth becomes more difficult. But if you don't confront what appears to be a lie, in effect, you condone lying.

Is it really a lie? What appears to be a lie may, in fact, be a different perception. Various studies have been conducted in which people are given a few seconds to look at a scene, and then describe what they saw. While there are typically some points of agreement, there are at least an equal number contested. People see what they look for, and typically don't see what they don't look for. Thus, witnesses to the same incident can truthfully give distinctly different reports.

Does your behavior prompt people to lie?   How you react to situations can have a bearing on how honest people are with you. Some people only stretch the truth when they fear your reaction to it. If the consequences for telling the truth are worse than for lying, then lying is rewarded, and vice versa. So, people are less apt to twist things if they discover that you are a reasonable person to deal with and don't punish them for their honesty.

What do you want to accomplish?   So, what do you do when something doesn't "smell right?" First, recognize the distinction between a difference of perception and intent to deceive. Next, decide what you want to accomplish by confronting. Are you after the truth? Do you want to find grounds to fire someone? Then, you determine your strategy.

Clarify the situation   In the USA, you are presumed innocent until proven guilty. In that spirit, if your objective is to determine the truth, first approach a discussion assuming that he/she may see things differently. It is embarrassing when you treat what appears to be a lie *as a lie* if it isn't.

"Gee, I'm puzzled. You say you can't work overtime tonight because you have a dentist appointment. Does your dentist have late hours?"

"As a matter of fact, once a week she does. I scheduled my appointment at 7:30 PM so it would not interfere with work."

Get your facts   Make sure that you have the facts and that they are correct. If you have evidence that someone has been less than honest, present the evidence and let the person explain it.

"Last night Miguel and Fred saw you and your wife at the Sharks game. You told me you could not work overtime because of your dentist appointment." (Silence.)

"Yes, we did bump into each other at half-time, just after Janet and I arrived. My dentist appointment was over by 8:00 PM, so we went to the game after that."

If you confirm that someone has lied, try to discover why. *"Hmm! So you had a half hour dentist appointment and then went to the Sharks game. Why didn't you mention the game?"*

"I figured that telling you about the dentist appointment was enough."

*"The fact that your dentist appointment was so short, and that you went to the Sharks game right afterwards knowing about our critical need for you here, makes me feel that you were not completely above-board with me. In the future, please tell me the **whole** story."*

Termination Some people lie compulsively. Some are not even aware when they are telling the truth and when they are fabricating. They are like Jim Carey in the movie, ***Liar, Liar***. You don't know when to believe them and how much to believe. There is no good reason to keep them as employees or colleagues. The objective is to catch them dead-to-rights in order to terminate their employment.

*"I overheard Margaret remind you of your dentist appointment **tomorrow** evening at 7:30 PM, not last night. So I phoned Dr. West to find out if her office was open last night, and it wasn't.*

"I have to be able to trust the people on our team. I can no longer trust you. We have discussed and documented five other incidents when you did not tell me the truth. You have just demonstrated to me for the final time that I can't trust you. Paula will help you with out-processing while I get you your final pay check."

Confronting lying is not a joyous task, but it is essential. Lying destroys trust, and teamwork depends on trust. People who get by with lying to you are probably lying to others, too. And, someone who violates your trust is unlikely ever to regain it. You can't afford to have such people on your team. Investigate, and if necessary, confront people when it appears that one is lying. If you do not confront lying, you tacitly condone it. That undermines your credibility and encourages others to lie. You don't need that!

7.11

Preserving Individual Dignity in Terminations

You wouldn't hire someone you knew was not going to work out, but who "bats 1000?"

As a leader, you have an obligation to your team to provide them with competent co-workers, and to help them to resolve problems. Even with your support, not everyone works out. When someone falls short of expectations, you need to take timely and constructive action, for everyone's sake. The appropriate action sometimes is termination of employment.

Preserving dignity reduces risk Having to terminate someone's employment is not a pleasant task. It can be done with dignity, or it can prompt a wrongful termination suit or action to "get even." You cannot eliminate the risk of such a reaction, but you can reduce it through conducting a termination in a way that preserves one's dignity.

People who feel that they have been treated fairly and with dignity in the termination process seldom take action against a former employer or colleague. What is important to an employee whose employment is being terminated is:

Before Termination

- ❑ Knowing what is expected
- ❑ Having a fair chance to succeed

During Termination

- ❑ Humane/straight-forward treatment
- ❑ A way to leave that preserves "face"
- ❑ A fair severance package
- ❑ Assurance that one is "OK," even though the job didn't work out

After Termination

- ❑ Fair references

No surprises Except for situations of serious misconduct where a termination may be "on the spot," a termination should not come as a surprise. An employee should have been aware that he/she was in a situation where continuation of employment was at issue. He/she should know the standards required, and should have had the opportunity and support to meet those standards. And, he/she should know the probable consequences for failure to meet expectations.

When to terminate When you have lost hope that an employee will meet or surpass reasonable expectations and standards in a reasonable period, then prepare for termination. In most cases, this will be after you have provided him/her with coaching and an opportunity to improve. If he/she would make a good employee in another situation in your organization, then you might consider a transfer or reassignment. However, if termination is due to a character flaw, don't try to accommodate him/her elsewhere.

How to terminate Termination discussions need to be in a private setting without interruptions. Get to the point quickly. Don't keep the employee in suspense. Then explain your rationale as a follow up to your decision.

"Leslie, I'm terminating your employment effective _____. Over the past two months, we've worked to help you meet our expectations. We've met every two weeks to review your progress. After all our efforts, I've now lost hope that you will

be able to do ____ within an acceptable period. I believe that we will both be better off when you are in another job better suited to you."

Just because an employee doesn't work out in one job may not mean that he/she is a bad person or can't succeed elsewhere. If your organization would benefit by having him/her work elsewhere, consider reassignment. Help him/her to move into a job where he/she can perform competently. Then, get a replacement that meets your needs.

If, in the course of working with the employee, you have seen potential for another job in your business, you can add *"As we've worked together, I've been particularly impressed with ___. I've talked with ___ in HR about you for such work, and would like you to talk with him/her."*

Denial Sometimes an employee will be in a state of denial and want to negotiate one more chance. That is natural, but once he/she has had a fair opportunity to prove him/herself there is no point delaying a well-founded action.

Communicating a termination At some point, before the rumor mill runs wild, you will need to announce the employee's departure.

"As I mentioned, ___ will be your last day here. It is better for us to plan what we will say rather than to leave it to chance. What would you like communicated to the rest of the group about you leaving?"

Saving face is important to most people. Try to accommodate reasonable wishes. If the employee chooses to resign instead, and your company policy permits that, let him/her "resign." If he/she chooses not to resign, then work out a statement that is both honest and face saving.

"Leslie will be leaving. He/she has been working hard to master his/her job. We have valued _____. _____ continues to be a challenge. As we have reflected on all that Leslie has done over the past weeks it has become clear that his/her strengths are in _____. So Leslie will be leaving on _____ to pursue that line of work."

Document Discussions on such important issues as termination need to be confirmed in writing.

Not all terminations proceed as simply and smoothly as the above. It is important to know the person with whom you are dealing, and it is essential to prepare. Discussing a situation with an objective and knowledgeable confidant, and with people in Human Resources, can help you to reduce your risk of a wrongful discharge suit, and enhance your image as an effective, caring leader.

8

Building Your Leadership Credibility

8.1

Building Your Leadership Credibility

There are no, "Just add water, mix and bake," answers to building your credibility as a leader. Leadership credibility has several components: being believable, reliable and competent. You can't be credible just by expecting or demanding it; like trust, it can only be earned. It takes discipline, patience, and a strong belief in people. Here are 11 tips:

1. Show respect for, **and** extend **trust** to, the people with whom you work. You may not see eye-to-eye. Be open to differing views. They can be valid, too. Don't talk about people behind their back. Though they may not find out, those with whom you talk may wonder, "What does he/she say about me behind my back?"

2. Care about the people you lead. Get to know them individually. Ask what you do that helps bring out the best in them and what you do that hinders them. Listen! Continue to do that which brings out their best, and change what you do that hinders them. This is "market research" among "customers" for your leadership.

3. Treat people as *they* want to be treated Try to bring out the best in them and you'll create a self-fulfilling prophecy for their success and loyalty.

4. Tailor communications Ask the people you lead what information they need to be kept adequately informed, and what is the best way for them to receive it. E-mail and bulletin boards may be fine for general information. More personal communications (one-on-one or small group) may be needed for information that affects them more personally.

5. Involve the people you lead in solving the problems that affect them. They are more apt to accept solutions they have helped to create.

6. Share your vision Then, ask the people you lead to augment it so that you create a shared vision. A shared vision builds buy-in and commitment.

7. Honor your commitments Credibility = what you do ÷ what you say you'll do. Under-promise and over-deliver! Demonstrate that you can be counted on.

8. Own-up to mistakes It's a sign of strength. People are amazingly forgiving of mistakes you admit. Richard Nixon destroyed his credibility by denial and cover-up. Had he admitted his mistake right off, history probably would be different.

9. Avoid being defensive when confronted with "bad news" or challenges. This is not easy, but defensiveness only brings out the worst in you.

10. Accept responsibility for your decisions and actions, and those to which you contributed. If you deflect blame, you appear ineffectual and without influence.

11. "Tell it like it is." Be completely candid, even if you risk offense and hurt feelings. I have seen more people hurt by being shielded from the truth than from having to face it. But remember, "Praise in public, critique in private."

The people you lead choose how much trust to place in your leadership. The above points represent critical behaviors on which they judge your credibility.

8.2

"Best Practices" of Leaders

The role of leaders is to *inspire* and *enable* people to achieve common goals while earning their respect, trust and support. Based on interviews and focus groups with close to 5,000 leaders and the people they lead, it is clear that people want leadership that both inspires and enables them. They want someone they can trust, respect, support, and who supports them. These are some of the common themes of what leaders do who get the best, sustained results, and earn their privilege to lead:

What Leaders Do to *Inspire* People to Strive for Their Best

- ❑ **Vision** Help their team to create a shared vision and instill a passion for team goals. Help people see how they can advance their own goals by pursuing team goals.
- ❑ **Competence in the field of endeavor** Understand the business, the critical issues, and know enough technically to provide guidance and inspiration.
- ❑ **Role model** Lead using behavior that others want to emulate.
- ❑ **Buy-in** Seek input from and involve people in decisions that affect them.
- ❑ **Believe in people** Care about people—make them feel important, empower them—look for and bring out the best in them. Welcome people with diverse backgrounds and outlooks. Integrate new people rapidly into the team. Treat everyone fairly.

❏ **Expect the best** Inspire people to stretch, grow, excel, and be all that they can be.

❏ **Create hope** Radiate positive energy and enjoyment of life. Savor life as an adventure/experiment and opportunity to learn.

❏ **Demonstrate high principles** Develop and instill a strong set of values. Tell the truth. Behave ethically without being rigid, intolerant, or like a zealot. Act socially responsible—within and beyond their organization.

❏ **Common good** Place the good of the team/organization ahead of self-interest.

❏ **"Walk the talk"** Lead by example, do what they say they will, honor commitments.

❏ **Show respect** Let people be themselves, honor them for who they are, trust them to do what is right, and recognize them for what they add to the team. Listen attentively, non-defensively, and with empathy. Seek to understand before seeking to be understood. "Praise in public, counsel in private."

❏ **Accept responsibility** Own up to their mistakes and refrain from seeking to blame others or find excuses.

❏ **Recognition** Recognize people for their special efforts and contributions. Celebrate team accomplishments and create team spirit.

What Leaders Do to *Enable* People to Work Together in Pursuit of Their Goals

❏ **Provide focus** Keep the team focused. Don't lose sight of their objectives. Allocate time to pursue what is important to their team's success. Filter out competing distractions.

❏ **Provide clarity** Clarify and confirm roles, responsibilities, quality standards, authority, ground rules and expectations. Make sure that everyone is "singing off of the same song sheet." Test for understanding. Confirm understandings in writing.

❏ **Secure resources** Represent the team persuasively in resource allocation decisions. Provide needed training and support.

❏ **Take action without over reacting** Listen attentively and get the facts. Reserve judgment, place things in perspective, display grace under pressure, and act with a sense of what is appropriate for the circumstance. Support team member decisions, if possible.

❏ **Resolve issues and conflicts** Confront issues promptly, resolve conflicts creatively, and seek to transform problems into opportunities. Help people create "win-win" solutions.

- ❑ **Provide information and feedback** Provide people with the information they need for self-management. Provide timely and specific feedback. Communicate openly, honestly and understandably. Foster understanding between their team and the rest of the organization. Foster team learning.
- ❑ **Create change** Sell the need for change. Involve stakeholders in designing change. Introduce change as an experiment. Coach the team through challenging transitions.
- ❑ **Keep in-touch** "Management by wandering around" to learn about the issues of the people they lead. Accept unwelcome news without "killing the messenger."
- ❑ **Humor** Find the humor in a situation. Don't take themselves too seriously. Don't make jokes at the expense of others, or speak ill of others behind their back.
- ❑ **Self-awareness** Recognize their limits and what they don't know, and get help. Understand their impact on the people with whom they work and behave accordingly.
- ❑ **Be authentic** Come across as genuine, sincere, open, trusting and trustworthy; self-assured without being conceited.
- ❑ **Build the team** Build leadership skills in their team and prepare potential leaders for succession. Build on people's strengths and help them to minimize the effects of their weaknesses.

What to do with "best practices" "Best practices" are distilled from a broad sample of feedback about leaders. They serve as a reference point. It is unusual to find someone who is a master of all the "best practices."

Every leadership role has its unique needs. First, get feedback (Chapter 13) from the people you lead about what behavior they need from you to bring out the best in them. Compare their feedback to the "best practices." Then, look at what you do currently. What do you need to do to bring out the best in the people you lead and get better results? If you were to change what you do, what might be the effect?

Experiment with changes that will improve your results as a leader. Let the people with whom you work know what you are seeking to improve. Ask for their support and feedback as you experiment. Not only will you benefit as you hone your leadership skills, so will they.

8.3

Passion—Don't Try to Lead Without it!

"Frank knows his stuff and all of us like and respect him. We work hard and usually get good results. But there is something missing. He lacks a spark, a passion for what we're doing. As a consequence, so do we. We miss out on the excitement and commitment we need to achieve our full potential as a team."

Passion If you don't have passion for something, how can you foster it in the people you lead? Passion is an intense, compelling emotional drive, "fire in your belly," for something you believe in. It cannot be feigned or bought. It has to be authentic. It is a quality of the heart that emanates from your values and beliefs. It is the application of your purpose in life to a goal with which you identify strongly. With passion, you conquer the obstacles in your path. When you have passion for your pursuit, other people who share your values, beliefs and goals want to join you.

Do you really need passion to be a leader? Yes! Leadership is the art of inspiring and enabling people to perform at their best to achieve a common goal. It is not just a care-taking function. It is getting them to buy in to a vision of a better future and leading them on a journey to the goal. I have yet to see a team win the Superbowl or World Series without a passion for the game and their goal. I have not seen a great teacher without a passion for his/her subject and imparting it to students. Passion separates the extraordinary from the ordinary.

Know yourself Not every leadership opportunity will have what it takes to "switch you on." What can you do if you are being asked to lead, but lack passion? First, clarify your own beliefs and values. What is really important to you? Then, examine the leadership challenge and the goal of your opportunity. How can you advance what is important to you if you accept the challenge? What can you add that is unique and that will rally your team to achieve its goal? Look at it positively and thoroughly! Discuss it with a confidant who has no vested interest in your decision. Does your pulse rise? Do you have enthusiasm for the goal and leading people to it? Can you envision the possibilities? How will your life, the business, or society be better off when the goal is accomplished?

"Lead, follow or get out of the way!" Sometimes a leadership opportunity is not for you. I was asked recently to be the president-elect (president the following year) of a non-profit organization. I had been president of it a decade before and had helped infuse new life into it then. After attending a meeting of their board of directors, I realized that what was important to me ten years before no longer fired me up. Been there, done that! As awkward as it was to admit that I had made a mistake, and as much as I hated to let my colleagues down, I reneged. I lacked passion for their challenges, so it was better to bow out and make way for someone who could be "switched-on" to inspire them to surmount their challenges.

Leading people to accomplish a goal down a road with obstacles and detours can be daunting, even with passion. If you lack passion for the goal and journey, don't try!

8.4

Assuming a Leadership Role

Congratulations! Assuming a leadership role can be the fulfillment of your life's dream. Condolences! Your dream could turn into a nightmare. How you launch yourself is critical.

Your first challenge is to establish yourself as the new leader. Just because you were offered and accepted the role doesn't guarantee that you have the support of the people you will lead. You may be following a dearly beloved leader who is a hard act to follow, a Machiavellian person who was distrusted, or someone who was not up to the job. To complicate the situation, there may be someone reporting to you who also sought the job you got.

Strategy Convert your constituents into allies. (Constituents = the people who you will lead and those with whom you will need close working relationships.) By getting to know your constituents, getting their views on the issues, and then taking action to address their concerns, you will begin the process of earning your right to lead. (See Chapter 7.7 for an example.)

Short "Honeymoon" You don't have much time to establish yourself as a leader, especially if you have to perform triage in a turnaround situation. Nonetheless, if you short-change the process you will spend more time trying to "get the toothpaste back in the tube." "Shooting from the hip" is a sure way to "shoot yourself in the foot." You have only a short "honeymoon" in which to earn the confidence of your constituents—in short, your right to lead.

Establishing yourself is a form of negotiation. As in other negotiations, you really can't begin to make progress until you understand the positions of the people with whom you are negotiating. Thus, meet with them individually or in small groups. Find out what's on their minds, and what's important to them, before you state your positions or take actions. Get to know them. Listen to what they have to say. What's working well? What are the issues? What are their ideas of what needs to be done? What do they support? What do they resist? How full is their "reservoir of good will" for making changes? What brings out the best in them? What "pushes their hot buttons?" What are their expectations and needs for your leadership? Who have they worked for who they respected as a leader? How did he/she earn their respect, trust and support? Vice versa. These are all questions to which you need the answers in order to demonstrate that you understand the challenges, and that you are competent to deal with them.

Emergency triage If your organization is "bleeding to death," you'll need to perform triage to stop the hemorrhaging. The process of getting to know your constituents described above must be cut to the quick initially and then completed once the hemorrhaging has stopped. You will need a quick reading from your constituency of the vital signs to know whether you need to amputate a leg or perform an appendectomy, figuratively speaking. In an emergency room, one of the first questions asked is, "What's going on? What are the vital signs?" While taking action is important, it is equally important to get the *right* information and take the *right* actions. You will have to make some decisions with less information than you might like. Get the most current relevant measures of the vital signs immediately. After taking your actions, be sure to place your patient in intensive care where you can closely monitor the recovery.

In triage, there probably won't be time to explain the reasons underlying your action in advance or concurrently. As soon afterwards as you can, explain your assumptions and reasoning. Your constituents need to understand your rationale so that everyone may learn from the experience. What if you make a mistake? People are more apt to cut you some slack when they understand your assumptions and reasons.

Help your constituents to understand you People want to know and trust their leader. Tell them about your background and why you have accepted your leadership role. Clarify your role and expectations. Tell them about your dreams and what excites you. Tell them about your hobbies and special interests. Let them know what they can do to bring out the best in you, and what "pushes your hotbuttons." As a leader, you want your constituents not only to be excited about what you can accomplish together, but also to support you as their leader. The more they understand the real you, the easier time they will have committing to your leadership, assuming that you are a worthy leader.

Involve your constituents in planning and action When you have completed your interviews and small group meetings, report what you have learned to your constituents. Discuss the issues. Ask for their input on priorities and suggestions of key people for teams to resolve issues. They will appreciate the opportunity to add their expertise and input, and will feel greater ownership of the results. Tackle a few easy-to-solve problems immediately to get the ball rolling and demonstrate that you mean business. Not everything has to be addressed at once. Years ago when I joined Duty Free Shoppers, my boss told me, "It has taken us years to get things this screwed up. Don't feel that you have to fix everything at once." He was right. People understood the need to sequence and accepted that.

Communicate your plan and report progress As partners in your plan, your constituents need to understand it. Meet with them individually or as a group to explain it and field questions. In your plan, include times for reporting progress. Then, report progress at the appointed times and celebrate your accomplishments.

Moving up Assuming the leadership of a group of which you have previously been a member presents a special challenge. You need to communicate that your role has changed. *"I am pleased and honored to be your new leader. As your leader, I will serve in a different role, and that will take a bit of getting used to for all of us. I am now your person to turn to for _____. I will now have to make decisions about _____. I will seek your input for many of the decisions, but it won't be possible, nor would you want me, to involve you in all. There will be times when I will have to communicate unpopular news or work with you on a problem. That comes with the job. In such situations, I will be trying to achieve a balance that is fair for the company, the team and you. If I do something with which you take issue, I'd like to know about it. I promise to listen without becoming defensive and to give you honest answers."*

Working with someone who didn't get your job You may have someone on your team, or as part of your constituency, who was considered for the job you got. Some people feel threatened and become paranoid in this situation. Their paranoid behavior makes life miserable for themselves, the person they consider a threat, and the rest of their constituency. People don't exhibit their best qualities when they are scared and fearful. Other leaders are relieved to find that they have someone on their team who is good enough to have been a serious contender for their position. They treat the person as a tremendous resource and an ally. They demonstrate through their ability to bring out the best in a previous contender why they were chosen for the leadership role. They prepare the person to move up when it comes time for them to move up. Clearly, it is better for everyone concerned to treat the person who lost out to you as your ally.

Feedback As a leader, you do some things exceptionally well, and you probably make a few mistakes. You probably have a sense of what goes well and what doesn't. Like the emperor in the fable, *The Emperor's New Clothes,* you need occasional reality checks. Feedback is essential for your learning and growth. Thus, ask people in your constituency:

- ❏ *How am I doing?*
- ❏ *What have I done that has helped you in your job or as a colleague?*
- ❏ *What have I done that has made life more difficult for you?*
- ❏ *What changes could I make that would improve how we work together?*
- ❏ *What else do I need to know for my learning and growth as a leader?*

Listen, listen, listen without interruption! Learn from both what is positive and what is critical. If someone has a perception with which you disagree, bite your tongue! You may ask questions to learn more about how a person got a particular perception. Don't try to defend yourself or argue a point while you are getting feedback. If you do, you will cut off further feedback and squelch honesty. If someone has a perception that you believe is based on only partial information, you may later reference the perception and say, *"As I was thinking about our conversation regarding _____, it occurred to me that you might not have been aware of _____. I accept your perception. I just want you to have a more complete picture."*

Thank anyone who provides you with the feedback, whether it is positive or critical. You need both. Anyone who provides you with feedback cares enough about you and your organization to make the effort to share it with you. That, in itself, is a compliment. And, if the feedback is critical, it is even more of a compliment. It communicates that they care enough about you (your organization) and trust you enough to risk giving you information that may be upsetting.

Most people you deal with want you to succeed. It makes life much easier and more fun for them when they can be on a winning team. And they will accept occasional mistakes so long as you admit them, try to prevent them from happening again, and are responsive to their concerns. They are unforgiving of arrogance, insincerity, favoritism, manipulation and deceit (as several Presidents of the United States have discovered). By demonstrating that you understand the issues, seeking expertise you lack, knowing what you are doing, creating an exciting shared future, taking steps to resolve problems, and making the people you lead feel valued and part of the team, you will start out on the right foot.

8.5

Changing Roles Within an Organization

People put you in a box. Their intent is not malicious. It is just that putting you in a box, like stereotyping, is convenient for them. So, when you change roles within an organization, you have to extricate yourself from the old boxes in people's minds and create new ones for them.

Example

Amelia began working in the office of her family's business at age 13. After completing her degree in business at college she became the office manager. At 27, she was promoted to VP of administration. To her dismay, in her new role, some people still thought of her as the girl in jeans and thongs that she was as a teenager. Unlike Houdini, she had been unable to escape from the box into which she was cast earlier.

When you change roles within an organization, you have to communicate to your constituents, through symbols and actions, that things have changed. A memo and organization chart, while important, are not enough. People need to *experience* a difference. This is what Amelia did:

1. **Changed location** Amelia moved out of the "bull pen" and into her own office. A different space communicates a change physically.

2. **Changed appearance** Amelia changed her hairstyle to a more sophisticated look and her wardrobe to be more professional.

3. **Introduced successor** She introduced the new office manager to the people with whom she used to work. This helped her not only to step out of her past, it also helped him to establish himself in his new role.

4. **Stepped out of old role** When people came to Amelia about matters that she handled as office manager, she took them to the new manager. This reinforced the point that she was no longer in that role and strengthened the role of her new office manager.

5. **Made new alliances** She met with the people with whom she needed to work in her new role. She noted issues that were causing problems and worked with them to solve the problems.

6. **Made changes** Amelia quickly made some visible, easy-to-implement changes to show that she could listen to concerns and take appropriate action.

7. **Created a shared vision** A facilitated one-day off-site meeting of key people resulted in a draft vision for her area. It was subsequently reviewed and refined by her staff and the rest of key management, and shaped how they provided their services.

8. **Reported progress** Amelia prepared a progress report that she shared with her constituents at the end of her first 30 and 90 days, and quarterly thereafter. She summarized the challenges she had faced, the actions she took, and upcoming priorities.

Amelia succeeded! Her actions earned her respect and demonstrated to everyone that she was, in fact, in a new role.

Placing people in boxes is normal organizational behavior (legitimized by organization charts). Accept that you will always be placed in some form of box. Make sure that when you change roles that you also take action to create your new box and escape from your old one.

8.6

Telling the Truth

Truth pays! It is much easier to live with the truth than it is try to hide it. People are not stupid; sooner or later, they see through efforts to lie or hide the truth. And when they do, someone who has lied has many more problems than just what he/she lied about!

Painful truth No matter how you look at it, the truth is not always joyous news. People are more apt to be truthful about joyous news and more reticent to communicate unpopular or upsetting news. However, people want and need to know the truth—even when it hurts. They can face up to it and deal with it better than they can deal with "white lies" and manipulations.

"White lies" Some people use "white lies" or euphemisms to protect others and avoid facing up to problems. In the process, they undermine their credibility. Why should anyone believe someone who "sugar-coats" the truth with such terms as "down-sizing," "right-sizing," or "redeployment of assets?" Who is being fooled?

If anyone is, it is probably the person using such terms. Like in the *Emperor's New Clothes,* everyone else sees right through.

Doctoring the truth What does withholding or "sugar-coating" the truth communicate? Some people believe that it communicates caring about others' feelings. While that might be the intent, it is more apt to come across as a lack of confidence that the person will accept the truth and deal with it constructively. Withholding the truth is a form of paternalism. It presumes that the other person is dumb enough not to see through what you are saying. *"You are incapable of dealing with reality, so I will protect you."* It is, in effect, an insult! Too many people's careers have been undermined by not finding out about a career-defining issue until it was too late.

Truth as a compliment The greatest compliment you can pay someone is to provide him/her with information that he/she needs to know, whether or not it is good news. It communicates, *"I care enough about you to make sure that you have information you need, even if it upsets you."*

Telling the truth The objective of telling the truth is to help others understand a situation by giving them accurate information. It is not to destroy them. You may be challenged from time to time with how to communicate an unwelcome message. I have found that it helps to set the context for what you have to say, get to the point, be factual, be caring, and avoid value judgments. *"Fred, I need to get back to you on your candidacy for the VP of sales. We have decided to promote Angelica. I know much you wanted that job, and I'm sorry to have to tell you that you did not get it. There is no question about your value in sales. You have had the highest sales in the last seven out of ten quarters, and we certainly value that! What kept us from promoting you this time are the four fights in the past year that you have had with your team members. A VP of sales must be able to work out disagreements more constructively than you have demonstrated. I'm hopeful that the training we are investing in for you in creative problem solving and conflict management will help to pave the way for you for future promotions."*

What if you have already lied Suppose, in a well-meaning effort to protect someone, you told a "white lie." How do you correct the situation? It takes some courage to own up to what you have done, and it's usually better to own up sooner than later. State that you need to correct a misimpression that you created or a mistake that you made. First, tell the reason why you did what you did, and then set the record straight. *"Last week I told you that there would be no layoffs. I'm sorry that I misled you. With all the pressure you were under, I did not want you to have to worry about your jobs. I was sure that we would get the contracts from IBM and HP. We lost both and don't have any prospects on the horizon for such major pieces of business. We are going to have to make some cuts to survive, and* *that includes a layoff."* People don't like to find out that they have been led astray, shielded from the truth, or that their trust has been violated. They are more forgiving if they are told the truth, and the truth about the misrepresentation, in a contrite manner by the person who told them without any further attempts to hide the truth. They will be wary of what they are told until trust is rebuilt. Trust can be rebuilt relatively quickly for an isolated instance of a "white lie." It probably will never be rebuilt for repeated, self-serving misrepresentations.

Leadership and truth To be effective as a leader, you have to be trusted, and trust requires that you are believable. I have found that the most effective and respected leaders face up to and communicate the truth, no matter how difficult it is to accept. Though hearing the truth may upset the people who hear it, they appreciate knowing the truth, and can deal with it. And when you tell the truth, you never have to worry about remembering what you said to whom.

8.7

Ethics—Doing the Right Thing, at the Right Time, for the Right Reason

- ❑ The CEO of your company wants you to hire his son for a job you don't need done.
- ❑ You are asked to ship products that you know have not met quality standards, so as to make quarterly sales meet the expectations of the stock market.

Organizational life is no stranger to situations that can test your ethics. Doing what is right can be costly. Recalling Tylenol during the Tylenol scare cost millions of dollars. Likewise, for Odwalla juices a few years later. Lives were at stake. Both companies, without hesitation, recalled their products. They could have delayed until more people had died to make sure that the deaths were directly attributable to their products before recalling them. That would have been too late. The right time for their recalls was immediately. They were genuinely concerned about the life and health of their customers and did not want any product of theirs to make ill or kill anyone (the right reason).

You may not be faced with life and death dilemmas, but you are sure to be confronted with situations that will test your character; such as use of copyrighted material and intellectual property, disclosing or taking advantage of confidential information, manipulating data, taking credit for the work of others, etc. When you are confronted with such situations, take the "high road." Make sure that you do what is right, at the right time, and for the right reason. You have to be able to live with yourself, sleep nights, and earn the respect of the people who are important in your life.

John's dilemma John, as Director of Information Technology for his employer, was in charge of reviewing proposals for a major IT initiative and recommending a vendor with whom to contract. Elegant Solutions (Pseudonym) clearly had the best grasp of the challenges and what was needed. Their bid, though not the lowest, was competitive. They also promised John the use of their corporate vacation home at Lake Tahoe for two weeks each year of their contract if they were awarded the contract.

John did not want to appear to be bribed for recommending Elegant Solutions. He considered eliminating them from further consideration to avoid the possible appearance of a conflict of interest. As he thought about the situation, he realized that he had a responsibility to his employer to recommend the best vendor for their needs. Elegant was the front-runner, regardless of the cabin offer. John decided to keep Elegant in the running. He told them that he appreciated their offer of the cabin, but that he could not accept it. There could be the *appearance* of a conflict of interest if he were to recommend them and also benefited from the use of their vacation home. He did the right thing (decline their offer), at the right time (before presenting his recommendations), and for the right reason (to make sure that there was no perception of the possibility of personal gain in his recommendations).

Legal versus ethical "Who cares, so long as it's legal?" People sometimes think that anything legal is also ethical. The Law creates the lowest common denominator of what is acceptable in our society. Ethical standards are higher. In the example of John, accepting the vacation home might not have been illegal if he could prove that it was not a bribe. It certainly had the appearance of a potential conflict of interest, and the appearance is as bad as though there were a proven conflict. Whether or not President Clinton committed perjury in testimony about his relations with Monica Lewinsky, he certainly lost the respect of the American public and undermined his credibility. People look to their leaders for a higher standard than what is merely technically legal.

Ask yourself these questions when you are faced with an ethical dilemma:

- ❑ **What is the "right" thing to do?** Most people have a sense of what is "right" and "wrong." Other ways of asking this question are: "What is the selfless thing to do?" "How would it reflect on me if this situation were reported on the front page of the newspaper?" "How honest could I be if I were being interviewed about this by Mike Wallace on *60 Minutes*?" "What would my constituents (the people with whom I work closely) think?"

❑ **What is the "right" time?** In most situations, it is best to be up-front. John forestalled a problem with the offer of the vacation home by telling Elegant Solutions that he could not accept their vacation home offer before he made his recommendation. Had he waited until after his company chose Elegant Solutions, he would have appeared to be trying to repair damage rather than doing what was right. Had the makers of Tylenol waited with their product recall until more people had died, their motive would have appeared as damage control rather than doing the right thing.

❑ **What is the "right" reason?** An employer acceded to employee requests for making health insurance available to them because it heard rumors of a union organizing drive and wanted to take action to ward off the union. Their move actually encouraged employees to vote for the union. The company's move communicated that they would only respond to employee needs when they were under pressure. As far as employees were concerned, management finally did the right thing, but for the wrong reason.

Help from a trusted confidant Ethical dilemmas can place a lot of pressure on you. You may not make the best decisions on your own under such pressure. In such situations, it really helps to discuss your dilemma with a trusted, objective, good listener who can help you clarify your thoughts and options.

As a leader, you live in a fishbowl. Your constituents constantly scrutinize your behavior and hold you to a higher standard than what is merely legal. They want to respect and trust you. They want you to do the right thing, at the right time, and for the right reasons. They will forgive you for occasional honest mistakes that you own up to. They will have a difficult time getting beyond a breach of ethics, so your credibility depends on doing the right thing, at the right time, and for the right reasons. If you are faced with an ethical dilemma, discuss it with a confidant you respect before you take action.

(Also see Chapter 7.9, Standing up for What is Important to You, and 8.6, Telling the Truth.)

8.8

Respect—A Key Element in Leadership

"I like my boss as a person. As a leader, he does things that create problems for me."

"How is that?"

"He's fun, has a good sense of humor, and is easy to talk to. We go bowling togeth-er and sometimes he gives me a ride to work. He's a good guy. As our leader, he seldom involves us in decisions where our input would contribute to a better deci-sion. He bawls me out in front of others, and when he says, `I'll get back to you,' he seldom does. He asked two of the women who report to him for dates, and they were afraid to say `No.'"

Leadership is the art of inspiring and enabling people to achieve a shared vision. People will support a respected leader in the pursuit of shared goals. They trust him/her to do the right things, at the right time, for the right reasons, and to support them in their quest. If they like their leader, too, all the better.

People are less willing to entrust themselves to a leader they don't respect, even if he/she is likeable. Too much of what is important to their values and lives is at stake to follow someone whose behavior they question.

Someone who is neither respected nor liked can lead only for as long as it takes people to bail out, if they have a choice.

I could cite a hundred examples of what leaders have done to *lose* respect. Instead, I'll focus on behavior that *earns* respect.

These Four Elements of Respect are Essential

1. Being scrupulously honest People want and can deal with the truth, even when it is painful. They have little tolerance for lies. President Clinton demonstrated that people have less tolerance for lying and/or obstructing justice than for his affairs.

2. Trusting others It is very difficult to respect someone who doesn't trust you. Micromanaging is a prime expression of not trusting others. Involving others in decisions that affect them and what they do builds trust. Empowering people not only communicates trust, it also increases the power of the leader through the addi-tional respect earned.

3. Being trustworthy Following through on promises, living up to values shared by the team, taking responsibility for one's decisions, treating others fairly, and giving credit where credit is due all help demonstrate that one is worthy of trust.

4. Competence Knowing what to do, and doing it with skill fosters respect. It is important in both the technical aspects of the job and the processes that enable people to work effectively. People look to leaders for a clear sense of purpose, direction, and support for reaching their goals.

Like a house, respect takes time to build, but can be destroyed quickly. Before respect can be rebuilt, as with a house, the debris must be cleared before rebuild-ing can occur. That takes time, as does the rebuilding process.

8.9

Trust and Relationships on the Job

90% of the people I know who have been fired in the past 35 years lost their job because of working relationship issues.

People go to school for years to acquire academic and technical knowledge, but life skills are shorted. As one person confided, *"I never learned how to work with others. I did not realize that is as important as my technical knowledge."*

You don't have to love someone to have a productive working relationship. You don't even have to like each other—but you do need mutual respect and trust.

You can't bring out the best in someone for whom you don't communicate respect and trust. When a relationship sours, mutual respect and trust are frequently a key issue. Why? They are universal needs. Their presence enables people to thrive and grow. Their absence is like pouring salt on a snail; people wither and shrivel.

Respect = showing consideration or courteous regard.

Trust = faith and confidence in what one says and does, including one's honesty, integrity, reliability, fairness, competence, and honoring commitments.

These are qualities of the heart. Can they be bought, borrowed, or demanded? No, they can only be earned through honesty, doing the right things for the right reasons, and at the right time. Notice, I said, "doing," not just "saying." Actions either reinforce or undermine what you say. And, people have a pretty good "nose" for distinguishing what is genuine and what isn't.

It is easier to build trust than to rebuild it. In building trust, you start at ground level. When you have to rebuild trust, you first have to climb out of a sinkhole of perceived betrayal. What can you do to build or rebuild respect and trust? Here are a few suggestions:

❑ Get to know the people with whom you work individually. Look for the good in them. The better you know them, the better you can understand and appreciate their unique gift. Each has a unique gift, and a personal style that may be different from yours. Suspend judgment. Keep an open mind, accept people as they are, and express *genuine* confidence in their abilities.

❑ Clarify expectations. Expectations are the benchmarks by which you are judged, and by which you judge others. Expectations are frequently based on assumptions. Faulty assumptions are the seeds of shattered expectations. In order to be trusted, you need to meet or exceed other's expectations, so make sure you know what they are and that you can live with them.

❑ When there are problems, investigate thoroughly. Avoid jumping to conclusions. When you take action, explain *what* you are doing and *why*. People are more accepting of what they understand, and know that you understand, too.

❑ Honor commitments you make. If you find that you can't fulfill a commitment, let the people to whom you made it know early on that you can't, and why. No surprises! Set a new commitment that you can meet, and meet it.

❑ There are no "white lies." Even though the truth may be painful, people want to know it and can deal with it. Even well intentioned lies undermine a relationship!

❑ Always be fair. Consistency is not always fair. People prefer what is fair. Feel free to ask, *"What do you think is fair, given these circumstances?"* People generally have an idea of what they think is fair. You don't necessarily have to go along with what they think is fair, but you need to know that and be able to explain your decisions in relation to that.

❑ Relationships are built on thinking first of the other person. Substitute the phrase, "what's in it for me" with "how can I help?" The more you do that, the more others will think of you—and all will benefit.

❑ Provide people with the information you have that they need to know. Information is power, and the more of it you share, the more you empower others. The more you empower others, the more power you have. Conversely, withholding information that others need only makes you appear insecure and untrustworthy.

❑ Don't talk ill about others behind their back. It harms them and you. When you bad-mouth someone, the people to whom you are speaking wonder what you say about them when they are not present.

❑ Forgive people for their mistakes and help them to learn from them. Seeking to place blame only puts people on the defensive and closes them to learning. That does not mean relaxing standards. Instead, it means that you recognize that people typically don't like to make mistakes. Your objective is to help them learn, and prevent a repeat incident.

❑ When you make a mistake, own up to it and try to learn from it. A little humility buys much more trust than denial and an attempted cover up. The more you own up to your mistakes, the more apt others are to own up to their mistakes.

❑ Encourage people with working relationships issues to get help. Such people are not necessarily bad people; they frequently do not know how to operate any differently. By discovering their "environmental impact," and learning alternative ways to interact, they can overcome or ameliorate their relationship problems.

Trust is a cornerstone for a productive working relationship. The people who work for or with you want to be able to trust your competence, your promises and your actions, and you want to be able to trust theirs. A strained working relationship can cut people's effectiveness by 50% and bring on health problems. Can you afford that?

Behaviors That Promote and Undermine Trust

Trust is built on respect and caring for others, and is the cornerstone for effective teamwork. People exhibit trust when they make themselves open to others whose subsequent behavior is beyond their control. Some behavior promotes a relationship of trust while other behavior undermines trust.

This survey can be used for a self-appraisal, or to obtain feedback about how people view your behavior. When used by both you and others, it will provide a profile of how you see yourself, and how others see you. There will be some areas of agreement and others of disagreement. The value of this survey comes from determining what behavior helps you to increase trust and team effectiveness, and what to avoid.

The behaviors listed below come from 35+ years of observing behavior in organizations, and from coaching people through issues related to trust, but they have not been validated scientifically.

Please circle your rating of the frequency of the described behavior for the person you are profiling.

Rating scale: 4 = exhibits this behavior *consistently*
3 = exhibits this behavior *usually,* but not always
2 = exhibits this behavior *occasionally*
1 = exhibits this behavior *rarely*
0 = *never* exhibits this behavior

A. Behaviors that *promote* trust

1. Looking for the good in people.	0 1 2 3 4
2. Assuming that people want to do a good job of what they do.	0 1 2 3 4
3. Accepting others as they are.	0 1 2 3 4
4. Extending the "benefit of the doubt" to people.	0 1 2 3 4
5. Listening attentively.	0 1 2 3 4
6. Reserving judgment until one has heard all sides of an issue.	0 1 2 3 4
7. Seeking to understand before seeking to be understood.	0 1 2 3 4
8. Keeping promises, or informing others in advance if one can't.	0 1 2 3 4
9. Keeping confidential information that is given in confidence.	0 1 2 3 4
10. Being honest and forthright.	0 1 2 3 4
11. Being open about one's values, intentions and actions.	0 1 2 3 4
12. Confronting difficult issues with integrity.	0 1 2 3 4
13. Doing the "right thing for the right reason."	0 1 2 3 4
14. Accepting criticism non-defensively and taking action on it.	0 1 2 3 4
15. Being the first to admit one's mistakes.	0 1 2 3 4

16. Laughing at oneself rather than laughing at others.	0	1	2	3	4
17. Accepting responsibility for one's actions.	0	1	2	3	4
18. Thinking of other's needs before one's own needs.	0	1	2	3	4
19. Supporting one's colleagues through adversity.	0	1	2	3	4
20. Treating others as equals.	0	1	2	3	4
21. Openly expressing one's feelings.	0	1	2	3	4
22. Showing consideration for the feelings of others.	0	1	2	3	4
23. Praising in public, criticizing privately.	0	1	2	3	4
24. Involving others in decisions that affect them.	0	1	2	3	4
25. Seeking "win-win" solutions to problems.	0	1	2	3	4
26. Making sure people have the info they need for their work.	0	1	2	3	4
27. Giving people freedom to get their jobs done.	0	1	2	3	4
28. Genuinely sharing recognition for team accomplishments.	0	1	2	3	4

Section A: Total

B. Behaviors that *undermine* trust

29. Stretching the truth for one's own benefit.	0	1	2	3	4
30. Sidestepping sensitive issues.	0	1	2	3	4
31. Putting one's own interests ahead of the team's interests.	0	1	2	3	4
32. Trying to win at all costs.	0	1	2	3	4
33. Playing political games, including "hidden agendas."	0	1	2	3	4
34. Talking about people behind their backs, or whispering.	0	1	2	3	4
35. Playing people off against each other.	0	1	2	3	4
36. Ridiculing people with whose thoughts/actions one disagrees.	0	1	2	3	4
37. Fostering rumors and misunderstanding.	0	1	2	3	4
38. Changing the "ground rules" without telling others.	0	1	2	3	4
39. Seeking to control the behavior of others.	0	1	2	3	4
40. Withholding information others need to do their work.	0	1	2	3	4
41. Passing blame to others, trying to justify oneself.	0	1	2	3	4
42. Taking credit for others' accomplishments.	0	1	2	3	4

Section B: Total

Net Total: Section A less section B

- ❏ Total your ratings for sections A and B, then subtract section B from the section A total for your net total.
- ❏ A net total of 70+, with no 0 or 1 ratings in section A, and no 3 or 4 ratings in section B, typically indicates that the person to whom this survey applies is viewed as trusting and trustworthy.
- ❏ A net total of less than 56 typically indicates that people are guarded in extending trust to this person.
- ❏ A net total of less than 28 typically indicates that people have serious concerns about extending trust to this person.

8.10

Special Relationships and Fairness

"Fred is my best employee! Just because we're dating doesn't mean that I give him special consideration. If the people who grouse about the way I treat him performed as well, I'd treat them the same."

Is Fred receiving special consideration? If so, does the fact that he and Francine are dating have anything to do with the way she treats her direct report? Do the other people who report to her have a fair chance?

Favoritism reflects a special relationship. Favoritism, according to Webster, is "the showing of more kindness and indulgence to some person or persons than to others." Nepotism, a form of favoritism, is about people being hired or promoted based more on an influential relationship than on what they can do. Family, significant others, and bosom friends are typically seen as having special influence. The new executive hires his/her team from another job. Junior is promoted to vice president when others are better qualified. Why is this a problem? Who likes to be treated as a second-class citizen—especially when advancing to a favored state is usually unattainable? Some people are categorically denied equal opportunity. That is a demotivator, and toxic to teamwork!

Prevention To prevent the perception of favoritism, people in special relationships should not have a reporting relationship to each other, and should not be involved in any personnel decisions that affect the other.

I recommend avoiding situations with the potential for favoritism. The costs to morale and performance of people who feel less well favored are just too great. Hiring family members, significant others, or bosom pals has the potential for being viewed as nepotism. Some such people are very competent and make good employees. It may not seem fair to exclude them from consideration just because they have a significant relationship with an employee. However, to avoid the perception of nepotism, any employee related to an applicant should be excluded from the hiring decision. If a selection panel that excludes the employee chooses the applicant, the applicant and the employee will have much higher credibility.

How about family businesses? They present a special challenge. In many, family considerations outweigh business considerations. Non-family members joining a family business hopefully understand and accept that they are going to be "outsiders." So long as they are working with people they respect, and feel that they are treated fairly, they may be able to live with knowing that they probably will never be part of the inner circle.

Dating and favoritism   People in the workplace typically spend more time working with each other than they spend with anyone else. In such a setting, it is not surprising that dating and romances occur. Once there is a dating relationship, neither person should be involved in any personnel decisions affecting the other.

Fairness is a deeply ingrained value in American culture. Special relationships, such as favoritism and nepotism, are seen as enemies of fairness. They are like termites that gnaw away at one's sense of fairness, and undermine trust and respect. The best strategy is to try to prevent situations conducive to favoritism. When that does not work, timely and fair action to correct them is essential.

9

Relationships with Your Boss,
Peers and Others

9.1

Managing Your Relationship with Your Boss

The comic strip, *Dilbert,* portrays the legendary boss for whom you *don't* want to work. If you are like most people, you've experienced bosses who brought out the best in you, and some who brought out the worst. The right boss (the person to whom you report directly) will be an ally. Don't even bother with one who is an adversary (unless he/she has the potential to become an ally). Life is too short for that!

Know your boss In a healthy relationship, people care about and value each other. They have to count on each other for mutual support in pursuit of their goals. Their success is intertwined, so they need to know how to bring out the best in each other, and what *not* to do. Thus, the first step in building a positive relationship with your boss is to get to know him/her.

Invite a new boss to meet with you in a setting that promotes open and informal communication. Indicate that you'd like to know more about his/her vision, values, aspirations and what works best for him/her in your relations with him/her. The objectives are:

- ❏ To discover what works and what doesn't in managing your relationship.
- ❏ To let him/her know what to do to bring out the best in you, and vice versa.
- ❏ To discover what works best when/if you have to communicate unwelcome news.

In the meeting, ask your boss to describe what people did who have worked out well for him/her, and what those did who did not work out. Conversely, share what others have done to bring out the best in you, and what they have done to "push your hot-buttons."

Is meeting with your boss to ask these questions "brown-nosing?" No, so long as you have an open and honest exchange of information. Most people I know who are bosses, even those who are short on people skills, actually want to bring out the best in the people they lead. 90+% of the time when they have rubbed someone the wrong way, they did not intend to. So, they need the information from this meeting as much as you do.

An alternative that I have used coaching teams is to ask each member to prepare a "Guide for Getting Along with Me." On one side of a page each lists what it takes to bring out the best in him/her. On the other side is his/her list of behavior that really upsets him/her (hot-buttons). Each presents his/her list and answers questions of clarification. Each team member gets a copy.

Communicating unwelcome news Organizational life has its surprises, and not all are good news. You need to be able to communicate with your boss without fear on issues that may be upsetting. As a management consultant, I frequently have to tell clients about issues that they wish they did not have to deal with. Clients and bosses have a lot in common. When I begin an assignment, I ask my client how he/she wants me to deal with unwelcome news if/when I come across it. First, I state: *"During the course of working with you, there is a chance that I will learn about information that you need to know and that may be upsetting."* Then I ask, *"When I come across such information, what is the best way for me to communicate with you about it?"* When I learn of disquieting news, I state: *"You may not like what I have to tell you, however, you need to know about this. Is now a good time?"* If it is, then I proceed to present the information as he/she has requested. If it isn't, then we schedule a time that will be better.

Problems are seldom welcome news. However, you are employed to solve problems. So, when you inform your boss about a problem, if you can, also propose some alternatives, your preferred solution, and the reasons you recommend it. Your news of a problem will be appreciated more if you also recommend a viable solution to it.

Commitments Your relationship with your boss involves commitments to each other. Commitments create expectations. You are judged by how you live up to what is expected of you—but not all expectations are realistic or reasonable. If you are facing an unrealistic or unreasonable expectation, negotiate expectations that you can live with. *"You know, Frank, I understand that you would really like this by Wednesday of next week. I wish I could be encouraging about the prospect of meeting that deadline. But I'd rather be honest with you and give you a date you can count on than to delude you into thinking we can meet that deadline. I can guarantee that we will have this for you by the following Monday. Can you live with that?"*

Once you make a commitment, "walk over glowing coals in bare feet" to meet it. Your reputation depends on it. If it becomes obvious that, even if you move Heaven and Earth you can't make it, let the person to whom you made the commitment know in advance. There is a fine line between explaining the reasons and making excuses. Take responsibility. Treading over the line to excuses "shoots you in the foot."

Specific feedback When your boss does something that helps you, or helps bring out the best in you, acknowledge it. In addition to expressing thanks, cite specifically what he/she did and why it was helpful. *"Thank you for intervening with Mr. Smith. You calmed him down, supported what I had told him, and explained our policy in terms that made sense to him. I learned from your example a good lesson in how to deal with an upset customer."* Likewise, when your boss makes life more difficult for you, give specific feedback, too. *"I'm sure that you didn't intend to embarrass me at our team meeting today when you called me your 'star player.' I am fortunate to have great support from the rest of the team. I looked good because of what they did, so I felt that I was getting the credit they should have gotten. Can you understand that?"*

Creating and nurturing a strong relationship with your boss is mutually beneficial. The keys to such a relationship are getting to know, respect, trust and support each other, and communicating openly on the issues and information of importance to both of you. It is time well spent.

9.2

Managing Expectations—No Surprises!

Managing expectations is key to satisfying customers and colleagues. They judge your performance in relation to what they expect of you. When you meet or exceed their expectations, they are happy. If your performance falls short, they are unhappy. You can express this relationship in an equation:

Happiness = What You Get ÷ What You Expect

This applies to anyone with whom you interact: clients, customers, investors, students and even your family and friends. So, in order to satisfy them, you need make sure that they get at least what they expect.

Expectations vary. Expectations for shopping at Costco are different from shopping at Nordstrom's. Earnings expectations for dot.com businesses are different from industrial companies. To have satisfied customers and investors, a happy spouse, or motivated employees, set expectations that you can meet or exceed.

Managing expectations requires a conscious effort to negotiate arrangements that increase your chances of success. It is better not to paint yourself and your team into a corner than to have to walk across wet paint.

What does it take to manage expectations?

1. Know your capabilities and what's important to you. Avoid assignments that do not play to your strengths, or that are marginally important, if you can.

2. Find out what's expected and important:

   ❏ What is the purpose?
   ❏ What is the expected outcome?
   ❏ Within what period of time?
   ❏ At what cost and level of quality?
   ❏ Who else will be involved?

3. Define what you can commit to:

   ❏ Accomplish
   ❏ By when
   ❏ Using what resources
   ❏ To what quality standards

   State assumptions that could affect the outcome. Be realistic and honest. You will have to live with what you commit to.

4. Negotiate arrangements:

   ❏ Know what is important to you
   ❏ Listen carefully to other's needs
   ❏ Seek creative ways balance your needs with those of others for arrangements you can "live with"
   ❏ Confirm in writing the essence of your understanding

5. Inform others promptly when circumstances change. People tend to judge how you do based on their expectations at the time you deliver, so make sure their expectations are current. Don't procrastinate!

6. "Under promise and over deliver," but not by too much. If you always deliver much more than was expected, you may inadvertently raise future expectations.

7. When you deliver, present your accomplishments in reference to expectations. *"I'm delivering this a day earlier than we agreed to, but I thought you might like it sooner."*

Expectations are a by-product of living in an interdependent world. With the pressures of a "faster, better, cheaper" mind set in our society, it is imperative for one's sanity and relations with others to manage expectations.

9.3

Working With Someone You Don't Respect

You don't always get to choose the people with whom you work—at least in the short run. You get a temporary assignment or someone is assigned to work with you. Someone new becomes your boss. Whatever the circumstances, if your values and/or style are at odds with your boss, a coworker, or someone who reports to you, you can experience agony. Your agony will be greater, and the situation trickier, if the person you don't respect is your boss.

When you work with someone you don't respect, you are likely to become fixated on his/her behaviors that rankle you. That does not bring out the best in you, so you become part of the problem, too.

Options

1. Adjust your outlook You can't control what others do, but you can choose how you respond. You see what you look for. If you look for behavior that you don't respect, you find it. If you look for behavior that you respect, you are more apt to find it. Thus, look for the good points in someone you don't respect and you may find some. If you can find enough, you may be able to place the behavior that bugs you in perspective.

Some years ago, I worked with someone whose values and behavior literally made me sick when I was in his presence. Fortunately, that was not every day. What got to me was that he did not listen, would interrupt, over dramatized situations, gushed superlatives and came across as condescending, especially to minorities. After coming to the realization that I was going to have to continue to work with him, at least a little while longer, that it was unlikely that he would change much, and that I was letting him bring me down, I decided to look for what was good in him. I found some things for which I could actually respect him. So I adjusted my outlook. He moved up the scale from "complete idiot" to "mixed bag." That helped me to live with having to work with him a while longer.

2. Confront issues of importance to you Confrontation is a form of negotiation. As in other negotiations, the better you understand the other person's outlook and motivation, the more effective you can be. In confronting someone, first determine what you want to accomplish. It is presumptuous to think that you can change someone's way of thinking, so don't even try to do that. You may be able to influence outward behavior. Someone who becomes aware of an effect that he/she is having on you and others may decide to act differently. At least he/she should understand better your reactions to his/her behavior. By confronting, you may create a better understanding of each other, even if there is no change in behavior. (This is easier to do with a peer, or with someone who reports to you, than with your boss. Your boss wields more power and is in a position to make life even more miserable if he/she feels threatened when confronted.)

❑ When confronting someone, describe exactly what he/she did or said. Avoid judgmental terms or labeling behavior. They increase defensiveness and decrease openness to considering other ways of acting. Then, test for understanding. Ask whether that is the message he/she intended to communicate. *"Yesterday, in the employee meeting, you said, 'Anyone who has complaints about working here should leave. We don't need anyone who is not a team player.' Did I hear you correctly? Do you actually want good employees who have valid and constructive concerns to quit?"* If the answer is, "No," then ask what he/she meant. If the answer is, "Yes," explain how the statement affected you and ask what he/she was trying to accomplish. *"What were you trying to accomplish? I couldn't believe my ears. Our corporate values encourage employees to look for ways to improve how we operate and to tell us about them. The issues they raised were just what we needed to hear. Please help me to understand what's wrong with that.'"*

❑ Paraphrase the person's answer to confirm that you heard it. Then state why it creates problems for you, and state your position. *"Let me make sure I understand you. You believe that anyone who raises issues is disloyal and that we don't need disloyal employees. Is that correct?*

"I see things differently. We have a good place to work, but we still have some issues. The issues raised were, for the most part, valid, and the suggestions well thought out and appropriate. It was obvious to me that the employees in that forum care a lot about our business and want to make our company stronger. Moreover, we are in the tightest job market we have known. The last thing we need is to have employees feel that we have a deaf ear for their legitimate concerns. For someone in your position to make the statement you did invites turnover and makes it harder for us to recruit and hire the people we need."

❑ Close the loop. Summarize the situation and ask for different behavior in the future. *"I understand that you don't think employees have any business bringing up issues that affect the work place. You believe that is the role of management. Even though I understand your position, I take exception with it. If you want us to be able to attract and retain the people we need, will you please refrain from making statements that challenge people to leave?"*

❑ Confirm the essence of your conversation in a memo with a copy to the person you confronted. People for whom you have low respect may also have a selective memory. A contemporaneous memo may be needed for future reference.

3. Change jobs If someone gets to you enough, especially your boss, after having tried the above options, and the prospect of having to work with him/her is unsavory if you stay, change jobs. The problem is that you are letting someone else influence your career decisions. But, that is preferable to enduring someone who brings out the dark side of you.

Continuing to work with someone you don't respect can be "hazardous to your health"—both physical and mental, and to your career. If you look for the good in such a person, and/or are able to work out the important issues that undermine your respect for the other person, you may be able to create an acceptable working relationship. You don't have to like the people with whom you work, but you need to have a basic level of respect for them. If you can't, do your homework and find a job where you can respect the people with whom you work.

9.4

Building Your Network

The three most important factors in real estate are location, location and location. In business the three most important factors are relationships, relationships and relationships. The Beatles sing, "I get by with a little help from my friends." The opportunities that open up for you in your life are most likely to come through the people who know you and trust you—your friends. They are people with whom you have enough of a relationship that they automatically and instinctively want to help you. They constitute your network.

Long-term relationship Building your network is a long-term proposition. You don't just meet people once at a chamber of commerce mixer or professional society meeting and expect to establish a significant relationship based on a three-minute encounter and exchange of business cards. With repeated meetings, over time, you may develop a relationship and friendship. If you do, it will be because you get to know each other more than superficially.

Cultivate before you harvest You build a network because you connect with certain people and want to get to know them better. They are people with whom you have common interests. You look for ways in which you can help them because they are people you respect, trust and want to believe in. To paraphrase President Kennedy, "Ask not what they can do for you; ask what you can do for them." When you help them, they look for ways to help you. But, if you approach people only interested in how they can help you, they will see through you. No one likes to feel used. They will avoid you like the plague! People want to feel that your interest in them is as a friend, rather than as someone you want to tap for what they can do for you.

To build your network First, determine what you are genuinely interested in. Relationship building with others needs to be authentic. Then, find opportunities at work or in the community to become involved in a team effort with people you can respect, want to help, and for whom you have something of value to offer. Get to know each person on your team as an individual and look for ways in which you can help them advance toward their goals. Help them when you find appropriate opportunities. Always follow through on commitments you make so they see that you are a person they can count on. In the process of you getting to know them, they will get to know you. Some will be able to help you sooner, some later, and others, even though they may want to, may never be in a position to help you. Similarly, you may never be in a position to help some people you would like to. That's OK. "What goes around comes around."

Keep your relationships alive As your network grows, you cannot be in frequent contact with everyone. Nevertheless, keep thinking of the people you know. When you find an article that you think would be of interest, cut it out and send it along with a note. Phone up your friends from time to time to touch base. Meet them for lunch or coffee or something else where you share a common interest. Try to have at least three significant contacts per year with each person.

Building a network of people who are your advocates and allies is as essential an investment in your success as getting a college education, or developing your resume of work assignments to make you attractive in the job market. All three require work. All are worth their investment. Invest generously! In the words of the Beatles, "And in the end, the love you take is equal to the love you make!"

9.5

Navigating Organizational Politics

Organizational politics is about how people in organizations acquire and maintain power, influence and status. Every organization has its formal organization, as expressed in its organization chart and policies, and its informal organization that reflects the real world relationships of power, influence and status. For example, in the military services, a junior officer has more official power than a master sergeant, but the master sergeant may have more informal influence and status. Why do you need to know about this? Politics is endemic to organizational life. Politics can range from healthy to dysfunctional political games. If you don't recognize and decide how to deal with political land mines, you can step on one and have it explode on you.

I have yet to find an organization in which politics doesn't play a role. I have talked with some people who claim that their organization is apolitical. On examination, politics did play a role, albeit a generally healthy one, in their organizations. The actions people take to acquire and maintain power, influence and status are, in a very real sense like games. Whenever some people in an organization have more power, influence and status than others, you find political games.

The political behavior of people in an organization is part of its culture and generally reflects the behavior of top management. The games played at the top are likely to be replicated throughout the rest of the organization. If the top leaders seek inclusion and consensus in decisions, others will follow. If they are insecure and authoritarian, their games will proliferate. As I was once told, "If you are trying to understand the behavior of a neurotic dog, first look at its master."

Some people are genuinely oblivious to organizational politics, and some act oblivious, which is actually a political game in itself. At a minimum, you probably need to recognize political games. Once you recognize them, you can decide how you want to deal with them.

Some political games Here are eleven political games frequently found in organizations:

1. You are beholden to me The message of this political game is, "Look at all that I do (have done) for you. You should be grateful! You owe me! Without me, you'd be nothing." The objective is to extract appreciation, acknowledgement, dominance and control. People who play this game want you in their web. They prey on people new to the organization who are still naïve about them. Sometimes they engage in blackmail, and sometimes in martyrdom to get you and keep you beholden to them. The people who play this game actually do things that can be quite helpful. Though they can pull strings for you, their generosity has an ulterior motive. In return, they want recognition and adulation, and if they don't get what they want, they withhold support and may bad-mouth you behind your back.

2. Rites of passage Just as fraternities and sororities have their hazing rituals, and the military has its Basic Training, some organizations require people new to them to be "tested" for their "fit" and loyalty before they are accepted into the group. This is found more in patriarchal organizations where it is important to be part of the "family." We're talking about more than just a normal orientation. One organization I know of asks everyone with whom a new employee has interacted during his/her first two weeks on the job for any negative feedback (nothing positive) they can think of. The new employee's boss compiles their negative trivia and relates it to him/her in a dump session, after which he/she is completely demoralized. If the new employee can take it, and "atones" for his/her "sins," he/she becomes a member of the "family." He/she then is entitled to dump on subsequent new hires. If he/she balks at such treatment, or doesn't shape up, he/she is judged not to fit in and is let go.

3. Indispensable This is a game in which people try to create the impression that they are critically important. They are late to meetings because they were needed to solve a crisis. They come to work early and stay late, whether or not they have anything to do, to create the impression that they are overworked. They spend more time talking about being overworked and under appreciated than they spend actually working. They constantly imply blessings by higher-ups for their activities in order to appear powerful. They typically take themselves very seriously. They insinuate that people who make them feel threatened are incompetent. They twist situations to promote themselves.

4. What does the boss think? In this political game, people are afraid to make a decision until the boss has stated his/her position on an issue. This is usually a symptom of an autocrat with weak staff. No one wants to make a decision that might be at odds with what the boss thinks for fear of humiliation and possible loss of one's job. This game is closely akin to *The Emperor's New Clothes,* in which people are afraid to confront an obvious issue. It is also akin to "Trial balloon," in which people pose an issue or action in draft form for discussion purposes only in order to see how it flies.

5. Sacrificial lamb In this game, people recognize that the organization seldom approves what is proposed without making some changes. Thus, they include something that is not especially important with the idea that it will be "sacrificial lamb" to be cut so that they will get what's important to them. This is especially prevalent in negotiations for budgets, and with suppliers and unions where less important issues are included in proposals, so that something can be given away in order to get what is really desired.

6. Poor me! In this game, people tell you about something that is troubling them, not so much to get help solving it as to invite sympathy. They will tell everyone else about what's troubling them except the person who can do something to solve the problem. They are less concerned with getting the problem solved. If you try to help them, they will find innumerable reasons why what you suggest won't work. I am told that there is an old Russian saying, "How miserable it is to be happy, and how happy it is to be miserable." They embody this saying.

7. They do it too! The underlying message in this game is that everyone else does what you are accusing me of, so it must be OK. Why single me out? You must have something against me. You can find this game from the playgrounds of elementary schools all the way to corporate settings. *"What's wrong with reporting this as a sale now? I know that they will buy, and our team needs to reflect this sale now so that we can get the trip to Maui. Other people do this all the time. Why pick on me?"*

8. Micromanagement The basic message of this game is, "I'm better than you are because I find and correct all your mistakes." It also communicates a lack of trust besides a sense of superiority. It is the opposite of empowerment. Bosses and people who check the work of others play this game. They try to validate themselves by putting others down. People in central administrative offices play this game with people out in operating units.

9. Destructive compliance In this game, people do *exactly* what they're told, whether it makes sense or not, and regardless of the consequences. Then, when something goes wrong, they say, *"Well, I did exactly what you told me to."* And they did, even though they knew it was wrong. This game is generally in reaction to micromanagement. The message is, *"If you think you are so damn smart and insist that I do this your way, I'll show you. I'll do just what you tell me to—no more, no less—and I'll show you up!"* They can do a lot of damage in the process, and all they are guilty of is doing exactly what they were told.

10. Cast system While this political game is found in family businesses, it is also found in organizations where there is an "anointed" group of people (the patricians) who seek to maintain power and advantage, and the rest (the plebeians). It is used to justify unequal treatment when there are high barriers to entry into the anointed group. In academic institutions, you have the FACULTY and the staff. In some businesses, you have MANAGEMENT and employees. In the medical community, you have DOCTORS and nurses. In libraries, you have LIBRARIANS and clerical staff.

11. Seeking consensus The objective of this game is to build support and commitment among constituents for taking an action. It recognizes that people resist what they don't understand, so education and building coalitions are essential strategies. When the action is for the greater good of an organization and the strategies used to build consensus are ethical and appropriate, it is constructive. However, consensus building can also be a dysfunctional game. Sometimes, distortion of facts is used to achieve a consensus for a personal agenda. Sometimes, seeking consensus is used as a crutch when a leader feels insecure about making a decision. Sometimes, a consensus is sought when none is needed. At Hewlett-Packard in the late 1990s, seeking consensus was a way of life. Decisions that did not need consensus were subject to the consensus-building process. The result was that some new products were late to market, placing H-P at a strategic disadvantage. Thus, in the game of building consensus, it is critical to make sure that consensus is important to a decision (see Chapter 5.1). It is also essential that it be used for the benefit of the organization and not for pressing a personal agenda.

As I said, some political games, those that help build support and consensus, can be beneficial. Some are innocuous, and others are plainly dysfunctional. If a political game serves an organization and its people well, then playing the game is fine. If a political game fosters behavior that undermines an organization or harms its stakeholders, such as destructive compliance, then you are faced with a choice of what to do about it. What you decide to do will be influenced by what effect you think you can have, and how your action to deal with a game can affect you and your career. Here are some options:

Play the game This may be the easiest option, at least in the short run. By playing, you blend in with the others who are playing. However, as in any game, you need to understand the rules and have the skills. You also need to devote the energy and attention to make sure you don't get swept away by the undertow. Jonestown and the Death March in Saipan are examples of people who played a deadly game and got swept away. In games that have win-lose outcomes, you will either win or lose.

Ignore or choose not to play the game If you don't understand how the game works, and/or if you don't have the skills or a good reason to play, this may be the safest choice. However, if you don't play, you probably won't have an opportunity to influence the outcome. If everyone else plays the game and you don't, then you will stand out. In opting not to play, you may call attention to the fact that there is a game, which is a form of calling people at their game. Nor does opting out assure you that you won't be affected by it. The actions of the people playing a political game may impact you. For example, labor-management negotiations are a game. Though you may not be on the negotiating committee, you will be affected by the outcome of the agreement. If you are covered by the contract, and the union goes on strike, you will either have to picket, decline to participate, or cross the picket line to go to work.

Call people at their game   When you call people at their game, you expose the fact that they are playing a political game. Calling the game usually stops it, at least temporarily. People who are benefiting from playing a game generally don't like to have it called because it foils them and may embarrass them. They may deny that a game is being played. People who have been caught in the undertow of a game may be relieved, and also anxious. For example, sexual harassment is a power game with an element of blackmail. The alleged perpetrator is apt to be furious when he/she is exposed and charged. Not only does the game stop, he/she is then held accountable for his/her behavior. Though the person who has been harassed is usually relieved to have the game cease, he/she is also filled with anxiety about publicity, possible retribution, having to testify, etc. Undoubtedly, some people who have been harassed decide not to call the game because the action of calling the game, and the associated follow-up, is equally repugnant. They choose "flight" over "fight."

Calling people at their game, especially a high stakes political game, takes courage and a clear understanding of what you want to accomplish by doing it. If time permits, it usually helps to discuss the issue, your objective and your strategy with a trusted, level-headed confidant.

If you choose to call people at their game, there are several important principles to consider:

1. Know what you want to accomplish   Do you just want to stop the game? Do you want to change behavior? What is your motivation for calling it? Will calling the game make things better?

2. Focus on behavior   Behavior is observable and can be described. Describe what you see. Avoid ascribing motives or assigning labels to what you see, as they can only be inferred. Ask a person involved to describe what is happening, or has just happened. It is more powerful if you can get someone to describe the behavior. If the person can't, describe what you have observed. *"Time out! During the past fifteen minutes, you have stated five reasons why you don't have the time to answer Mr. Baskin's letter. Answering his letter should take no more than twenty minutes. What's going on?"* I have found that some people involved in playing a game were not paying attention to behavior of others. They were intent on pressing their agenda. If someone can't describe what has happened, or if you observe relevant behavior that no one mentions, then describe what you have observed. *"John has restated his position on this four times, and Frank has restated his position three times. Everyone else is just sitting listening to them, except for Marlene who rolls her eyes every time John begins restating his position. What's going on? Is this the best way to run our meetings?"*

3. Set new norms Ask the person (people) to define their ideal way of interacting. Most people will define a standard higher than what they have been exhibiting. If they don't know, you can ask, *"How do you want to deal with _____ behavior?"*

4. Get commitment People are more apt to "live up" to what they say they can "live with." Ask people, *"Do these new standards make sense? How can you benefit from them? What changes do they imply? Can you live with them?"* If anyone has issues with the proposed new norms, ask him/her to elaborate on his/her concerns. Seek consensus. Unanimous support may not be possible but majority support (51%) is not enough.

5. Build monitoring into the process Just defining new behavior and gaining commitment is not enough, as anyone knows who has ever made New Years resolutions. When there is a plan of follow up, and people know that they will be held accountable for their behavior, they are more likely to take responsibility for their actions. When I work with a group, I ask them to set ground rules that will enable them to work together effectively. I always post them for any group meeting, and I ask one of the people to read them to the group each time we meet in order to refresh everyone's memory. Then I ask them if they need to add, delete or modify any and remind them that we will revisit them in the meeting review. At the end of our meeting, I ask the group to review how they behaved in relation to their ground rules. If they fell short on any, I ask them what we need to do so that future meetings will be even better. This process becomes standard practice and makes a noticeable difference in how well the group works together.

As a management consultant who specializes in issues of leadership and organizational life, I have had my share of assignments that involved calling people at their game. One of the reasons I am brought into an organization is to help people stop a political game when they are not sure how to, or are afraid of the possible consequences. Thus, my objective is to help them find and adopt ways of interacting that will be better for them and their organization, and will make it easier for them to stop games in the future.

Not all political games are played in group settings. I worked with a client where, after interviewing a significant sample of people, it became clear that the VP of administration was playing the political game of "Torpedo the Boss." In all his interactions with others, he tried to undermine the authority and credibility of the president. No one felt confident enough to call him at his game. Using what I had learned in the interviews, I met with the VP one-on-one and described a consistent pattern of feedback about his behavior. He had not realized how people were perceiving his actions. We discussed how his behavior would need to change if he chose to stay. He concluded that it would be easier for him to get a fresh start in a new job elsewhere. Why was I able to call him at his game? First, in confronting him, I approached him as an ally trying to help him make sense of a confounding situation. Our meeting was in private. I had done my homework and the feedback I had on his behavior was sufficiently consistent that he could not dismiss it. Second, it was easier for me, as an outsider, to confront him. People had spoken with me more openly about the issues than they would have to an insider. Third, I let him know clearly that his past behavior was considered unacceptable, and defined what I thought he would need to do to change his behavior if he wanted to try to mend the situation. Fourth, we explored his options so that he understood them before making his decision. I helped him find a way to bow out and save face. Though he did not like what happened, at least he felt that I had been fair, respectful, helpful and professional in dealing with him in his situation.

Games to acquire and maintain power, influence and status are a fact of organizational life. You need to recognize them for what they are and decide how you want to respond to them. Games that empower people and advance the purpose and mission of an organization can be beneficial. Those that subvert an organization or foster dysfunctional behavior are destructive and need to be stopped. Calling people at their game is dicey, yet, essential for the health of an organization. If you are going to call someone at a political game, make sure that you know what you want to accomplish and that you have your facts straight. You will be engaging in a win or lose contest. Be prepared. Test your perceptions and confrontation strategy with a confidant. A confidant should be able to help you to determine whether you are, in fact, observing a political game and help you to try out several approaches to confronting it. Because confronting a political game is a challenge to your power and that of the person you are challenging, and such struggles can suck you into a downward vortex, make sure that you don't lose sight of what you seek to accomplish.

9.6

Negotiating an Agreement

Life is a series of negotiations. Some are formal, such as negotiating a contract with a supplier. Others are casual. A husband wants to go to the football game; his wife wants them to see *The Bridges of Madison County*. Through the process of negotiations, they arrive at an agreement.

The central premise of negotiations is that the people involved *want* to come to an agreement that meets their needs on issues of mutual concern. Negotiating is a specialized process of discovery in overcoming obstacles in the path to an agreement. Issues that are important to one person may not be of equal importance to others, and vice versa. Through discovery and weighing options, people can reach an agreement that satisfies their priority interests, while satisfying those of the others. Of course, if there is no desire to reach an agreement among the parties (a fatal obstacle), negotiations won't work.

For some people, negotiating is a "zero sum," adversarial game (like in court room law) where in order for one person to "win," the other has to "lose." A more creative approach is to view negotiating as a collaborative exercise in which people work together to find a mutually satisfying solution to a problem. A number of manufacturers have negotiated agreements with their suppliers through this process. Using this approach, the people involved determine their interests and objectives in the issue under negotiation. After stating their interests and objectives, they all participate in brainstorming to create options that will satisfy everyone's needs, as much as possible. Frequently, there is a facilitator who takes the people through the process and keeps them focused on how to achieve a solution that maximizes everyone's needs.

Regardless of whether you are in adversarial or collaborative negotiations, here are some tips that can make the process work better for you.

1. Determine your objectives What do you want to accomplish? What is your "ideal" outcome? What can you "live with?" What is unacceptable? Why? If you're not clear about what's important to you, you won't get it! Some years ago I was buying a used car. The owner was asking $9300. I had done my research. Midpoint between high and low Kelley Blue Book was about $9000, and I was prepared to pay that. In talking with the owner, I discovered that he was eager for a cash offer. That was no problem for me. I asked him what the best price was that he could give me for an all-cash deal then and there. He dropped the price to $8700. I knew I had a good deal and was able to act on it.

2. Prepare your position This is your statement of what you are seeking and what is important to you. In adversarial negotiations, this may be called a proposal and is usually a written document. Whether negotiations are adversarial or collaborative, formal or informal, you need to think of how you want to express clearly and persuasively what you are seeking. It will become what is subject to discussion and problem solving. In adversarial negotiations, you generally have a strategic advantage if you can negotiate using your document rather than your adversary's. It becomes the focal point. More of what is important to you is apt to be in your document.

3. Present your position vividly Part of the challenge of negotiations is to help people see an issue from a different perspective. Think of appropriate analogies and metaphors that help the people with whom you are negotiating to see things out of their typical perspective. You need to search for a way of expressing your position in such a way that the people with whom you are negotiating say, *"Ah hah! I never thought of things this way before."* I was working once with the CEO of a business whose sales and profit had been declining for three years and who was facing major new competition. It was not until I likened his business to the Titanic sailing at 22 knots into a field of icebergs that he realized he was in danger and could no longer operate on a "business as usual" basis.

4. Listen for understanding Listening is an essential communication skill. When you think of great communicators, you probably think first of people who express themselves clearly and persuasively. That's only part of communications. You learn when you listen, not when you talk. You cannot negotiate successfully what you don't understand. In negotiations, you need to concentrate on listening for understanding. What is the other person trying to communicate in words, in what's not said, in facial expressions, gestures, tone of voice, pitch, volume, modulation, etc.? To make sure that you understand, you need to synthesize and summarize the other person's position in your own words. This is known as testing for understanding. *"Let's see, Bill. If I understand you correctly, this is what is important to you. _____. Am I correct?"* When you do this, you confirm that you listened, understood, and were able to summarize correctly what you heard. You have taken a significant step in building trust. You communicate that you thought it was important enough to try to understand the other person's concerns that you invested yourself in the process. It is a compliment that is appreciated. Of course, if you missed the mark, you can seek clarification before proceeding.

5. Look for and acknowledge points of agreement There are always some points of agreement. Look for them and confirm them. Create an "agreement pool." Place what you agree on in the "agreement pool." Your objective in negotiations is to drain the "disagreement pool" and fill the "agreement pool." Taking issues on which you achieve agreement out of the "disagreement pool" and placing them in the "agreement pool" symbolically communicates progress.

6. Seek creative alternatives to outstanding issues Some people have a disease that I call "hardening of the categories." They believe that 2+2 is the only way to arrive at 4 when, of course, there are many other ways. Keep your objectives clear and in sight, and don't become blinded to the many ways to achieve them. Listen to and consider alternative routes to achieve your objectives. Look for how they could work, not just why they can't. Once you have tested for understanding, and you know that you understand an alternative, and you still doubt that it can meet your needs, ask, *"Can you help me see how what you are proposing will meet my objective of _____?"* In asking this question, you are communicating that you are still open, yet have some concerns that have not been addressed satisfactorily. You enlist the people with whom you are negotiating in an effort to meet your needs with their proposal. If you can't go along with a proposal, state that you can't and explain why. *"I appreciate your creative thoughts on this issue and your effort to try to make it work. I still am not sold on it for these reasons: _____, _____."*

7. Be patient The process of negotiating an agreement can take time. It is better to negotiate the right agreement than a fast agreement. The goal is to negotiate an agreement with which you and the people with whom you are negotiating can "live." It is actually faster to work out the details beforehand than to have to revisit and possibly renegotiate an agreement born in haste. Especially in an adversarial negotiation, if you communicate urgency, you divulge a vulnerability that will be taken advantage of.

8. Ponder an offer before accepting it You want the person with whom you are negotiating to believe that he/she has negotiated the most favorable agreement possible. If you accept an offer without pondering it, the other person may suspect that you got the best of him/her. Even if you only take 30 seconds, look like you are going through a serious thought process. *"Hmm! $8700 is the very best price you will accept for an all-cash deal this afternoon?"* *"Yes, I already have an offer of that from another buyer, but he can't pay me until tomorrow."* (Pause and look over your notes.) *"OK. We have a deal."* (Shake hands.) Remember: negotiating is a type of game.

9. "You've got to know when to hold them, know when to fold them, ..." As the song implies, you may not always be able to achieve a win-win outcome, or even a win-lose one. You may, at times, need to pack up and leave—at least temporarily. When you reach a stalemate, especially in adversarial negotiations, you may need to say, *"We've been over this ad nauseam and are making no progress. Life is too short to waste any more of it here. Call me if/when you are willing to get serious."* This is not a tactic that you use very often, otherwise you blow your credibility. It should be reserved for only when other efforts have failed to refocus a deteriorating negotiation process.

Life requires crafting agreements—from simple, informal ones to major mergers, acquisitions, and divestitures. Such negotiations can be adversarial or collaborative. They can be fun and creative, or they can be like warfare. Whatever the characteristics of the negotiation, you need to know what you are trying to achieve, what's really important to you and what isn't, and you need to be prepared. Listening and testing for understanding are as important as persuasive expression of your position. An open mind is essential for arriving at creative solutions that enable all parties to feel satisfied with the outcome. My personal preference, and what I am finding popular among my clients, is collaborative negotiations. I have facilitated negotiations where *everyone* felt that the outcome was far better than they had any reason to hope for. That's win-win!

9.7

Improving Relations With Your Non-Traditional Customers

STOP! Please take a minute to list people who are your customers.

You probably identified your traditional customers/clients, but did you list the following?

- ❑ Your "boss" (who can replace you if he/she is not satisfied with your services)
- ❑ People on your team (who can withhold cooperation and assistance)
- ❑ People who report to you (customers for your vision, knowledge and leadership)
- ❑ Your students (who can tune you out) and their parents, if you are a teacher
- ❑ Your spouse or significant other (customers for your love and companionship)
- ❑ Your children (customers for your love, knowledge and guidance)

These people may not be customers in the traditional sense, but you need to please them in your roles with them as though they were customers. They make decisions, with their head and their heart, whether to "buy" what you offer. You can't force them. As with your traditional customers, if you don't treat them as valued customers, you will not have their loyalty and business for long.

"Satisfactory" customer service is not enough! What does "satisfactory" mean to you? Would you choose to marry someone who was "satisfactory?" Is an employee whose job performance is "satisfactory" giving your business a competitive advantage? Do customers refer other customers to your business because your customer service is "satisfactory?" Will your business survive if all that you strive for is "satisfactory" service to your constituents?

Customers refer others to your business when they are delighted with the service/treatment that they receive. They tell dozens of people about you and become your "champion." On the other hand, if they are displeased, they will bash you for years. When they are merely "satisfied," they are passive. They may not bad-mouth you, but neither will they promote you. "Satisfactory" is not enough! A higher standard is needed. Seek to delight your customers, whether they are traditional and non-traditional.

Delighting customers What does it take to delight customers? For starters, how about:

- ❏ Listening to their needs and making sure that their best interests are served
- ❏ Providing exceptional value
- ❏ Integrity: Honest representations and answers
- ❏ Meeting commitments ahead of schedule
- ❏ Making them feel special and valued

Are customers always right? No! But give them the benefit of the doubt.

Why delight your non-traditional customers? Your success is a function of their success. When they are delighted, they are your champions and advocates. They will sing your praises in ways you never could. That is invaluable!

9.8

Keeping Others Informed

"How come you didn't tell me about the Zyzex problem and how you solved it? What you did was commendable!"

"Hey, no big deal. I was just doing my job. I didn't want to seem as though I was 'tooting my own horn'."

In organizational life, people are interconnected. Much of the time, the people with whom you work need to know what you do that may affect them and the team—and vice versa. The principal of an elementary school shielded her staff from all financial matters so they could focus on teaching. Instead, all she heard was constant carping about her allocation of resources. So she opened the books, shared the budget information with them and asked for their input. Once they understood the trade-offs, their carping stopped. They pulled together to make recommendations for the betterment of the school as a whole.

Managers and employees ask the same question: How much information should I share concerning what I do? They work on issues that affect each other.

Some information is important and other may be inconsequential. How do you keep others informed without it seeming like you are "tooting your own horn" or providing a boring list of details? There is no magic formula. The basic principle is to share information that the people with whom you interact need to know and think is significant. How do you find out? Ask them:

- ❑ What information do you need to perform your job?
- ❑ What information do you need to feel connected and part of the team?
- ❑ How do you want me to treat information that you probably should know if it doesn't fall into the above categories?
- ❑ What is the best way for me to communicate with you about this?

Ask these questions of the people in the groups with which you interact (your boss, your team members, the people who report to you, etc.). Try for a consensus in each group to make communication easier.

Create a matrix of the groups and their information needs. Code the preferred communication method into each cell.

Transmitting information is not communication until the receiver receives the message. Thus, ask for feedback periodically:

- ❑ Is the information I am providing you useful and what you need?
- ❑ Is it timely and easy to understand?
- ❑ What should I add, delete or change?

Communication is more than having a matrix of people to whom you send messages. It is a mindset that constantly asks about each decision or event:

- ❑ Who needs to know about this?
- ❑ Why and what do they need to know?
- ❑ What don't they need to know?
- ❑ What is the best way to communicate this considering the purpose?

While some people may be telepathic, thoughts are not enough for most. A memo, an e-mail, a phone call, a meeting, etc. is needed to transmit a message.

The process of asking these questions has value. It prompts people to think through their needs and methods of communication. In most businesses, communication is an afterthought. This approach places communication as forethought.

9.9

Becoming an Excellent Communicator

Communications are the vital fluid of leadership—like what blood is to the body. There is no way you can inspire people in the pursuit of common goals without good communication skills.

Excellent communicators—who comes to mind? Perhaps you think of high profile names like Ronald Reagan, Martin Luther King Jr., or Franklin Delano Roosevelt. It is possible to be an excellent communicator without being a legend. In addition, excellent communicators are not just speakers; they are writers, too.

What makes someone an excellent communicator? What do they do?

They know their subject and audience, and how to connect with them.

- ❑ They view each audience as a target market for their message, and research the issues and interests important to them.
- ❑ They listen with undivided attention and actively try to understand what is being said.
- ❑ They tailor the message to their audience.
- ❑ They test and fine-tune their message.
- ❑ When speaking, they practice using a video camera or a coach for feedback.

They get their message across in terms that their audience understands and can relate to.

- ❑ In crafting their message, they use the vocabulary of their audience.
- ❑ Their opening engages their audience and previews their message.
- ❑ There is a logical flow from start to finish.
- ❑ Their closing summarizes their message memorably.
- ❑ They use questions to engage their audience or to demonstrate a point when a question communicates their message more powerfully than a statement.
- ❑ They use appropriate analogies, anecdotes and humor to relate to the realities of their audience, cut to the essence of an issue, and underscore noteworthy points.

❑ When speaking to a group:
They use their whole body to communicate.
Their movements, gestures, expressions are consistent with their words.
They modulate their voice and pace.
They move easily around the stage or room.
They appear spontaneous and comfortable before the audience.
Their visual aids are readable, and they are used strictly as aids.
Their handouts underscore what they want their audience to remember.
They summarize and restate questions before answering them.

They inspire people to believe them and believe in them.

❑ They appear as people with integrity—respectworthy and trustworthy.
❑ They come across as knowing what they are communicating about.
❑ What they say makes sense to their audience.
❑ They exude an infectious energy and belief in what they are saying.
❑ They are confident, without being arrogant.
❑ They show people how they can be part of a compelling future by "joining in the journey."
❑ They are honest and will say they don't know an answer, rather than "winging" it.
❑ They will expose their vulnerabilities and share a personal experience to demonstrate a point.
❑ They confront and resolve issues, and own up to those for which they have some responsibility.
❑ They don't speak ill of others to make themselves look good.

Just as it is easier to enjoy a piece of music played by a musician than it is to be a musician, it is easier to appreciate an excellent communicator than it is to be one. Some people have a natural talent for communications, and others have to work at it. Some people have the talent to become a virtuoso pianist. Many more can learn to play the piano reasonably well. But, anyone who is going to succeed at either playing the piano or at becoming a better communicator has to work at it. Practice, practice, practice! A pianist needs a piano teacher for instruction and feedback. A leader developing communication skills needs a coach for the same reasons.

How about someone who is really shy? Shyness presents a challenge, but not an insurmountable one. As a kid I was shy—really shy. I still am to a certain extent, but I have made progress. I decided that I wanted to change. To do that, I decided to put myself in situations that would stretch me. So, I took a job interviewing job applicants. That was fairly structured, my role was clear and I got some training and coaching. As I gained proficiency in interviewing, I became more comfortable in that type of situation. To become more comfortable speaking publicly, I became a radio disk jockey. I could speak to an audience that I did not see. As I became more confident and competent in that role, I moved into conducting seminars and workshops where I could see my audience. I'll not get into all the details, but now I speak in public at least once a month. I am comfortable now speaking to groups. Though I still have a way to go before becoming an excellent communicator, the feedback I get indicates I have come a long way.

If I could become a better communicator, so can others. But, it is not possible to master everything at once. What is needed is to concentrate on developing one or two skills at a time, as I did, with the aid of someone who can model, observe, and provide constructive feedback. Some people find Toastmasters helpful, others use a coach, and others have a skillful colleague to coach them.

In the interdependent world in which we live, one's influence as a leader is a direct function of one's ability to communicate. Improve your ability to communicate and you will have much more influence, and influence is power.

10

Creating Organizational Change

10.1

Mastering Organizational Change

The poster states, "Change or die." Change is a fact of life, but many change initiatives go awry. Why? Most frequently, the reason for failure is disregard for, or unawareness of, these principles:

- ❑ People fear and resist loss of control, loss of power, or what they don't understand. They will oppose what they fear
- ❑ People will be attracted to (support) changes that benefit them
- ❑ Change is disruptive—even change that one wants
- ❑ It takes time and support to achieve full implementation of a change
- ❑ People want a voice in what affects them

Fear is a natural and healthy reaction to danger in the environment. It sensitizes the mind and body to danger and puts one on the defensive. That's all well and good when there actually is physical danger. What do people fear about change in an organizational setting?

- ❑ Loss of control over their work, relationships and environment
- ❑ Loss of competence while moving from the familiar to the new ways
- ❑ Loss of influence and power
- ❑ New ways of working that may not seem to make sense

Fear of loss of control is a major reason people resist change. They don't like the transition from a state of competence in old ways to temporary lower competence in the new. It takes time to become proficient with something new. Just think of how long it takes you to become proficient with new software!

When you are trying to bring about change in an organization, you want people to be open minded, imaginative, and willing to experiment with new ways. Thus, fear, and its accompanying defensiveness, is not the state of mind you want for people in a change effort.

Diminish fear by providing people with as much control as possible over the change process. Ask for input. Provide them with information, training and coaching to help build competence and confidence during their transition.

Involvement You can't solve an organizational problem without involvement of the key stakeholders. Identify these people and bring them into a change effort early-on. When they are involved in a change effort where they will be implementing the change, they can:

- ❑ Understand the need for change

❑ Have input into it
❑ Help debug it early-on
❑ Begin preparing for it themselves
❑ Begin preparing others for it

People need time to prepare mentally for change. They resist what seems foisted on them. They are less apt to resist that in which they are involved.

Constructive dissatisfaction According to Richard Beckhard,* change occurs when:

Dissatisfaction with the Present × Vision of Future × Steps (strategy) > Resistance.

All three multipliers must be greater than zero for change to occur.
In other words, if you want to bring about change, you have to create:

❑ Dissatisfaction with what exists now (convince people that there is a problem)
❑ An attractive vision of what it will be like with the new
❑ A road map (strategy) of how to get there

Support vs. opposition Any change will have support *and* opposition. The better you understand who supports and who opposes a change, the more effective you can be in bringing it about. One helpful tool for analyzing support and opposition is the Force Field Analysis, created by Kurt Lewin.** Take a piece of paper and draw a line down the middle. Label one side "Support," and the other "Opposition." Brainstorm what support and opposition there may be, and list these on their appropriate side of the line. Then draw arrows pointing toward the centerline. Make the length of the arrows proportionate to your estimate of support or opposition. This creates a graphic picture of what you are facing. Then brainstorm what you can do to transform opposition into support, or at least diffuse it, and adjust the length of the arrows accordingly. The objective is to create strategies to maximize support and minimize opposition.

Support   Opposition

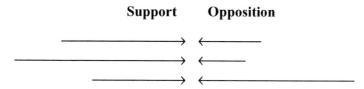

*Richard Beckhard, *Organization Development: Strategies and Models* (Reading, Mass.: Addison-Wesley, 1969)

**Kurt Lewin, *Field Theory and Social Science* (New York: Harper & Bros., 1954)

Vision   While dissatisfaction with the present repels people, a compelling vision of a desired future attracts them. Create a vision of what life will be like when a change is fully implemented. People accept change more easily when they can see what's in it for them. A vision of future benefits can be a powerful influence to help overcome resistance.

Experiment   Change, when introduced as an "experiment," may have a greater chance of success. People are more willing to risk change when they know it is not "cast in concrete" and that they can influence the final outcome. Trying something as an experiment provides the freedom to try it without losing face if it doesn't work, and then try something else. Moreover, if people try a new way and like it, they will do what they can to assure its success.

Select a trial group of people willing to experiment. Help them understand the needs and objectives. Let them try the new ways with full support, then evaluate the results and be open to modification. Don't worry about creating system-wide change all at once. Learn from the "pioneers" so that you can work out the bugs on a small scale first. "Pioneers" can become "champions" who serve as role models and mentors when a successful experiment is implemented throughout the organization.

Welcome objections   They help you to "find the flies in the ointment," and lead to a better solution or decision. You can't resolve an objection you don't know about, and people won't buy into a change until their objections have been addressed. Don't, however, let people grovel in objections. You can say, *"Thanks for expressing your objections. We now have a healthy set of them. The question is, given our goals and these objections, what we can do to resolve these issues and move forward?"* At that point, only accept ways to resolve the issues. If people continue to harp on the objections, call a "time out." *Say, "Wait a minute! We're not here to kill this. We're here to find ways to **make it work**. Let's focus on how we **can** do that!"*

Be open   to other ways to accomplish an objective. There is seldom just one right answer. A solution that people buy-into has a better chance of success.

Interrelationships   An organization is a system in which everything is interconnected. Change can't be made in isolation—it is bound to have effects elsewhere. When you weigh options, look for the "unintended" consequences. For example, what behavior and results do the pay system and other forms of recognition provide as reward for people? Individual commissions reward individual sales, but may destroy teamwork. Make sure that what you reward is consistent with your goals. "The solution to today's problem can be the seed of tomorrow's."

Transitions   It's not change that causes people trouble as much as it is the transition. To master change, you must understand the nature of transitions. Let's look at a graph, Effect of a Change (adapted from a presentation by John Adams and

Effect of a Change

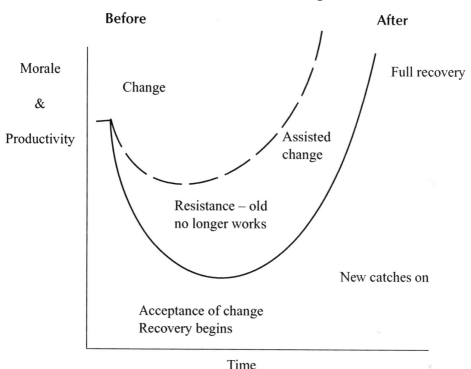

Sabrina Spencer), that plots morale and productivity through time before and after a change. Morale or productivity is usually relatively constant before a change. Sometimes these decline with the premonition of a change. Then a change occurs. If it is welcome, there may be a temporary euphoria; but whether it is welcome or not, morale and productivity drop. They drop because of denial and resistance, and because it takes time to work out the problems with the transition, and because it takes time to gain competence and confidence with new ways.

As the bottom of the curve is reached, people begin to accept a change and rebuild their competence and confidence. As competence and confidence increase, so do morale and productivity. In a successful change, morale and productivity exceed their before-change level.

As you can see from the transition curve diagram, it is natural, even under the best of circumstances, to see a decline in morale and productivity after a change. It takes time to let go of the old and become proficient in the new. Many change efforts are abandoned or declared a failure prematurely, especially when there has been inadequate support for the change. In public education, a new program is introduced in the summer. Teachers are given an in-service day of training in the new program and told to march with it. Then, before the end of the school year, it is abandoned because the desired results have not yet been achieved when, actually, three to five years is a more appropriate period for evaluation.

Why is it is important to grasp this almost universal pattern?

- ❏ Your need to have realistic expectations
- ❏ Understanding the nature of transitions can keep you from becoming dispirited during the decline, and help you to recover faster
- ❏ Depth of the trough and time it takes to recover can be minimized (dotted curve) by achieving buy-in and commitment among people who are responsible for implementing a change, and providing them with support during the change process
- ❏ You can monitor your progress in implementing a change

Celebration To rise out of the transition trough, recognize people for progress, as well as accomplishments. Celebration adds a dimension of recognition and joy, and helps reinforce people's efforts.

Many of my consulting assignments have involved helping clients recover from failed efforts to implement change. Though a proposed change may have been technically sound, it met with debilitating resistance because the process used was out of step with the above change principles.

10.2

Organizational Change Analysis

Mastering change involves applying change principles, learning from each experience, and applying your learning to future initiatives. In learning from or planning for a change initiative, the following principles and questions apply. Use them as a checklist for analysis and planning. Change the tense of the questions to *past* for *analysis* and *future* for *planning*.

1. **People fear and resist what they don't understand or see a need for.**

   - ❏ What is being done to make the people who have a stake in the change aware of the problem and the need to change? What data is provided to enable people to discover the need?

❑ What is being done to help people realize that "business as usual" won't work?

❑ What is being done to create a compelling vision of a better post-change future?

❑ What is being done to create a "road map" from the present to the desired future?

2. **People who need to be part of the implementation need to be involved in the problem solving and planning process.**

❑ Who are the people who have a stake in the problem?

❑ Who is being involved in planning the change initiative?

❑ Who is being left out who believes he/she has a stake in the problem?

❑ How significant a role are the stakeholders playing in the change process?

❑ How much is their input influencing the outcome of the initiative?

3. **People fear and resist loss of power, influence control and competence.**

❑ Who loses power, influence and control as a result of the change?

❑ Who gains power, influence and control as a result of the change?

❑ What is being done to allay their concerns and minimize negative impact?

4. **People are more accepting of change when they can see tangible benefits.**

❑ Who benefits from the change and in what ways?

❑ What is being done to sell the benefits of the change?

❑ Are these changes desired by the people affected by them?

❑ What do constituents desire that can not be provided?

5. **Change is disruptive—even change that people want.**

❑ What is being done to introduce the change as an "experiment?"

❑ What is being done to introduce the change to a "pilot" group first?

❑ What is being done to convert people in the "pilot" group into "champions" or "missionaries" to help spread the change throughout the organization?

❑ What training is being provided in the new ways?

❑ What is being done to facilitate grieving for the loss of the old?

6. **It takes time and support to achieve full implementation.**

❑ Considering the time it takes people to adapt to change, how much time is needed for people to regain full competence in their work after the change?

❑ How much time must be provided for the transition from the old to the new?

❑ What other changes requiring adaptation are happening concurrently?

❑ What metrics make sense to use to evaluate the success of the change initiative?

❑ What support is being provided to help people through the transition?

Force Field Analysis In any change initiative, there are forces that support change, and forces that oppose change. Identifying and understanding these can be of great help in learning from and planning for change. The tool for this analysis, developed by Kurt Lewin, is called a Force Field Analysis. In the two columns below, first identify all the forces supporting and opposing a particular change. Then draw arrows pointed toward the center (equilibrium) line proportional in length to the support or opposition you estimate for each force. This will give you a graphic representation of what you have working for and against a change. In order for change to occur, the forces supporting change need to exceed those opposing change. Look for what can be done to transform opposition into support.

Equilibrium

Forces supporting a change	*Forces opposing a change*
5　　4　　3　　2　　1　→	←　1　　2　　3　　4　　5

10.3

"If It Ain't Broke, Don't Fix It!"

How many times have you heard, "If it ain't broke, don't fix it?" Would you fly on an airline with that philosophy? I wouldn't! It's hard to pull over to the side of the sky when an airliner breaks down! If you live the "If it ain't broke, don't fix it," mindset, then you doom yourself to a life of recovering from breakdowns!

Un-American The "If it ain't broke, don't fix it" philosophy is actually un-American! It is the antithesis of the American spirit: looking for a better way. Ole Evinrude's wife loved ice cream. He used to row across the lake to the store to buy it for her. By the time he got it home, it was melted. Thus, he invented the detachable rowboat motor to get the ice cream home faster. There are millions of other examples where people did not accept the *status quo* and took risks that have paid off. The American way, and a key element of leadership, is looking for opportunities with promise and seizing them. Unfortunately, there are also many businesses that have folded because they were lulled into complacency by the "If it ain't broke, don't fix it" myth.

Sell the problem One of the challenges of leadership is getting people to take action *before* a situation becomes a problem. That requires challenging the *status quo* with information and questions. Questions can be much more powerful than statements, as they require people to think and come up with answers. *"What if investors decide that current profit really is important? What could happen to our business model? If you were a consultant, what would you identify as our vulnerabilities? What action must we take to protect against them? What actions must we avoid?"* When people have information and penetrating questions to answer, they usually get the picture and start the process to solve problems creatively.

Focus on the potential benefits People mired in an "If it ain't broke, don't fix it" mindset can always find reasons not to try something different. They need to be listened to. They typically won't open their minds to possibilities until they feel they have been heard. Once they have, they have an obligation to listen. Say, *"Thanks for expressing your concerns. We need to take them into consideration as we move forward. However, if we **could** make this work, what would be the benefits?"* By asking them to search for and articulate benefits, you engage them in a process that requires a positive outlook. A vision of a better future is needed to overcome resistance.

"How can we make this work?" A vision, however, is not enough. People need to see how to get there. By asking them what it will take to make it work, you are enlisting them in a process to make it work. Though some will cling to the *status quo,* emphasize that you are looking for ways to make things work, mindful of their concerns. When people can see real benefits, and define the process to achieve them, you get results.

The *status quo* is easier. It is known, and adventure involves risks. To dispel people of their "If it ain't broke, don't fix it" mentality, first help them to understand that what may not seem broken is, in fact, heading for the breaking point. Let them define the possible consequences, and the benefits of addressing the situation proactively. Some people need to see a path out of the forest before they will move. Help them to discover and define that path. The more experienced they become with this process, the less you will hear, "If it ain't broke, don't fix it."

Your Life and Career

11.1

Making the Most of Your Life

You never know how long you'll live until it is too late. Most of us live through our work years as though we were immortal, but we aren't. If you knew that you had only one year to live, what would you do differently? Now is the time to reflect on your life and make changes if you want it to be different in the future.

Your choices Making the most of your life is a personal challenge. No one else can do it for you. Your life is a composite of the choices you make, the big ones and the small. The big ones are obvious: going to college, choosing a major, a job, a spouse, etc. Where you are most apt to lose control is in the everyday choices that consume your life: "putting out a fire" instead of taking a leadership course, watching a sitcom instead of reading a book. Life can dribble away!

At sea, you need a guiding star, compass or global positioning system to stay on-course. In life, you need as your guide a sense of purpose, values, goals, a vision of how you want to live your life, and criteria for sorting through the many opportunities to use your time here on Earth.

What is the purpose of your life? Making decisions about how to use your life is easier when you have a sense of purpose. For me, life is about making a difference. I endeavor to make life better for the people whose lives I touch. This guides my use of time. What I choose to schedule must either "make a difference" for something important to me, help someone important to me, or add to the quality of my life and that of my family. What criteria do you use for such choices?

Manage your life! Create a sieve for screening requests for your time. Stephen R. Covey, a noted author on management (*First Things First*), distinguishes between what is important and urgent. "Important" activities advance you toward your major goals. "Urgent" ones seek immediate attention. Many people respond to what is "urgent" because it is screaming for attention and never make time for what is "important." Making the most of your life requires you to invest your time in what is "important," whether or not it is "urgent."

Do you need a way to manage your life? Yes! Does it need to be complicated? No! A simple system that you use is better than a sophisticated one that you "never have time for." As Covey suggests, create a matrix ranging from "important" to "unimportant" on one axis, and "urgent" to "not urgent" on the other. Review your past week to see how what you have done falls on the "important" and "urgent" matrix. How satisfied are you with your results?

Calendars and electronic organizers can be magic. What gets on them is more apt to happen. They can also be a tyranny. It is typically harder to cancel what has already been scheduled than not to schedule it in the first place. You will always have more to do than you have time for. So be careful what you schedule. Before you schedule anything, ask:

- ❑ How does this fit with what is important to me in my work and vision of life?
- ❑ Is it the best use of my talents and limited time?
- ❑ Would I do it if I had just one year to live?
- ❑ What will happen if I say, "No?" (Frequently, someone else could do it.)
- ❑ How much time am I willing to commit? (Set limits.)

Working in an organization is replete with opportunities to be distracted and sucked into the priorities of others. It can be hard to say "no," especially to someone with whom you work closely. Here's an approach that has worked for me:

1. Listen attentively to a request for a slice of your life.

2. Before giving your answer, ask yourself the questions above.

3. If the request meets your criteria for getting involved, specify the limits of your commitment.

4. If it doesn't, you can say something like, *"I understand the importance of what you want to accomplish, and I applaud your endeavor. With what I have 'on my plate,' I cannot devote the time I would need to do the quality of work you need."* If you know of someone better suited, suggest that person.

5. If the person asking for your involvement is your boss, you can ask, *"Considering what I already am working on, where does this fit in to our priorities? What gets bumped if this becomes top priority?"*

"Parking lots" Not everything you take on has to be done at once. Create three "parking lots." In "metered" parking, place what you choose to focus on this week. In "short term" parking, place what you choose to work on in the next month. And in "long term" parking, place what doesn't require attention for more than a month. "Parking lots" can help you keep focused on the present. They can also help you manage expectations of the people whose requests are "parked" by communicating your time frame for devoting your attention to them. As with real parking lots, they can become full. Periodically check the expiration or due dates of what's parked. Have those that are no longer important "towed" out of "parking" to the dump!

Your life equals how you use your brief time on Earth. In order to have your life amount to something, you have to make conscious decisions about your use of time in support of what is important to you. You can't turn the clock back and live your life differently, so use your time wisely. It's all you've got!

11.2

Work-Life Balance, or Life Management

Work-life balance may be like the ever-receding pot of gold at the end of the rainbow: sought after and always a little out of reach. Part of the problem may be your expectation of what constitutes a desirable balance between work and the rest of life. That varies among people. The other part of the problem is gaining a sense of control of your use of time. So, can you achieve a satisfactory balance? Over the long term, you probably can. In the short term, you may not be able to if you are involved in a time-critical project, or if your use of time is beyond your control.

In our society, for a considerable portion of our life, our work defines much of who we are, and it occupies a very significant portion of our waking hours. If you are in an important position, enjoy your work, and don't have many competing demands for your time outside of work, you may want to devote a significant portion of your life to your work. If work is just one of your many interests, you will judge the amount of time you devote to work by different standards.

Satisfaction with your work-life balance is a function of what percentage of your time you have to work in relation what percentage you expect to work. If you expect to work 40 hours a week, and have to work 50, you are likely to be dissatisfied. If you expect to work 55 hours a week and only have to work 50, you are more apt to be satisfied. Thus, your expectations are critical in determining your happiness.

Life management A key to "having a life" is to determine what's important to you, and how much of your life you want to devote to each sector of what is important. Then, manage decisions about how you use your time accordingly. Think of this as *life management,* not *time management.* You *can't* manage time. It happens regardless of what you do. You *can* manage decisions about your use of time. So, your decisions that affect your use of time are critical to achieving a balanced life.

Look at your life Each week you have 168 hours available to you. Some of the time you sleep, some of the time you work, some of the time you commute, and some of the time you do other things like eating, watching TV, getting ready for work, household chores, socializing, etc. Your life is composed of different segments of the 168 hour week.

Think of your typical week, list the segments of it you allocate to your 168 hours, and estimate how much of your week you typically devote to each segment. If there is a segment of your life for which you are not currently allocating time, include it on your list at zero.

Level of satisfaction You are probably more satisfied with some segments of your life than others. Using a scale of 1–5, with 1 = unsatisfied and 5 = very satisfied, rate your level of satisfaction with each segment of your life that you listed.

Your life—graphically Sometimes a graphic representation helps you see things in a different light, so draw five concentric circles (like a target). First draw lines from the center to the outer-most circle (pie-style) to represent the segments of your life you listed. Each segment should be approximately proportionate on the circle to its proportion of your life. Now apply your satisfaction rating to each segment. The innermost circle = 1, and the outermost = 5. Shade the area of the segment covered by your rating. When you finish, you will have a representation of your level of satisfaction with the various segments of your current life for a week.

How does your life look? Are you devoting your life to what is important to you? Which segments are getting more than their importance warrants? Which are suffering? What do you want to de-emphasize? What do you want to increase? Set goals for how you want to change your life over a given period. Now, construct a new visual incorporating your goals for the reapportioned segments of your life and for improving your level of satisfaction with the segments you want to change.

Repeat this exercise periodically. What is important to you will change, as will the amount of your life you devote to each segment. So will your level of satisfaction. Congratulate yourself for your progress. Try to learn from shortfalls. Fine tune your goals and try again.

Creating a support system You have an effect on the lives of others, and they have an effect on you. Setting life goals is much easier than executing them, especially when others can influence what happens in your life. Changing your life requires their support. They can be your allies or enemies. They cannot help you unless they know what you are trying to accomplish and how they can help. Thus, meet with the people you need as allies in your quest to change your life. Tell them about what you seek to change. Tell them how they can help and ask for their support. Ask what you can do to reciprocate. When they are supportive, thank them. When they aren't, remind them of the changes that you are trying you make. I have found most people want to be supportive.

Your calendar/scheduler can be your friend What gets scheduled in your life is more apt to happen than the unscheduled. Be sure to schedule time for the segments of your life that you are trying to increase. Block out time for your priorities *before* you have competing requests. If you need time to plan a project, schedule it. If attending your daughter's soccer game is important to you, schedule it. If watching the Superbowl with a friend is important to you, schedule it. When something is already on your calendar, it is less apt to be bumped for something else. When you are asked for time that you have already scheduled, weigh the importance to you of the competing uses. If you choose to bump what you have scheduled, reschedule it if you can. If you choose to stick with your previously scheduled use, tell the person who requested your time that it is already taken.

"Scope creep" and time overruns It can be difficult to estimate accurately how long an assignment or project may take. Meetings and phone calls can take longer than you anticipate. How do you deal with such challenges? Tell people up front how much time you have available.

> *"Do you have a minute to discuss _____ with me?"*

> *"Yes, I can devote 10 minutes to that now. Will that be enough?"*

As the end of your allocated time approaches, remind the person of your need to end the conversation at the appointed time. People generally get to the point faster when they know that there is limited time. If you decide to extend your conversation, set a new limit.

> *"We're running out of time. How much more do you need? Can we finish in five minutes?"*

If you need to extricate yourself from a meeting or conversation where you have set a limit, say:

> *"I'm sorry. I have to leave (end our conversation). As you know, I have another commitment and we have run out of time."*

People may not like this, but you are following through on what you committed to do. When people realize that you are serious about keeping your time commitments, they respect you for it and associate a higher value to your time.

Intensive, time-critical projects are especially challenging. During participation in such projects, it is unrealistic to try to achieve your full work-life balance goals. That does not mean discarding them. Instead, readjust them for what is important to you during the project. Seek to balance your life between projects and during less intense periods.

Achieving a balanced life is a constant challenge. Periodically, review how you use your 168 hours per week in relation to what is important to you. Set goals.

Enlist support of colleagues. Allocate time to what's important. Experiment. Pursue what works for you.

11.3

Keeping Your Focus Through Distractions

"A fanatic is a person who, having lost sight of his objectives, redoubles his efforts."

—Unknown, via Walter C. Petersen

The danger of becoming a fanatic is real. Our post-downsized, just-in-time, faster-better-cheaper, world creates pressures that make it easier to become a fanatic. Many competing demands, all of which seem immediately important, may vie for your attention. But, the harder you work on immediate issues, the less time you have to pursue strategic objectives.

Focus, like a lens bending rays of light, concentrates one's activities on a goal. It is created by clarity and intensity of purpose and mission, and aided by self-discipline. While organizational focus does not guarantee accomplishment, at least it enables people "to sing off of the same song sheet," and helps them to set priorities. Here's what I have found that helps people stay focused:

- **Compelling purpose, clear mission** Everyone needs a reason for existence and a clear goal to accomplish. I keep mine on the cover of my notebook as a constant reminder. When leading a team, I always have our purpose and mission posted prominently. If we begin to stray I ask, "Where does this fit in with our purpose and mission?" If it doesn't fit, it gets zapped or placed in a "parking lot" of ideas/issues for future reference.

- **Limited number of strategic objectives** In spite of emphasis on increasing people's capacity to work on multiple tasks simultaneously, the more "on one's plate," the less attention each gets. It is better to accomplish 2-3 objectives well than to attempt many and do a mediocre job on all. The thinner you spread yourself, the less you can provide quality concentration, and the more mistakes you make.

- **Filter out distractions** The opportunities to be distracted are legion! In organizational life, people such as your boss, customers, team members and people who report to you have a legitimate claim on your time. But you can probably negotiate some "sacred time" when you are uninterruptible in exchange for some "sacred time" for them. Even so, you will still be interrupted from time to time. Interruptions only grow into distractions when you let them derail you.

Anticipate that you will be interrupted. When you are, harken back to your purpose and mission. Ask, *"How does this fit in with why I am here?"* If it doesn't, and you can think of someone better suited to the situation, say, *"If I understand correctly what you want, _____ (somone else) is better suited to this than I am."* You can also say, *"I appreciate your situation, but with what I currently have on my plate, I can not devote the attention you need until _____."* If you are the appropriate person and you must deal with a situation immediately, set a limit on your time. *"I can devote ___ minutes to this now."* As you approach the end of the allotted time, say, *"We have another five minutes. Can we finish now or do we need to schedule some time later?"* If the situation does not require immediate attention, try to schedule it at a better time, or "park" it for a later date.

❑ **Recover quickly** A "bookmark" enables you to find your place where you left off and resume. You can say, *"Just a minute. I need to make a note here to help me resume when we finish."* Most people will cooperate.
❑ **Learn from each day** As you start each day allocate a few minutes to plan what you want to accomplish and how you will deal with the issues. In the evening, review how it went. How did you stray from your plan? What could you have done differently? What can you learn and do differently to make tomorrow better?

Focus brings clarity and concentrated energy to a subject. Think of yourself as a lens bringing those dimensions to what you do. Don't let the siren call of urgent and unimportant needs distract you, and you will be pleased with your results.

11.4

Are You in the Right Job?

When you are in the right job, you look forward to a good day of work when you arise, and end your day with a sense of satisfaction with how you met the challenges of the day—at least most of the time. You identify with your work, work team, and the organization for which you work. You have a sense of purpose that is in harmony with what you do, and you are pursuing goals in keeping with the future you desire. You are respected, appreciated, and growing in your career.

Not everyone is in the right job. If the previous paragraph describes your work situation, be thankful! If it doesn't, you may want to analyze the strengths and shortcomings of your situation. There may be some things you can change to improve it, or you may need to look for alternatives. For your analysis, I recommend taking a piece of paper and making three columns:

Job Satisfaction Analysis

Job components	*Strengths*	*Shortcomings*
Work that interests you		
Work that develops you		
A business with a future		
Opportunity to grow in your career		
A boss you respect		
A boss who respects and supports you		
Colleagues you respect		
Colleagues who respect and support you		
Appreciation for your contributions		
Competitive pay and benefits		
Opportunity for a life outside of work		
Etc.		

In the components column, list those things about your work situation that are important to you. I have listed a few for you to consider. Then, for each listed component, describe briefly what you find attractive about it in your present situation in the Strengths column, and what you find unattractive in the Shortcomings column.

Importance Some components of your work situation are critically important, and others are less so. Now, go back to each component and rate its level of importance to you. Rate as "+4" components that are critically important, and "+1" for those that are only slightly important.

Satisfaction Now go back to each entry and rate your level of satisfaction with it. "+5" = passionately satisfied and "+1" = slightly satisfied. Conversely, "–5" = passionately dissatisfied, "–1" = slightly dissatisfied.

Importance-weighted satisfaction Now, multiply your ratings of satisfaction by your ratings of importance for each component to arrive at an importance-weighted rating. Look at the top and bottom rated components, and at the overall pattern of your ratings. Do the pluses outweigh the minuses? Are the top and bottom rated components really as important as their scores suggest? Is there something you can do to help change the bottom rated components?

If the profile of your ratings is positive for the company as a whole, but low for your immediate leadership or work group, are there other opportunities for you within the organization? If your importance-weighted ratings are low for the organization's purpose, mission values and ethics, there is probably little you can do to change those.

Only you can decide what is right *for you*. This is a tool to shed a different light on the components of the right job for you. It should be helpful in evaluating your current situation, and it should help you evaluate alternatives, if you need to.

Being in the right job *for you* is key to your motivation, productivity, health, happiness and career. If you are not in the right job, not only do you suffer, so does the organization for which you work.

11.5

Benefiting From a Mentor/Coach Relationship

There is nothing like having an excellent mentor to help you grow in your career. Someone who takes an interest in you, someone in whom you can confide, and someone who inspires you as a role model can make a tremendous difference to you and your career.

I have been fortunate! I've benefited from excellent mentors. In my early years, Gene Grant, Joe Scroggs, Bill Pedersen, and Emil Sarpa helped me with their caring, patience, and wisdom.

Why Have a Mentor or Coach?

Though you learn from reading and classes, you really learn to develop skills by doing. Think about swimming. It is one thing to read about it, but it is not until you get into the water that you can actually swim. A coach can observe, instruct, give you feedback and encouragement, and help you hone your skills.

If you expect to earn more, you have to increase your value in the job market continually. That means lifelong learning. A coach can:

- Help you to be focused
- Be honest and objective with you

❑ Help you recognize and develop your true gifts
❑ Connect you with others who can help
❑ Listen to your challenges and help you to find your way through them
❑ Encourage and inspire you

Finding a Mentor/Coach

Your boss   Sometimes the person to whom you report can serve as a mentor, but there may be a conflict of interest. What may be best for you and your career may not always be best for him/her, or the organization. He/she may not be able to be objective and free of vested interests in discussing decisions in which he/she has a stake. Also, you may change bosses frequently, while you'll probably want a more lasting relationship with a mentor or coach.

Another insider   When you don't know of anyone in another part of the organization to be your mentor, ask people in your Human Resources department to suggest possibilities. Some organizations, like HP and Sun, have designated people to make matches between mentors and mentees.

An outsider   An alternative is to ask someone else you know and respect outside your organization to be your mentor. Most people are flattered to be asked to serve in that role, but first both of you need to determine whether there is a good fit between you. Whoever you choose needs to understand the environment in which you operate and the issues you face.

Business owners and CEOs may not have anyone within their organization free of vested interests with whom they can confide. (Sometimes a director can fill that role, but there may be a conflict of interest.) In that case an external mentor/coach may be needed.

Professional mentor/coaches   There are a growing number of people who specialize in coaching. They can be very good, and they may be more accessible than someone for whom coaching is an added duty. They can be located through the Institute of Management Consultants and other professional organizations.

Choosing a Mentor/Coach

"Chemistry" is critical. Look for someone you respect, someone who has something to offer you, and someone to whom you can relate easily. Will the mentor be honest, constructive and supportive in helping you conquer your vulnerabilities? Does he/she have any vested interests in your decisions? Can you talk freely without worrying about what you say? Is he/she an attentive, non-judgmental listener?

Does he/she ask the right questions? Does he/she help you to explore, learn and make your own choices, or does he/she prescribe answers? Is he/she committed to helping you be all that you can be, even if that means changing employers? Will he/she make time to coach you when you need it? Choose your mentor carefully!

Working With a Mentor

Negotiate your arrangements with your mentor/coach, and commit them to writing. Both of you need to verify that you agree to the arrangements and sign an acknowledgement. This formalizes the arrangements for a more professional relationship. In the arrangements, there should be an "escape clause" that permits either of you to opt out if the relationship isn't working. The agreement should cover confidentiality so that there are no misunderstandings, and so that you can talk freely with your mentor about sensitive and confidential issues.

I have found that it helps to have a set schedule of meetings, with the opportunity for phone conversations or e-mails on issues that arise between meetings. Scheduled meetings are more apt to happen. It usually helps to have "homework" that the mentee completes before a meeting to further the action.

Finally, I recommend periodic mutual assessments of what's working in the relationship, and what needs to change. A healthy relationship grows, and that requires periodic recalibration.

Two-way Street

In a healthy coaching relationship, both people learn. Each learns something different, but both benefit. That is why a mentor/coaching relationship is of benefit to both people.

11.6

Preventing Burnout

"I'm exhausted! I've averaged 80 hours a week for the last six weeks. I can no longer think straight or creatively. And to make matters worse, we're having to redo half of what we thought was completed because of errors and quality issues. I thought this was a great place to work only a year ago, but all I can think of now is escaping from this prison!"

Six month product life cycles, "better, faster, cheaper," a shortage of talented people, and cumbersome work processes have created situations where people are pushed beyond their limit.

Culture of burnout Some organizations create a culture of burnout. They create social pressures where people are expected to be at work early and stay late whether or not they have something important to do. People not at work on weekends are considered slackers. People brag about the hours they work—at least for a while. But after the adrenaline rush is bankrupt, they become zombies. They lose their creativity and judgment, and errors compound. They become frustrated, lose their enthusiasm for their work and become apathetic and unproductive. Though a shell remains, they have been "strip-mined" and "burned out." Eventually, they bail out or are discarded. And the effect on a business is:

- ❏ Decline in quality and productivity
- ❏ Late-to-market product introductions
- ❏ Increase in absenteeism and employee turnover
- ❏ Escalating increases in stress related illnesses, worker's comp and health care costs
- ❏ Decrease in creativity, innovation and problem solving ability

Businesses that burn out their employees experience increased difficulty competing in their market because they have squandered their prime renewable resource—their talent.

Burnout is not a personal character flaw Burnout is usually a symptom of weak leadership and an unsupportive and disorganized organization. The function of leadership is to create a work place that inspires and enables people to perform at their best in pursuit of important organizational goals. The comic strip, Dilbert, epitomizes conditions for creating burnout.

Burnout is preventable Burnout is easier to prevent than it is to correct. Rebuilding an organization with exhausted and dispirited people is starting from *below* "ground zero." Preventing burnout is possible by implementing the following:

- ❏ **Goals** Involve the team in setting goals that, though challenging, can be attained.
- ❏ **Resources** Provide the resources needed to do the job right the first time.
- ❏ **Team training** Provide teams with the training they need to work together productively and deal with stress and conflict.
- ❏ **Work processes** Let the team participate in designing the work processes they will use.

❑ **Process check** Allocate time each week for reviewing what is working and what is getting in the way. It may seem like there is no time for this, but neglecting to conduct this review is like not checking your map when you are lost because it takes time.

❑ **Recognition** Recognize people for their special efforts. Express genuine appreciation.

❑ **"Instrument panel"** Create a panel of meter dials, about 2 feet in diameter, with one end being high and the other low. One is to measure stress, one is to measure burnout, one is to measure teamwork, one is to measure management support, and the fifth is to measure job satisfaction. Give each team member a color-coded sticky dot for each meter. Ask them to place the dots each day at the points on the dials that represent their relative levels of stress, burnout, teamwork, management support and job satisfaction.

❑ **Monitor** the workload and meter dials. Look into situations where the stress and burnout levels are increasing, or where the perceived teamwork, management support and job satisfaction levels are decreasing.

❑ **Take action** to correct problems that contribute to overwork, frustrating work processes, lack of support, and other causes of decreased morale, productivity and work life balance.

❑ **R & R** When the pressure lets up, *require* people to take time off for rest and recharging.

❑ **Celebrate** milestones, accomplishments and significant events for the team.

Retention of talented people is of strategic importance in today's economy—and, it is of equal importance to make sure that the talent one *has* is renewed, refreshed, creative and productive. A culture that fosters burnout is a cancer that will eventually hobble an organization, and if left unchecked, will kill it.

11.7

Dealing With the Loss of Your Job

Why would you want to read this? You don't plan on losing your job, and I certainly hope that you don't! Nevertheless, welcome to the 21st century job market! People in leadership roles are not immune from being laid off or fired. There is at least a 50/50 chance that you will lose your job at some point during your career.

Layoffs, "right-sizing" and other efforts of employers to reduce payroll and head-count are a fact of life in our turbulent economy. Reorganizations, organizational politics and personality conflicts can happen any time. No matter what the reason, it is no fun when you discover that someone has decided that you should leave. No matter what the reason, you are just as out of work. It is better to know in advance about how to deal with this eventuality if you discover that you are "heading toward the exit."

Premonitions You may have a premonition of change. You may see business decline or drop off. The "jungle telegraph" may have word of an impending reorganization. You may have "crossed swords" with a "higher-up" who is displeased with some aspect of you or what you have done. Even if you have an inkling of impending change, being told that you will be out of your job will likely come as a shock. At one point in my career, as I was making plans to leave my employer for a different opportunity, I was called into my boss' office and fired. I knew that there was one executive with whom I had had several run-ins, but I was surprised to be fired.

If you see signs that do not bode well for you, review your resume and prepare to update it. Even if you don't have to use it, there is value in reviewing your resume periodically to chart how you have grown in experience and value. Hold off, however, on contacting the people in your network about new opportunities until you can give them a clear picture of what you are seeking in a different job. People in your network can be of great help when they know specifically what you are looking for. Their helpfulness will be limited if you are not sure of what you want.

Emotions you will experience There is the typical pattern of emotions people feel during the transition from the loss of a job through landing a new one. Knowing this can help you monitor your emotional progress. The first natural reaction to being let go is a feeling of anger, disbelief and denial. *"How can they do this to me? I've really busted my buns for the company! This just isn't fair!"* This feeling normally lasts from a few days to a few weeks. It's OK to pass through this state: just don't get stuck in it. Once you accept that the clock will not be turned back and your termination rescinded, it is time to move on. Life is ahead of you, not behind. You can't create your future looking out the tailgate window; get into the driver's seat. You will, at some point, come to this realization and begin taking your next steps. You may be provided with outplacement assistance and job counseling, and these services can help you move on to launch your campaign for a new job. As you realize how much value you have to offer a prospective employer, your outlook will improve. Your emotions will experience a roller coaster as you go through interviews. Then, when you get and accept the job offer you want, you will reach a new high that will extend until the full impact of the challenges and pressures you face in your new job hits you. Finally, as you make progress conquering these challenges, your emotional state will return to, and probably exceed, the high you experienced when you accepted your new job.

What to do when you discover you're losing your job Listen, listen, listen, and take notes. Ask questions for clarifications. Avoid confrontation or negotiations until you have had a chance to process the news and decide rationally how you want to proceed. Though you may feel like expressing anger, this is not the time to do it. You will need to negotiate the best severance package that you can, and strategically, you are not at your best as a negotiator when anger and disbelief may get the best of you. It makes no sense to "burn your bridges behind you." Don't sign any severance agreement at this time, either. You will want to review it carefully when you have regained your composure, and you may want an attorney to review it, too. Instead, just say, *"This really stuns me! I am not in a position to respond on the spot. Let me have a little time to regain my composure and focus, and to think of the questions I need answered, before we agree to the terms of my departure."* Ask for at least a few days in which to review the proposed terms before you meet to negotiate your departure.

If you are given a severance agreement to sign, read it carefully. Write your questions on Post-it notes and stick them to the appropriate section. These notes will refresh your memory when you get into your meeting to negotiate your severance package. If you have an employment contract, compare the proposed terms with what's in your contract. If there is anything that is confusing, or that appears unfair, consult an employment law attorney. Though you will probably not want to take legal action, you may need clarification and a legal opinion on some issues.

Negotiating your departure The most important issues in this negotiation are your reputation and the financial aspects of the agreement. As in other negotiations, make sure that you know your priorities and keep focused on your objectives. Discussing a potential negotiation with a trusted and knowledgeable confidant or mentor in advance can help you prepare for the meeting.

If you are being let go with a number of other people, it may be difficult, but not impossible, to negotiate around a standard package being offered. To succeed, you will need a compelling reason for your employer to treat you differently. An employment contract with severance provisions would be a compelling reason, as might a recent relocation across country or internationally. If you are being let go individually, or with just a few others, your employer may be more open to negotiation. Your employer will be concerned about treating everyone equally, so you will need to demonstrate that what you are seeking deserves fair and different treatment.

Your employer does not want to be sued, and legal action on your part should only be a last resort for something really unfair or egregious. Legal action anchors you in the past. A prospective employer may be put off if you have taken legal action against your past employer.

Issues for Clarification and Negotiation

Reputation-Related Issues

1. Are you being laid off or terminated? If you are being laid off, the implication is that when the economy improves, you may be asked to return. If you are being fired, there is no such expectation. You need to know this. The answer will affect your communications with colleagues about your departure, and what you will say in seeking another job. If you are being fired, don't resign. You may lose your eligibility for unemployment benefits.

2. What will your employer be communicating to your colleagues and contacts outside the business about your departure? The message should be consistent with the answer to the above, and with what you say. This is a situation where it may help if you draft the message you would like said. You are more apt to get more of what you want when you negotiate from your proposal than from your employer's standard document.

3. What reference information will be provided when a prospective employer contacts your employer for information about you? Some employers will only confirm your dates of employment and job title. That does not help you much. You may want to draft a reference letter as part of your negotiations. (See Chapter 4.6). Though some employers limit the information they provide for reference inquiries to your employment dates and job title, they may sign a factual reference letter that you can take with you, if it is fair and accurate. Factual information could include:

- ❑ Your starting and ending employment dates
- ❑ The job titles you held and a brief description of your responsibilities for each
- ❑ Your history of pay increases, bonuses, stock option awards
- ❑ Special commendations, patents
- ❑ Performance review ratings
- ❑ Sick leave usage, safety record

Your employer may shy away from the information about the quality of your leadership and statements about your performance.

4. When will you be required to vacate the premises and return company property? This may happen when you are notified of your termination. If not, negotiate for a dignified departure.

Financial-Related Issues

1. Pay   When is your last day of work? Are you receiving pay in lieu of notice? How much severance pay will you be getting and what will be deducted from it? How about bonuses or incentive compensation for which you were eligible?

2. Insured benefits   How long will company-paid benefits continue? What can you continue to pay for through the company's group plans, and what can be converted? There are COBRA provisions for these, but you may be able to negotiate a more favorable deal.

3. Vacation and sick leave   How will unused accrued vacation and sick leave be treated? You have a right to your accrued vacation. Your right to unused sick leave depends on your employer's sick leave policy.

4. Retirement/401(k) plans   What happens to these? What is vested? What can be rolled over?

5. Stock   What happens to the stock you own in the company, and your stock options, if applicable?

6. Tuition assistance   If your employer is subsidizing any tuition for you or your family, what happens to it? Will it be forgiven, or do you have to reimburse the company?

7. Childcare   If you have been receiving childcare assistance, what happens to it? If the company has a childcare center, how long will your child (children) be allowed to attend?

Other Issues

Will you get outplacement assistance? Career coaching/counseling? If you have been out of the job market for some time, these can help point you in the right direction for marketing yourself for your next opportunity.

"Landing on your feet"   Yes, losing your job is unnerving. Yes, it is normal to feel upset. Yes, it is normal to wonder how you could have averted losing your job.

Yes, you need to take a little time to assess where you are going and what you want to do next. These are part of the process that people move through in their transition from the loss of a job to the start of another. If you find that you are getting stuck in your transition process, seek help from a trusted mentor, confidant or person with career transition expertise. Just make sure that whatever job offer you accept, you are being attracted to the *work,* the *opportunity,* the *people* and the *company.* You'll do much better when you are enthusiastic about all four of these.

11.8

Interviewing for a Job

Your career depends, in part, on how well you "come across" when you are interviewed for a job. You will undoubtedly be interviewed a number of times during your career, so you need to know how to negotiate the maze of the interview process.

When being interviewed, your first order of business is to determine what you want to accomplish in the process. Most job interviews have at least two objectives:

❏ To convince the person (people) making the hiring decision that you are the right candidate.

❏ To determine whether you would want to accept the job if it were offered to you.

If the first objective is not met, the second becomes irrelevant. Let's focus on the first.

To convince a hiring manager that you are the answer to his/her prayers, you need to know what he/she is looking for, and why. If there is a job posting with a job description, read it carefully, noting the stated requirements. What do you bring to it? What abilities (knowledge, skills, experience) and motivation do you possess? Why are you the right person for this job? You need to provide answers to these questions to convince the interviewer that *you* are the right person. With a basic idea of the job, its requirements, and the sort of person desired, you are in a better position to frame your answers to the interview questions.

A job interview is a chance for your prospective employer to see you think "on you feet," and respond to questions thoughtfully and articulately. If you are involved in a group interview, it is also an opportunity for the group to see how you relate to them under pressure and for you to see the group in action. Even though an interview is not referred to as a test, in essence, it is one. As with most tests, the better prepared you are, the better you are apt to do.

Preparation

In an interview you are providing information, and you are also seeking information. Usually, the first part of the interview is providing information. In providing information, you need to decide how you want to present or package it.

1. What are your strengths to emphasize? What examples of relevant situations do you have to demonstrate your strengths? It pays to plan how you want to come across. Then, no matter what situation you find yourself in, you can keep focused on your objectives.

2. Have you had any moments of which you are not very proud? While you may not want to lead the people interviewing you into problems you have had, you need to be prepared to answer their questions truthfully and explain the circumstances. (*Actually, I left Whizzit because I had a disagreement with Mr. Smith over how to deal with a product recall. I believed that a recall of our model 2300 was essential for safety reasons and for our credibility as an ethical business. I was overruled and lost my job as a result.*)

3. Given the position for which you are interviewing, what questions are you apt to be asked? If you can anticipate and answer the questions you are apt to be asked, then you will have an easier time answering them.

Types of Questions

Knowing how to respond to questions is part of negotiating the maze. Let's review some basic types of questions used in job interviews. Understanding these types of questions will help you know what type of answer is being sought.

Closed questions seek a brief, factual answer. (*In your career, who is the best supervisor for whom you have worked?*) They are appropriate for verifying data, confirming one's understanding, and for prefacing a probing question. Answer them succinctly. (*Fran Jones at Electrofoam was the best supervisor I've had.*)

Open questions seek to draw out your views. (*What aspects of your job did you enjoy most?*) Answer them with some detail. If it is important for the interviewer to understand the context, explain it, too. (*Mr. Jones at Electrofoam traveled about* *two weeks a month. I was in charge of our group in his absence. I really enjoyed the challenges of leading a project team.*)

Probing questions prompt you to expand on a previously stated answer. (*And what were some of those challenges?*) This type of question is used when the interviewer is interested in digging deeper into what you have said. (*We had a couple of engineers who always were seeking the perfect design. We could not have gotten our products to market on time if we had worked to their standards. I was able to keep them focused on what our customers were telling us that they want. It was a delicate balance. I wanted them to stay motivated and also meet our schedule.*)

Test questions pose a situation you may have to face in the job, and ask how you would handle it. (*While in Maria's cubicle, you note that she is downloading confidential files to her laptop computer. It is strictly against company policy to do that. What would you do?*) For some test questions, there is a right answer and a wrong one. For others, there are a variety of acceptable answers. You can try to "psych" out the desired answer, but the best policy is to give your honest answer. If it is not acceptable, then there is no use trying to be someone you aren't.

Questions You May be Asked

There is no universal set of questions that you will be asked. The following non-technical questions are asked frequently in one form or another. By answering them before your first interview, you will be prepared for them when they, or similar questions, are asked.

- ❑ *Why did you leave your last job? Or, Why are you considering leaving your present job?*
- ❑ *What new knowledge and skills did you learn from your last job?*
- ❑ *Describe for me what was one of your most challenging assignments, and how you met the challenge.*
- ❑ *Describe a situation that did not turn out as you planned. What was your reaction? What did you learn from it?*
- ❑ *What was the most difficult (or unpleasant) part of your last job?*
- ❑ *How do you feel about (some unpleasant aspect of the work)?*
- ❑ *What were some of the pressures you experienced in your past jobs? How did you deal with them?*
- ❑ *What are your career goals? How do you see this job fitting into your career?*
- ❑ *What has given you a sense of satisfaction in your last three jobs?*

❑ *What would you have changed, if you could, about your last three jobs?*

❑ *What have your previous supervisors done to help bring out the best in you?*

❑ *What have your previous supervisors done that made your job more difficult?*

❑ *What has been your experience in working as part of a team? What do you find satisfying about being part of a team? What problems does being part of a team create for you?*

❑ *What have you learned about working with people from your previous supervisors, co-workers, customers or clients?*

❑ *Please describe a situation at work where someone created a problem for you. What did you do to resolve it?*

❑ *Who has had the most influence in shaping your work habits? How?*

❑ *A friend with whom you work has been reprimanded for too many late arrivals and is on warning. Another late arrival this month and she may lose her job. A few minutes before the start of her shift, she phones you to say she will be fifteen minutes late. She asks you to clock in for her so that it will not look as though she was late. This is contrary to policy. How would you handle this?*

❑ *What information do I need to know about your references to understand the point of view of the people giving them?*

❑ *Is there anything else I need to know in considering you for this job?*

Some Questions You Will Want Answered

You will probably have questions about pay, benefits, hours, etc. But, there are some questions you need answered because they will give you clues about the specific work environment for which you are interviewing.

❑ *Why is this job open now?* If it is newly created, but someone else did the work previously, ask, *Who did this work before? How did you decide to add a new person? How have you drawn the line between what he/she does now and this new position?* It is not unusual for jobs to be created without much thought regarding who will be responsible for what in the new structure. If the job was filled before, and someone left, you need to understand why in order to evaluate whether it is the job for you. *What are the reasons why _____ left? How long was he/she in the job? Why have others in your work group left?* If turnover is because people are being promoted, that's a positive sign. If people are leaving because of the work-load, or because they did not get along, beware! If people are leaving because they received a pay increase to move to another job, there may be a problem with the compensation plan, or people may be just giving an "acceptable" reason for leaving as opposed to their real reasons.

❑ *Please describe the people who have worked for you who have been excellent employees, and those who didn't work out. What did they do that made them stand out in your mind?* The answers to this question are essential for understanding your prospective boss. They give insight into what he/she values.

❑ *What prompts the people in your work group to derive pride and satisfaction, and what are their sources of irritation and frustration?* Usually, there are both in any work group. The question is whether the sources of pride and satisfaction are what give you the same feeling. Can you live with the sources of irritation and frustration?

Tips

These tips are primarily common sense; however, it doesn't hurt to be reminded of them.

1. Be on time for your interview. Arriving late creates concern about your punctuality.

2. Dress one step up from what you expect that your interviewer(s) will wear. Look attractive, not distractive. *You* need to be the focus of attention, not your clothes or accessories.

3. Look at the person interviewing you as the question is posed, and as you answer it. If you are in a group interview, as in other forms of public speaking, make eye contact with your audience as you answer questions. *Note,* however, that in some cultures eye contact is considered rude. So, observe how the people with whom you are interviewing relate to each other and take a cue from them.

4. Be yourself, as much as possible, given that you may find a job interview to be stressful.

5. Ask how and when a hiring decision will be made, and when you can expect further word on your candidacy.

6. Before leaving, ask, *"How do I compare with the other candidates for this job?"* The answer to this question may give you a clue regarding your

chances of a job offer. If they have a misimpression of you, you have an opportunity to correct it.

7. If you are asked any question that you consider inappropriate, ask for a clarification. Sometimes an interviewer may not realize that a question is inappropriate until he/she is asked for a clarification. At that point, the question may be restated of retracted. If, after clarification, the question is still inappropriate, point out that it doesn't seem related to successful job performance If you answer the question anyhow, note it, your answer, and the reaction of the interviewer. If you don't get a job offer, and you believe that the question and your answer had any bearing on not being selected, you may have grounds for legal action.

8. Thank the people with whom you interviewed for the opportunity to meet them. Send a thank you note to the person who invited you for the interview.

Job interviews are part of organizational life. They are also career-defining events. Not every job interview will result in a job offer. Coming across well in an interview is an acquired skill. View each interview as an opportunity to learn and develop your skill. What went well? What would you do differently next time? Then, apply what you learn to future interviews. The more experienced you become in being interviewed, the more comfortable and competent you will become.

11.9

Responding to a Job Offer

Being offered a new job is exciting! It poses new possibilities. If you are currently employed, you know what your present job has to offer. Key to sorting out a job offer is to obtain the information you need to make an informed comparison and a decision.

Choose your new employer carefully! Your career is too important to entrust to someone who does not have your interests at heart, or from whom you cannot learn. Before you can make an intelligent decision, you need information about the job, the expectations of the person to whom you will report, that person's style, and the compensation package. Remember, when you are being offered a job, you have more negotiating leverage than at any other time. Here are some questions to help you learn more about these issues, if they were not previously covered.

❑ First, thank the person who has made you the job offer. *"I really appreciate your job offer. I take it as a great compliment, and want to give it serious consideration. To help me make an informed decision, I have a few questions. May I ask them?"*

A job offer is a compliment. In expressing your appreciation, you pave the way for getting your questions answered, and for negotiation. Also, thoughtful questions enhance your attractiveness as a job candidate.

❑ *"What do you want accomplished within the next three months, six months, and year?"*

It is not just the job description that counts; it is what is expected of you. Will you be able to fulfill the expectations? Is too much expected? Will you be able to learn and grow? Are you a "sacrificial lamb" for an incompetent person?

❑ *"How do I compare with the other people you considered for this job? What do you see as my strengths? What concerns do you have about me for this job?"*

Anyone who has done his/her "homework" should be able to answer these questions. If he/she neglected the "homework," he/she may be a "shoot from the hip" boss. If the person holds back on answering your questions, you may have difficulty getting the information you need on the job. Honest feedback is critical for your growth and development, and to a mature relationship.

❑ *If I accept your offer, I want to do my very best for you. To help me gauge how well I may be able to meet your expectations, please describe for me people who have been your star performers, and those with whom you have had problems."*

Most managers have had someone who has been an outstanding employee, and one who has not. This information will enable you to determine whether your prospective employer will be someone who can help bring out the best in you. Avoid someone whose leadership style is inconsistent with your needs. Also, beware of someone who consistently bad-mouths previous employees.

❑ *"What is the salary range for this job? What are other people in this range paid whose qualifications are similar to mine? What were your considerations in arriving at $_____ per year as the offer? When would I normally be eligible for a salary review?"* (if there is a bonus or incentive pay plan). How does the bonus/incentive plan work? "Assuming I accomplish what you expect me to, what can I reasonably expect as a bonus?"*

The answers to these questions should help you understand how your prospective employer views compensation, and you in relation to their compensation plan.

A key is how he/she plans to pay you in relation to people of similar qualifications in the same range. If the proposed salary is lower than what you expected, but consistent with other people, your room to negotiate is limited. If the proposed salary is high in relation to the range and other people, your salary increase prospects are diminished.

Most employers offering you a job will extend the best offer they can to get you, assuming that they really want you. While you may be able to negotiate a higher offer, it generally is not to your advantage to go through more than one round of negotiations. If the employer won't offer a salary that satisfies you in one round of negotiations, you will probably feel underpaid, and the employer may feel that you are too aggressive about your salary. That is not healthy!

❑ If you have questions about benefits or stock options, address them.

❑ *"What else should I know in considering your offer?"*

Someone making you a job offer is probably trying to sell you on accepting it. This question is a "catch all" that enables the employer to add anything that may have been missed, and to summarize the reasons why you should accept.

❑ *"Thanks for your patience and candor in answering my questions. I now have the information I need to place your offer in context. I will give your offer very serious consideration. I would like to give you my answer on _____, if that is all right with you."*

From a negotiating viewpoint, you want the prospective employer to feel pleased that he/she has devoted time to answering your questions. Unless there is extreme urgency, you should be able to have 24 hours to reflect on the offer and make your decision. Don't feel pressured into making your decision on the spot. If it is the right job today, it will be the right job tomorrow.

Discuss the job offer with your spouse, significant other, or a close confidant. The process of discussing it with someone who is a good listener will help you to articulate and clarify what you see as the plusses and minuses (and there are apt to be both).

Your job offer needs to be confirmed in writing. If the person offering you a job does not confirm the offer, and you decide to accept it, write a letter of acceptance in which you confirm your understanding of the offer. Make sure that your understanding is accurate before you give notice to resign your from current job.

Remember, it takes at least two people to make a hiring decision. No one has as much at stake in the decision as you. It is your career and life!

12

Using External Resources

12.1

Outsourcing Services

To outsource or keep in-house—that is the question! Outsourcing is contracting to purchase services that you might otherwise have in-house. You may benefit from better services for less by buying them from a purveyor who specializes in them. In-house support services typically "play second fiddle" to the core business and are a distraction from the central focus of the business. They are not what defines the identity of a business or creates its competitive edge.

Is it a central competency? Every business has certain competencies that are *central* to its existence. They are what define and distinguish it as a business. They contribute directly to its competitive advantage. They should not be outsourced. There may be others that, though important, *support* the central ones. They may be candidates for outsourcing. In schools, custodial services and meal preparation, though important, *support* the learning experience. The academic performance of students is not defined by the quality of these services. However, janitorial services are a central competence in a building maintenance business, as is food preparation in a food service business. These services may be performed more effectively, efficiently, and at a lower cost when they are the central competence of another business.

When Outsourcing makes sense when there is a choice of purveyors, and when they can do a job better or at a lower cost than you could if you staffed the service internally. It also makes sense to outsource a competence that you need only occasionally. Apple successfully outsourced the design of its iMac computer's packaging. The design has been one of its defining features. It has won awards and customers. What they purchased was better than they could do in-house.

Choice of purveyors Choice is important! You benefit when there is competition for your business. You don't want to be a captive of just one source. Some businesses have spun off a service—they then purchase it as *outsourced*. That is unhealthy unless there is a choice of purveyors so that your business is not a captive of the spinoff. Additionally, a spunoff business needs other customers to which it can allocate its overhead and amortize its investments.

Partnering Outsourcing works best when there is a partnering relationship. Communication and coordination are critical for planning new products and services, designing work processes and interfaces, solving problems, creating the quality standards, monitoring quality and for inventory management. Invest the time and attention up front to create a solid working relationship.

Build in incentives for quality and delivery. Locate your quality inspectors where they can make timely inspections and decisions of whether to accept or reject what you are buying. For example, Cisco Systems locates their quality people at the end of their contract manufacturer's production line.

Outsourcing is not always appropriate If you can do it better and/or for less in-house, don't outsource. If there are strategic or security reasons not to outsource, don't do it. If you have the best talent and service already in-house, don't outsource. If you have spare capacity, you may be able to sell the services of your staff to other businesses and turn your service into a profit center.

Outsourcing, done properly, enables you to focus your business and deploy your resources more effectively and efficiently. Should you outsource? Do your homework.

12.2

Choosing to Use a Consultant

"We need help, but doesn't engaging a consultant signify that we have a weakness?" No! It recognizes that you have a need, and that you are intelligent enough to use the resources available to you.

If you needed triple by-pass surgery, would you do it yourself? If the air conditioner in your car broke, would you repair it yourself? Probably not. Heart surgery is sufficiently serious and specialized that you would turn to an expert. Though you might try to repair an air conditioner, you would probably find that it makes better use of your time to use a specialist with the right tools and know-how.

Consultants have specialized know-how that you need only occasionally. Seeking their help is actually a sign of wisdom and maturity. You cannot be all knowing and meet every challenge single-handedly. You are expected to marshal the resources available to you to accomplish your goals.

When to Engage* a Consultant

Engage a consultant when you need:

- ❑ One-time or occasional expertise
- ❑ A knowledgeable, independent perspective free of vested interests
- ❑ The benefit of experience you don't have
- ❑ Someone who will be listened to
- ❑ Focused attention for solving a problem
- ❑ To accomplish a project for which no one internally has the time
- ❑ To bring diverse views into agreement

Finding a Consultant

Many people call themselves consultants. Some may be professionals in their field but lack training and experience in the disciplines of consulting. If you don't already know a consultant who meets your needs, seek one who has earned professional certification or who at least has undergone a thorough screening. For management consultants, look for the CMC mark. Certified Management Consultants subscribe to a code of ethics and undergo a rigorous process of peer and client review that assures competence, trust and client satisfaction. They can be found on the Institute of Management Consultants' website (www.imcusa.org or www.cmcglobal.org).

The fact that a consultant has not earned certification does not mean that he/she is of lesser quality per se. Certification indicates that the holder of the mark has chosen to undergo the certification process and has passed. While certification does not guarantee the services of a consultant, it signifies that his/her clients and peers have deemed him/her to be experienced, trusted and recommended.

---

*I use the term, "engage," rather than "hire." You hire employees into defined jobs according to terms and conditions that have been defined by your business. (A consulting business may hire consultants for its consulting staff.) The relationship between a consultant and a client is normally a negotiated contract for a specific engagement. A consultant, unlike a hired employee, works with you through a process of engagement to determine the purpose, scope, desired results, methods, terms and fees for a unique assignment. You can fire an employee according to the provisions of your termination policy. You can only terminate a consulting engagement according to the provisions of the consulting agreement.

What to Look for

In selecting a consultant look for:

- ❑ Professional competence (knowledge, skills and experience)
- ❑ Integrity (ethics, straightforwardness, confidentiality, and willingness to face up to difficult issues honestly)
- ❑ Reputation (certification, references, track record)
- ❑ Approach (how they plan to tackle the issues, how suited their approach is to your situation, and who they plan to involve)
- ❑ Personal qualities (willingness to listen and reserve judgment, ability to work with your people, ability to communicate sensitive information)
- ❑ Business practices (clear-cut arrangements, responsiveness to your needs)

Engaging a Consultant

Engaging a consultant is much like much like selecting a surgeon for triple bypass surgery. There is usually a lot at stake that will affect you and your organization. You want to have confidence that the consultant you select will deliver the results you need and be a credit to you, especially for a career-defining project.

Some organizations require a competitive bidding process to select and engage consultants. If your organization uses a Request for Proposal (RFP) process, then follow it. Where there is no RFP process, meet face to face with prospective consultants. Explain your needs, efforts so far to solve your problem, desired outcomes, timing, and approximate budget. A good consultant, like a good doctor, needs to understand (diagnose) your situation before he/she can recommend (prescribe) an approach to solving it.

A prospective consultant will ask questions to clarify points and make sure that he/she understands your situation. Look for questions that reflect insight into your critical issues. How well does he/she listen and reserve judgment? How applicable is his/her knowledge and experience? Who will actually be performing the work? What is his/her track record? How open and honest is he/she in answering your questions? How does he/she deal with sensitive issues? How well would he/she work with you and your organization? Ask for examples of similar assignments conducted and their results. How appropriate is his/her recommended approach for your needs and situation?

If you are comparing several consultants, you may need written proposals from them. Written proposals take a lot of time for consultants to prepare and for you to evaluate. Only ask for them from serious contenders.

Unless a prospective consultant comes highly recommended by people you respect, check his/her client references.

If a prospective consultant meets your needs and you decide to engage him/her, you may only need a letter to confirm the arrangements for the engagement. Ask him/her to draft the letter. It will test whether you and he/she are on the same wavelength. If his/her draft corresponds with your understanding, and is acceptable to you and your organization, sign your acceptance. If not, discuss the differences and ask him/her to modify the engagement letter accordingly before you accept it.

Choose consultants who can achieve the results you need. Quality consultants working on a worthwhile engagement deliver value far in excess of their fee. That's a good investment!

12.3

When and How to Use Temporary Help

The staffing needs of businesses today, especially small businesses, are too fluid to warrant hiring "permanent" staff for all their needs. Temporary help can enable a business to achieve staffing flexibility and be competitive. Let's look at when it is appropriate to hire long-term employees, when to hire temporary staff, and how to make the best use of temps.

Businesses need a core of employees with regularly assigned, on-going responsibilities. They should be fully occupied whether the business is at a peak or in the doldrums. Long-term continuity in these jobs is important for teamwork and smooth operations. These jobs should normally be filled with "permanent" staff.

When is it appropriate to use temporary help? Use temporary help when you need:

- ❑ A short-term replacement for an employee who is out or on leave
- ❑ Additional employees to help you through a peak period of business
- ❑ A job filled temporarily while recruiting a long-term employee
- ❑ A project accomplished for which you don't have the time or in-house expertise

Temporary help is frequently thought of as coming from temporary agencies, and limited to non-exempt jobs. That is too narrow a view. While temporary agencies can be excellent sources of temporary help, there are other sources, too. Some businesses recruit and develop their own pool of people who return time after time to meet varying needs. Such people have been recruited to work only as needed. A good example of this is substitute teachers for school districts. Other businesses turn to "job shops" to farm out work, or "brokers" to "lease" specialized talent for projects or long-term assignments. Other businesses seek specialized expertise through the directories or referral services of professional organizations, such as the Institute of Management Consultants. It is now possible to obtain temporary engineers, accountants, CEOs, etc., so don't limit your concept of temps to the old stereotypes.

Several years ago, I helped a client who had tremendous employee turnover. I discovered that when they had a job vacancy, they hired the first available person because they "could not wait" to fill the job. That meant that their hiring was hit or miss. They had not considered using temporary help to keep the operation going while they defined their needs and recruited the right long-term employee.

Another client had seasonal needs for employees. They carefully recruited housewives, students and retired people to call on for their peaks or to fill in for employees on sick leave. The temps knew the company and liked having occasional work. Because of their familiarity with the company, they could fill in with a minimum of "start-up" time and are very productive.

A small start-up needed seasoned expertise to set up their manufacturing operation and train their operations supervisor. They considered hiring a manufacturing manager in the hope that their business would expand fast enough to warrant paying the salary that such talent can command. Instead, they contracted with an outstanding consultant to work part-time with them over a six-month period. He provided them with the expertise they needed and trained the operations supervisor to become the manufacturing manager. This cost them less than half of what it would have cost to hire a manufacturing manager.

Temporary help may be a useful staffing alternative for your business, but it is not a panacea. Here are some pointers to help you benefit from temporary help:

1. Know your requirements before contracting for a temp. Define the skills you need and for how long. Identify who will be responsible for supervising the temp.

2. Before you use temporary agencies, job shops or brokers, check their clients to determine how satisfied they are with the service and quality of employees they provide. Find out whether they are familiar with your requirements and can meet your needs.

3. Develop a long-term relationship with several sources of temporary help. It is a good idea not to rely on just one. Sometimes one won't have the people you need for an immediate need, while another will. On the other hand, don't work with too many. You want to be a significant enough client that they invest the time to learn about your needs and business. A good agency, job shop or broker will have its representative visit you to learn about your needs and the particulars of your work environment that are important to appropriate placement. Also, consistent business with one agency may provide you with a discount after you pass a certain threshold of billings.

4. Employees of agencies and job shops are not on your payroll. You are not responsible for their payroll taxes, insurances, and W-2s. You are responsible for these when you hire directly.

5. Invest time to brief temps about the job they will be filling and your business, and debrief them when they leave. They will come "up to speed" faster with a briefing. While they are working for you, they will also develop impressions of the work and work situation. Their perceptions can be very valuable. It is worthwhile investing a half hour to discover what went well for them, and what they experienced that could be improved. They may be able to help you improve your business, if you will listen to them.

6. If you have a problem with a temp, confront it as soon as you discover the problem. Don't procrastinate in the hope that the problem will improve. You hire a temp because you have an immediate need, so there is no reason to delay. Many temporary agencies will replace someone who doesn't work out free of charge, so long as you contact them within a prescribed period.

7. When hiring temps directly, hire people who are not looking for steady employment. When they are not working, you don't want them filing for unemployment insurance.

8. When engaging independent contractors, make sure that they are truly in business as an independent contractor. Ask to see their business license and other evidence that they are running a business. Make sure that you are not their only client. Treat them as independent contractors, rather than employees, and report their earnings on a Form 1099.

9. On the surface, rates for temporary or leased employees, and independent contractors may seem high in relation to what you pay your employees. Remember that their rates reflect their overhead. In order to make a meaningful comparison, you should also consider your overhead costs.

In this age of "just-in-time" manufacturing and supply chain management, think of temps as "just-in-time" staff. You can obtain the services of well-qualified people for only the time you need them, and when you need them, through planning and establishing relations with good purveyors of temporary help.

12.4

Leading Volunteers

As a leader, you have probably worked with volunteers or you will at some time. Whether you work for a not-for-profit organization, coach Little League, or serve on the board of a civic organization, leading volunteers requires as much, if not more, leadership skill as leading employees. While employees receive pay and psychic rewards, volunteers only get psychic rewards. If their rewards don't outweigh their commitment of time, they can walk away more easily than can someone whose rent and groceries depend on working for you.

Volunteer motivation People generally volunteer because they want to—because they feel that they are serving a higher purpose. They choose to invest part of their life in making a difference for something they believe in. To build their commitment and performance, you need to have a purpose and mission that moves them to want to help. Touch their heart and tap their spirit! If you don't, you will have only half-hearted commitment and performance until they become discouraged and leave.

What Volunteers are Looking For

- Something important and meaningful to accomplish
- Clear roles, expectations, guidelines and accountability
- A supportive organization and sufficient training to feel competent in what they do
- Respect, recognition and appreciation for what they do
- An enjoyable experience—camaraderie, fun, being on a winning team.
- Learning and personal growth

What Turns Volunteers Off

- Feeling that their talent and time are being wasted
- Seeing no important purpose to what they are doing
- Micromanagement or a non-trusting work environment
- Unrealistic or irrelevant goals or demands on their time
- Being treated as "second class" to paid staff, or in a parental (condescending) way

❑ Political games and in-fighting
❑ Lack of appreciation and recognition for their contribution

Assess your environment If you are leading or plan to lead volunteers, review your volunteer environment against the above points. Discover what is working well and where you see symptoms of problems. Ask current volunteers what parts of their volunteer experience they do and do not find satisfying. Ask how you can make their volunteering more rewarding.

Selecting volunteers Volunteers can be amazingly dedicated and effective, or deadbeats. Choose them carefully. Interview them to make sure that you have an appropriate fit between what they can do, their needs and wants, and what you have to offer. Ask what it takes to bring out the best in them as a volunteer. Only choose those for whom you can provide the sort of environment that will bring out the best in them.

Not free Don't accept volunteers just because they are "free." They are not. Though you don't pay them, you do need to provide meaningful personal and psychological rewards.

Give meaning to work How do you make stuffing envelopes seem important and fulfilling? Don't think of the work as stuffing envelopes. Communicate the purpose and context of the work. *"We are seeking to build a new performing arts center. To do so, we need to raise $75 million. We have pledges of $45 million to date, and our deadline for funding this project is December 31. Our purpose this evening is to contact people who have shown an interest in the performing arts and to solicit their contribution. We need to contact an additional 5000 potential donors. You are key to helping us make that contact by preparing 1000 letters to be mailed tomorrow."* Yes, the work is still stuffing envelopes, but for an important purpose.

Discipline Can you discipline or "fire" a volunteer? Yes, however, as with an employee, do your homework first. When you discover a problem, bring it to the volunteer's attention:

❑ Describe what you see and why it is a problem—explain what was expected
❑ Ask how he/she sees the situation
❑ Ask what he/she can do to remedy it or prevent a recurrence
❑ Ask what course of action he/she can commit to
❑ Set a follow-up progress review and confirm your discussion in a note to the volunteer

If progress is less than acceptable after several attempts, ask the volunteer to leave. *"George, I'm asking you to step down as assistant coach of our soccer team. We've discussed three times your temper outbursts at the kids when they make a mistake on the field. I know how involved you get with the game. As we discussed before, swearing at them and making inappropriate insinuations about their relationship with their mother is unacceptable behavior as a coach of our team. You have not demonstrated that you can control your temper, so I am asking you to leave."*

In essence, what constitutes good leadership and management of employees also works with volunteers. Just never delude yourself into thinking that they are "free," and remember that providing meaningful psychological rewards is critical to creating committed, productive volunteers.

Getting Feedback About Your Workplace and Leadership

13.1

Using Employee Feedback to Improve Employee Retention

The knowledge base of your business walks out your door at the end of each day. Will it return the next? Most will, but some won't. Some employees will choose to work elsewhere—perhaps for a competitor. When that happens, you lose—big time!

Turnover costs! Many businesses have no idea of what employee turnover really costs them. When asked, they mention recruiting costs and sometimes training costs. Those are just the tip of the iceberg. When an employee leaves, someone else has to do the work, or it doesn't get done. That costs. Even highly competent, trained employees take some time before they know the ins and outs of your business and can perform to full capacity. That costs. You can't grow your business as fast when you are missing people you need. That costs. When customers phone and talk with someone new each time, the credibility and service quality of your business are questioned. That costs. You need to estimate your true cost of employee turnover to your business. The typical cost is in the range of six to twelve months pay. Multiply that times the number of people you lose in a year and you may be talking serious money! Can you afford that?

Keeping people You can't manacle employees and chain them to their workstations. Instead, you need to create a work environment where they look forward to coming to work. Competitive pay and benefits, and stock options, while important, are not enough. Employees see a paycheck (or direct deposit confirmation) once or twice a month. They may use their benefits occasionally. They experience their work and the people with whom they work every day. Whether they decide to leave or stay is based more on their work and relationships than anything else.

Employees = "customers" Think of employees as "customers" for your work environment. When they buy, they work for you; when they don't, they leave. If you want to attract and retain the talent you need to grow your business, treat employees as you would your *best* customers.

"Market" research When you view employees as "customers" for your work environment, it only makes sense to conduct periodic "market" research. Before you create and introduce a new product or service, you probably conduct market research. You want to make sure there is a market, and you need to know what it takes to motivate customers to buy. The same goes for employees. You need to conduct your market research with them in order to understand what attracts them to work for you, what they find unattractive, and what inspires and enables them to perform at their best. Only with this knowledge can you tune your work environment for high employer attractiveness and outstanding performance.

How do you conduct market research among employees? Ask them. Ask them in your conversations (management by wandering around). Ask them in interviews. Ask them in focus groups. Ask them in periodic surveys. The tools are not new. Which should you use? Use all of them. Each has a slightly different purpose, and they complement each other.

- ❑ **Conversations and interviews** When Ed Koch was Mayor of New York City, he was always asking, *"How am I doing?"* As you talk with employees in the hall, in the break room, and in performance review discussions, ask them for feedback. *"How is your work coming along? What makes this a good place to work? What do we need to do to make it even better?"* These are simple, straightforward questions that show concern and elicit qualitative information.

- ❑ **Focus groups** From time to time, assemble groups of a dozen or so employees from different parts of the business to talk about "what its like to work here." Ask them the questions mentioned above. Take notes of what is said (but not necessarily who said it). When you get the same or similar feedback on an issue, you can ask whether it is a commonly-shared perception. One of the valuable contributions of a focus group is the breadth of perspective that you will get. You can mine a wealth of qualitative information from the dialogue.

Conversations, interviews and focus groups provide microperspectives of life in your business. These microperspectives may be rich with qualitative and anecdotal information, but they generally represent only a small sample of your workforce. Periodically, you also need a macroperspective in the form of a comprehensive survey of your work place. A survey affords broader participation on a broader spectrum of issues. It enables you to obtain a quantitative assessment to supplement the qualitative feedback.

- ❑ **Employee surveys** Employee surveys are generally a series of questions that employees answer, or statements that they rate, on a form. The form may be printed on paper or Internet-based (as is the Jacobsen Survey of Employer Attractiveness).

There are basically three types of surveys: those that are standardized, those that are designed specifically for your organization, and those that are a hybrid. The benefit of the standardized survey is that it enables you to benchmark with

230 *Leadership at Your Fingertips*

other employers who use it. You can see how you compare with your competitors. The drawback is that they may not reflect the uniqueness of your business and work place. However, if you choose a survey designed exclusively for your business, you miss out on benchmarking. In these days of mass customization, you have another option: a standard survey with an addendum design for the special needs of your business. This option provides the best of both worlds.

Sample Surveys

The remainder of this section of the book contains sample surveys.

- ❑ **The Organizational "Quick-Check"** (QC) is a checklist of factors that affect organizational climate. Completing it will give you a snapshot through your eyes of strengths and vulnerabilities of your organization.
- ❑ **The Work Environment Description** (WED) is a survey with 50 statements about the work environment that employees rate for accuracy and importance to bringing out the best in them. It can be used as a micro-survey with just a team, or with an entire organization. It is normally administered by an independent organization that compiles their responses, analyzes them, and reports results and recommendations.
- ❑ **The Team Environment Description** (TED) is a micro-survey instrument you can use with just the people on your team. It asks participants to rate the team on 30 characteristics of a well-functioning organization. Usually the completed forms are sent to a trusted individual outside the team for compiling and reporting.
- ❑ **The Leadership Self-Assessment** (LSA) is a checklist you can use to rate yourself in relation to 30 behaviors of well-respected leaders. It can be used independently of team feedback, or used to compare your perceptions of your leadership with those of the people on your team.
- ❑ **The Leadership Assessment—by Team Members** (LA-TM), like the TED, is a micro-survey for the people who report to you. The statements of the LSA are adapted for rating your leadership behavior by the people who report to you. It is also sent directly to a trusted individual outside your team for compiling and reporting.

Transforming information into action Surveys and employee feedback provide useful data and information. You can discover or confirm what employees find attractive and where you are vulnerable. The key is to make sense of the messages and then use them to guide your actions.

Survey results should provide you with information about what is important to employees for leadership and employer attractiveness. Some can compare responses from your business with those from similar businesses. While responses from other businesses provide a sense of how your business compares with your competition, the focus of your attention needs to be on life in your organization. Look at the factors survey participants have rated as most important to them. Look at what is generally rated highly. Those features may create a competitive advantage for you. Look at what is generally rated low. Those are your vulnerabilities. In surveys that are organization-wide, or cover a major segment of the organization, look at the discrepancies in ratings between organizational units. You may have a problem area. Look at the distribution of ratings on each question. Bimodal or skewed ratings may require further investigation.

What are your strengths and vulnerabilities? What strengths can you capitalize on? What are sore points that can be changed easily and with little expense? Which changes will be more complex or expensive that need to be scheduled for later action? Set priorities and a schedule to change what bothers people. Not everything can be done at once. Employees understand and are willing to accept that certain changes may take time, as long as they can see a plan and timetable for addressing important issues.

Share the results of the survey with employees. Accentuate what they find attractive. Tell them of your plans to make improvements. Then, update them on progress as it occurs. Employees think twice about "jumping ship" when they can see real progress on what's important to them.

Management credibility Conducting an employee survey raises expectations. It implies that you care. If you don't act on significant issues, employee morale and management credibility suffer. You, in fact, boost morale and management credibility when you act on employee concerns and issues—and, you improve your ability to recruit and retain talented people.

The competitive arena for talented people has become the nature of work and the quality of your work environment. While there is a similarity to what attracts and retains talented people from one business to the next, there are enough differences that you need to target market. That necessitates market research, followed by actions to make your work and work environment attractive to the people you want. When you are meeting the needs of what is important to employees, you will have a much easier time attracting talent and keeping the people you need.

Organizational "Quick-Check"

This is a tool to help a small business owner or CEO quickly assess his/her organization's "climate."

Please read each statement and rate how accurately it describes your organization.

1 = *not accurate* at all   3 = *partially* accurate   5 = *very* accurate.

1. Our position in our market (market share) is improving.	1 2 3 4 5
2. Our organization anticipates market changes and adapts easily.	1 2 3 4 5
3. We seldom lose customers/clients to competitors.	1 2 3 4 5
4. I devote part of each week to talking with customers and employees.	1 2 3 4 5
5. Continuous improvement and quality are a "way of life" with us.	1 2 3 4 5
6. Our purpose and mission are vital, and inspire us to pull together.	1 2 3 4 5
7. We have a flexible strategic plan that is helping us create our future.	1 2 3 4 5
8. A set of shared values guides the way we conduct our business.	1 2 3 4 5
9. Our policies are consistent with our values, and people comply with them	1 2 3 4 5
10. Employees enjoy and take pride in their work.	1 2 3 4 5
11. Duplication of effort, or "things falling between the cracks," is rare.	1 2 3 4 5
12. People in our organization honor their commitments and meet deadlines.	1 2 3 4 5
13. No one is treated as a "second class" citizen.	1 2 3 4 5
14. Grievances are rare, and are resolved quickly when they arise.	1 2 3 4 5
15. Performance expectations and standards are clearly communicated.	1 2 3 4 5
16. People get the information they need for monitoring their performance.	1 2 3 4 5
17. Performance problems have been confronted, documented and treated.	1 2 3 4 5
18. Employees get timely and useful coaching to help them grow in their job.	1 2 3 4 5
19. Employees are learning and gaining value as fast as technology changes.	1 2 3 4 5
20. We have a policy and process to prevent and confront sexual harassment.	1 2 3 4 5
21. No current or former employees have taken legal action against us.	1 2 3 4 5
22. People tell me about the "bad news" as well as the "good news."	1 2 3 4 5
23. People affected by a problem are included in the problem-solving process.	1 2 3 4 5
24. People focus on solving problems rather than on seeking others to blame.	1 2 3 4 5
25. People have access to the information needed for making good decisions.	1 2 3 4 5

26. Once decisions are made, they are implemented readily and with support. 1 2 3 4 5
27. Employee turnover is low and has had little adverse effect on our business. 1 2 3 4 5
28. We are able to fill vacant jobs in a reasonable period of time. 1 2 3 4 5
29. References and the background of new employees are checked thoroughly. 1 2 3 4 5
30. Employees reflect the composition of the surrounding workforce. 1 2 3 4 5

31. Payroll is a constant or decreasing percent of sales/revenues. 1 2 3 4 5
32. Our wages/salaries and benefits are reasonably competitive. 1 2 3 4 5
33. Pay relationships reflect worth, and are defensible. 1 2 3 4 5
34. Superior performance is recognized and rewarded appropriately. 1 2 3 4 5
35. Employees are paid on time, and in the correct amount. 1 2 3 4 5

Add your ratings and divide by 35. A 4+ average is exceptional! Statements rated 1 or 2 indicate a vulnerability worthy of your attention, and an opportunity for improvement.

Work Environment Description

This survey seeks your rating of 50 statements about your current work environment and how important each is for bringing out the *best* in you. Please read each and rate it.

	Level of agreement	**Level of importance to you**
Rating scale	5 = strongly agree	Extremely important
	3 = partially agree	Somewhat important
	1 = strongly disagree	Not important

In the *Agreement* column, circle your rating for your level of agreement with the statement as it applies to your current work environment. In the *Importance* column, circle your rating for how important the statement is to bringing out the *best* in you.

Your survey response is **CONFIDENTIAL.** Do not write your name on it.

Note: The term "leader" = the person to whom you report directly.
              The term "group" = the people who work with you for your leader.

Mission & values	*Agreement*	*Importance*
1 I understand our organization's purpose and mission.	1 2 3 4 5	1 2 3 4 5
2. I understand and support the values of our organization.	1 2 3 4 5	1 2 3 4 5
3. Our leader behaves consistently with our values.	1 2 3 4 5	1 2 3 4 5
Policies		
4. I understand our organization's policies.	1 2 3 4 5	1 2 3 4 5
5. Policies and rules are fair and realistic.	1 2 3 4 5	1 2 3 4 5
6. Our leader administers policies and rules fairly.	1 2 3 4 5	1 2 3 4 5
Personal support		
7. I have had the training I need for my work.	1 2 3 4 5	1 2 3 4 5
8. I know what performance is expected of me.	1 2 3 4 5	1 2 3 4 5
9. Expectations for my performance are realistic.	1 2 3 4 5	1 2 3 4 5
10. I get the information I need to do my work.	1 2 3 4 5	1 2 3 4 5
11. I have adequate freedom to do my work.	1 2 3 4 5	1 2 3 4 5
12. I am encouraged to try new ways of doing things.	1 2 3 4 5	1 2 3 4 5
13. Our leader is accessible for my questions.	1 2 3 4 5	1 2 3 4 5
14. I feel free to ask our leader questions.	1 2 3 4 5	1 2 3 4 5
15. Our leader answers questions promptly, or obtains the correct answer on a timely basis.	1 2 3 4 5	1 2 3 4 5

	Agreement	*Importance*
16. I can believe what our leader tells us.	1 2 3 4 5	1 2 3 4 5
17. When our leader has to communicate an unpopular decision, (s) he never tries to blame others for it.	1 2 3 4 5	1 2 3 4 5
18. I feel free to discuss problems with our leader.	1 2 3 4 5	1 2 3 4 5
19. If anyone in our group has a problem, our leader helps resolve it constructively.	1 2 3 4 5	1 2 3 4 5
20. I get recognition for the work I do well.	1 2 3 4 5	1 2 3 4 5
21. If I make a mistake, our leader helps me learn from it.	1 2 3 4 5	1 2 3 4 5
22. Our leader never criticizes me in front of others.	1 2 3 4 5	1 2 3 4 5

Trust & respect

23. Our leader communicates trust and respect for us.	1 2 3 4 5	1 2 3 4 5
24. People in our group trust and respect our leader.	1 2 3 4 5	1 2 3 4 5
25. People in our group trust and respect each other.	1 2 3 4 5	1 2 3 4 5
26. People in our group keep promises they make.	1 2 3 4 5	1 2 3 4 5

Work organization

27. I understand how my job interrelates with the other jobs in our group.	1 2 3 4 5	1 2 3 4 5
28. Our group's work priorities are clear.	1 2 3 4 5	1 2 3 4 5
29. Work is normally well organized and coordinated.	1 2 3 4 5	1 2 3 4 5
30. We normally have enough people to do our work.	1 2 3 4 5	1 2 3 4 5
31. People in our group willingly help each other.	1 2 3 4 5	1 2 3 4 5

Group goals

32. We are included in developing our work group's goals.	1 2 3 4 5	1 2 3 4 5
33. Our goals are important and challenging.	1 2 3 4 5	1 2 3 4 5
34. Our leader secures the resources we need to do our work.	1 2 3 4 5	1 2 3 4 5
35. Our leader inspires enthusiasm for our goals.	1 2 3 4 5	1 2 3 4 5
36. Our leader encourages and coaches us to do our best.	1 2 3 4 5	1 2 3 4 5
37. We are kept informed of our progress on our goals.	1 2 3 4 5	1 2 3 4 5
38. We celebrate as a group when we achieve our goals.	1 2 3 4 5	1 2 3 4 5

	Agreement	*Importance*

Meetings

39. We meet as a group as frequently as we need to.   1 2 3 4 5   1 2 3 4 5

40. Group meetings deal with important issues.   1 2 3 4 5   1 2 3 4 5

41. Our leader involves us in solving problems
important to our group.   1 2 3 4 5   1 2 3 4 5

42. Our leader encourages differing views.   1 2 3 4 5   1 2 3 4 5

43. We feel free to express our views.   1 2 3 4 5   1 2 3 4 5

Decisions

44. Decisions made in our meetings have our support.   1 2 3 4 5   1 2 3 4 5

45. Decisions made in our meetings are implemented
in a reasonable period of time.   1 2 3 4 5   1 2 3 4 5

Relations with other groups

46. I understand how our work group fits in with the
other parts of our organization.   1 2 3 4 5   1 2 3 4 5

47. Our leader keeps us adequately informed of news
from other parts of the organization.   1 2 3 4 5   1 2 3 4 5

48 Our leader gets the cooperation and support of
his/her leader, and others in management.   1 2 3 4 5   1 2 3 4 5

49. Our leader represents our group effectively when
decisions affecting us are made in other parts of
the organization.   1 2 3 4 5   1 2 3 4 5

Pride

50. My job helps me feel proud of myself and what
I do.   1 2 3 4 5   1 2 3 4 5

Team Environment Description

This survey is a tool to profile what it is like to be part of your team or work group in relation to 30 characteristics of well-functioning teams. Please read each statement and rate your level of agreement with it as a description of how your team *currently* functions.

Note: Your response will be treated confidentially.

Rating scale: 5 = *completely* agree
3 = *partially* agree
1 = *completely* disagree

1. We have an important purpose and mission to accomplish.	1 2 3 4 5
2. We are pursuing an inspiring shared vision.	1 2 3 4 5
3. We have the resources we need to perform our jobs.	1 2 3 4 5
4. We have all the information we need to perform our jobs.	1 2 3 4 5
5. We have adequate freedom to perform our jobs.	1 2 3 4 5
6. Roles, assignments, expectations, authority and accountability are clear.	1 2 3 4 5
7. Performance goals are measurable and inspire us to perform our best.	1 2 3 4 5
8. Our products/services consistently meet or exceed quality standards.	1 2 3 4 5
9. We willingly pitch in to do whatever is needed, whenever it's needed.	1 2 3 4 5
10. People on our team keep promises they make.	1 2 3 4 5
11. Policies and ground rules are realistic, understandable and accepted.	1 2 3 4 5
12. Policies and ground rules are applied evenhandedly.	1 2 3 4 5
13. Mutual trust, respect and commitment prevail.	1 2 3 4 5
14. Our views and feelings are important and treated with respect.	1 2 3 4 5
15. Political games are discouraged, and seldom occur.	1 2 3 4 5
16. Conflict is easily confronted, and resolved on a "win-win" basis.	1 2 3 4 5
17. Debate focuses on issues, not personalities.	1 2 3 4 5
18. Problems are identified and corrected rapidly.	1 2 3 4 5
19. People who have a stake in a problem are involved in resolving it.	1 2 3 4 5
20. Decisions reflect consensus of stakeholders, and are easily implemented.	1 2 3 4 5
21. We feel free to call *"time-out"* if we don't understand what is going on.	1 2 3 4 5
22. We are encouraged to take well-thought-out actions and risks.	1 2 3 4 5
23. Both success and failure are used as learning opportunities.	1 2 3 4 5
24. We are encouraged to challenge the system for continuous improvement.	1 2 3 4 5
25. We maintain our focus, perspective and humor, even under pressure.	1 2 3 4 5

26. Rewards reflect accomplishment.   1 2 3 4 5
27. Accomplishments, even small ones, are celebrated.   1 2 3 4 5
28. The atmosphere is relaxed, informal and comfortable.   1 2 3 4 5
29. New members are welcomed and quickly integrated.   1 2 3 4 5
30. I am recognized as an important member of the team.   1 2 3 4 5

Leadership Self-Assessment

This is a tool to profile what you do, as a leader, in relation to 30 statements of leader behavior that create a well-functioning team. Using the rating scale, circle the number that corresponds best to how accurately each statement describes what you do *currently*. (Note: "Team" and "people" = the people who report to you directly.)

Rating scale: 5 = Yes! This is what I do, *without*   2 = This is what I do *once in a while.*
                 exception.   1 = No! That's not me.
               4 = This is what I do *most* of the time.
               3 = This is what I do *some* of the time.

1. I have helped our team create a shared vision of our purpose/mission. 1 2 3 4 5
2. I create excitement for what we can accomplish together. 1 2 3 4 5
3. I make sure our team has the resources we need to accomplish our goals. 1 2 3 4 5
4. I communicate clear expectations for high quality and performance. 1 2 3 4 5
5. I make sure that goals are clear, measurable, challenging and attainable. 1 2 3 4 5

6. I make sure that our team celebrates "little victories" as well as big ones. 1 2 3 4 5
7. I encourage collaboration, and empower people to achieve their goals. 1 2 3 4 5
8. I have helped develop and instill a strong set of values to guide us. 1 2 3 4 5
9. I lead by example, and "practice what I preach." 1 2 3 4 5
10. I keep calm under pressure, and focused on our goals. 1 2 3 4 5

11. I help people solve their problems, rather than try to solve them myself. 1 2 3 4 5
12. I encourage and reward honest expression of feelings and thoughts. 1 2 3 4 5
13. I am in touch with my feelings and how they affect my behavior. 1 2 3 4 5
14. I confront problems as soon as I become aware of them. 1 2 3 4 5
15. I listen carefully and reserve judgment until I understand the relevant views. 1 2 3 4 5

16. I engage people who have a stake in a problem in solving it. 1 2 3 4 5
17. I strive for decisions reflecting consensus among people affected by them. 1 2 3 4 5
18. I "praise in public, counsel in private." 1 2 3 4 5
19. I answer questions truthfully and give honest feedback. 1 2 3 4 5
20. I discourage playing political games, and avoid them myself. 1 2 3 4 5

21. I respect and value diverse people with diverse views. 1 2 3 4 5
22. I do what I promise to do, or let people know in advance if I can't. 1 2 3 4 5
23. I encourage people to test their limits and take appropriate risks. 1 2 3 4 5

24. I reward people for results and taking risks, even when they don't
    work out.   1 2 3 4 5
25. I support decisions of team members, or help them save face if I can't. 1 2 3 4 5

26. I listen to criticism without expressing defensiveness.   1 2 3 4 5
27. I accept "bad news" without "killing the messenger."   1 2 3 4 5
28. I learn from both successes and failures, and foster team learning. 1 2 3 4 5
29. I view and treat team members as "customers" for my leadership.   1 2 3 4 5
30. I am honest and realistic with myself about my strengths and
    weaknesses.   1 2 3 4 5

Ratings of 4–5 = what you are doing that helps your team. 3 or lower = opportunities for your development. 1 or 2 reflect behavior that probably is restraining what the people who work for/with you can accomplish.

Leadership Assessment—by Team Members

This is a tool to help profile what your leader does in relation to behavior that typically helps bring out the best in people. Using the rating scale, circle the number that corresponds best to how accurately each statement describes his/her current behavior.

Note: Your response will be treated confidentially.

Rating scale: 5 = This is what he/she does, *without exception.*
4 = This is what he/she does *most of the time.*
3 = This is what he/she does some of the time.
2 = This is what he/she does *once in a while.*
1 = "No way does he/she do that!"

Our leader

1. Has helped us create a shared vision of our purpose/mission.   1 2 3 4 5
2. Creates excitement for what we can accomplish together.   1 2 3 4 5
3. Makes sure we have the resources we need to accomplish our goals.   1 2 3 4 5
4. Communicates clear expectations for high quality and performance.   1 2 3 4 5
5. Makes sure that goals are clear, measurable, challenging and attainable.   1 2 3 4 5
6. Makes sure that we celebrate "little victories" as well as big ones.   1 2 3 4 5
7. Encourages collaboration, and empowers us to achieve our goals.   1 2 3 4 5
8. Has helped develop and instill a strong set of values to guide us.   1 2 3 4 5
9. Leads by example, and "practices what he/she preaches."   1 2 3 4 5
10. Keeps calm under pressure, and focused on our goals.   1 2 3 4 5
11. Helps us solve our problems, rather than try to solve them him/herself.   1 2 3 4 5
12. Encourages and rewards honest expression of feelings and thoughts.   1 2 3 4 5
13. Is in touch with his/her feelings and how they affect his/her behavior.   1 2 3 4 5
14. Confronts problems as soon as he/she becomes aware of them.   1 2 3 4 5
15. Listens carefully and reserves judgment until he/she understands the picture.   1 2 3 4 5
16. Engages people who have a stake in a problem in solving it.   1 2 3 4 5
17. Strives for decisions reflecting consensus among people affected by them.   1 2 3 4 5
18. "Praises in public, counsels in private."   1 2 3 4 5
19. Answers questions truthfully and gives honest feedback.   1 2 3 4 5
20. Discourages playing political games, and avoids them him/herself.   1 2 3 4 5
21. Respects and values diverse people with diverse views.   1 2 3 4 5
22. Does what he/she promises to do, or lets us know in advance if he/she can't.   1 2 3 4 5

23. Encourages us to test our limits and take appropriate risks.   1 2 3 4 5
24. Rewards us for results and taking risks, even when the risk doesn't work out.   1 2 3 4 5
25. Supports our decisions, or helps us save face if he/she can't.   1 2 3 4 5

26. Listens to criticism without expressing defensiveness.   1 2 3 4 5
27. Accepts "bad news" without "killing the messenger."   1 2 3 4 5
28. Learns from both successes and failures, and fosters team learning.   1 2 3 4 5
29. Treats us as "customers" for his/her leadership.   1 2 3 4 5

In Conclusion

Work is a natural activity. It can range from something ennobling to dehumanizing. For most people who work, it occupies more waking hours than any other single activity. However, the way in which people have been led and managed in the workplace, for the most part, has not tapped their true potential. People, the organizations they work for, and society as a whole have all lost in the process.

Can you imagine what this world would be like if everyone could:

- ❑ Look forward to a good day of work as they roll out of bed at the start of their day, and
- ❑ Feel a sense of pride and satisfaction with their work at the end of their day?

Can you imagine how much more profitable business would be by tapping the full potential of their *people* resources?

Can you imagine how much better off society as a whole would be if the full creative potential of people were engaged in the workplace?

Changing the world starts with you. In *Leadership at Your Fingertips* I have tried to provide you with useful tips on how to begin to bring out the best in people, and hence, improve your workplace and the performance of your organization. As a leader, you can make a difference for the people you lead—both in their work environment and as a role model. My hope is that you will become a leader whom people seek out, and that you, the people you lead, your organization and society will prosper as a result.

Let me know how it goes for you. Send me an e-mail (ian@jacobsenconsulting.com) with your feedback on this book. Let me know what issues of leadership and organizational life you would like addressed in the future. I'll be pleased to add you to my quarterly letter, IanSights, if you would like.

About the Author

Ian Jacobsen is the owner of Jacobsen Consulting, based in Santa Clara, California. He coaches people with potential to become effective leaders, and helps them create a work environment where talented people *want* to work. He feels fortunate to have worked in settings where he could look forward to a good day at work. He firmly believes that everyone should be able to enjoy their work, so he started Jacobsen Consulting in 1983 to help clients create that sort of environment.

Ian's career began in 1963 on the staff at Stanford University. He joined Duty Free Shoppers in 1976 to head personnel for their Hawaii Division. While at Duty Free, he was promoted to Corporate VP of Personnel and Organizational Planning. For all the positions he has held, save one, he saw a need, convinced management of that need, and then created the job. He describes himself as "having infinite patience for a very short time." In other words, he enjoys a creative challenge and digging into a project where there is a beginning and an end.

Ian holds an AB Degree in Economics from Stanford University and completed a year of graduate study there in the Social Sciences. He is a Certified Management Consultant, and was elected a Fellow of the Institute of Management Consultants in 1997, a distinction accorded to only 27 management consultants in the USA at that time. He has been recognized repeatedly for his leadership and community service.

Ian and his wife, Bonnie, live in Santa Clara, CA. For his leisure time, he enjoys motorcycling, travel, cars, hiking, camping, music and home improvement projects.

Ian's quarterly letters on leadership, *IanSights,* can be found on the Jacobsen Consulting web site, www.jacobsenconsulting.com.

Reference List

Numbers listed refer to chapter references.

Bold numbers indicate primary references among the choices.

Numbers listed refer to chapter references.

Bold numbers indicate primary references among the choices.